PEARSON

Math
Makes Sense

Practice and Homework Book

Author Team

Ray Appel

Robert Berglind

Susan Ludwig

David Sufrin

Publisher
Claire Burnett

Publishing Team
Lesley Haynes
Enid Haley
Ioana Gagea
Lynne Gulliver
Stephanie Cox
Judy Wilson

Design
Word & Image Design Studio Inc.

Typesetting
Computer Composition of Canada Inc.

Elementary Math Team Leader
Diane Wyman

Product Manager
Kathleen Crosbie

Copyright © 2008 Pearson Education Canada, a division of Pearson Canada Inc.

All Rights Reserved. This publication is protected by copyright, and permission should be obtained from the publisher prior to any prohibited reproduction, storage in a retrieval system, or transmission in any form or by any means, electronic, mechanical, photocopying, recording, or likewise. For information regarding permission, write to the Permissions Department.

ISBN-13: 978-0-321-43176-9
ISBN-10:   0-321-43176-6

Printed and bound in Canada.

2 3 4 5 -- WC -- 11 10 09 08

Contents

Patterns and Relations

Integers

Math
Makes Sense 7 — Practice and Homework Book

Welcome to *Pearson Math Makes Sense 7*. These pages describe how this Practice and Homework Book can support your progress through the year.

Each unit offers the following features.

Activating Prior Knowledge provides a brief introduction and Examples to refresh your skills, and Check questions to let you reinforce these prerequisite skills.

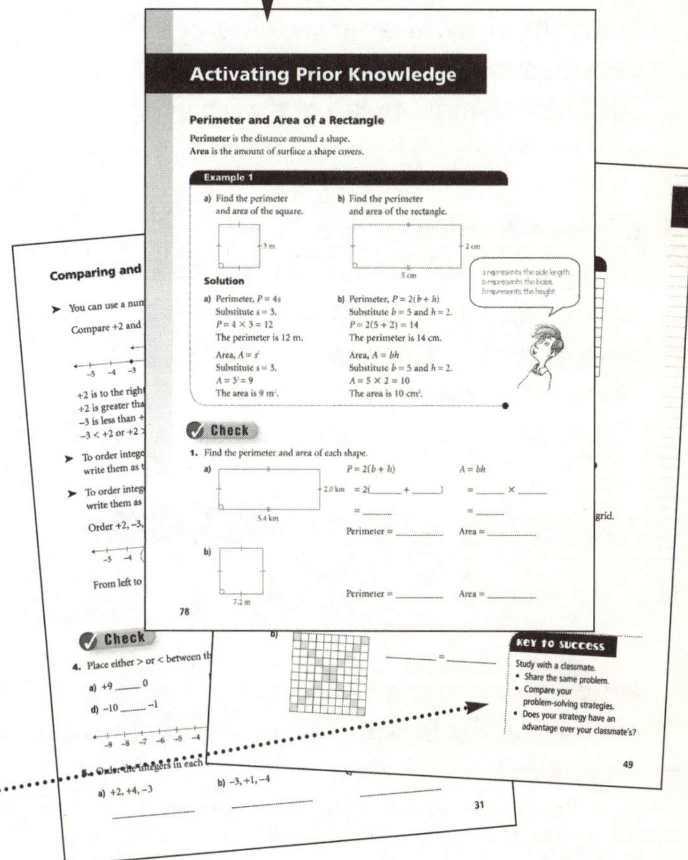

Just for Fun presents puzzles, games, or activities to help you warm up for the content to come. You may work with key words, numeracy skills, or creative and critical thinking skills.

Key to Success highlights ways you can develop your study skills, test-taking skills, and overall independence as a grade 7 student.

For each lesson of the Student Book, the workbook provides 2 to 4 pages of support.

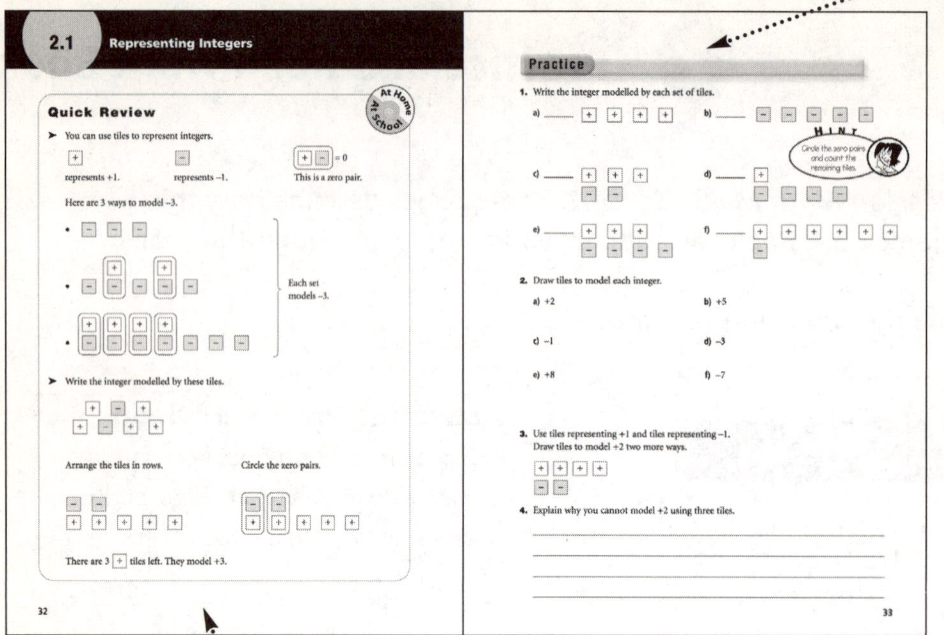

Practice questions provide a structure for your work, gradually leaving more steps for you to complete on your own.

Quick Review covers the core concepts from the lesson. If used for homework, this Quick Review lets you take just the Practice and Homework Book home.

In Your Words helps to close each unit. This page identifies essential mathematical vocabulary from the unit, gives one definition as an example, and allows you to record your understanding of other terms in your own words.

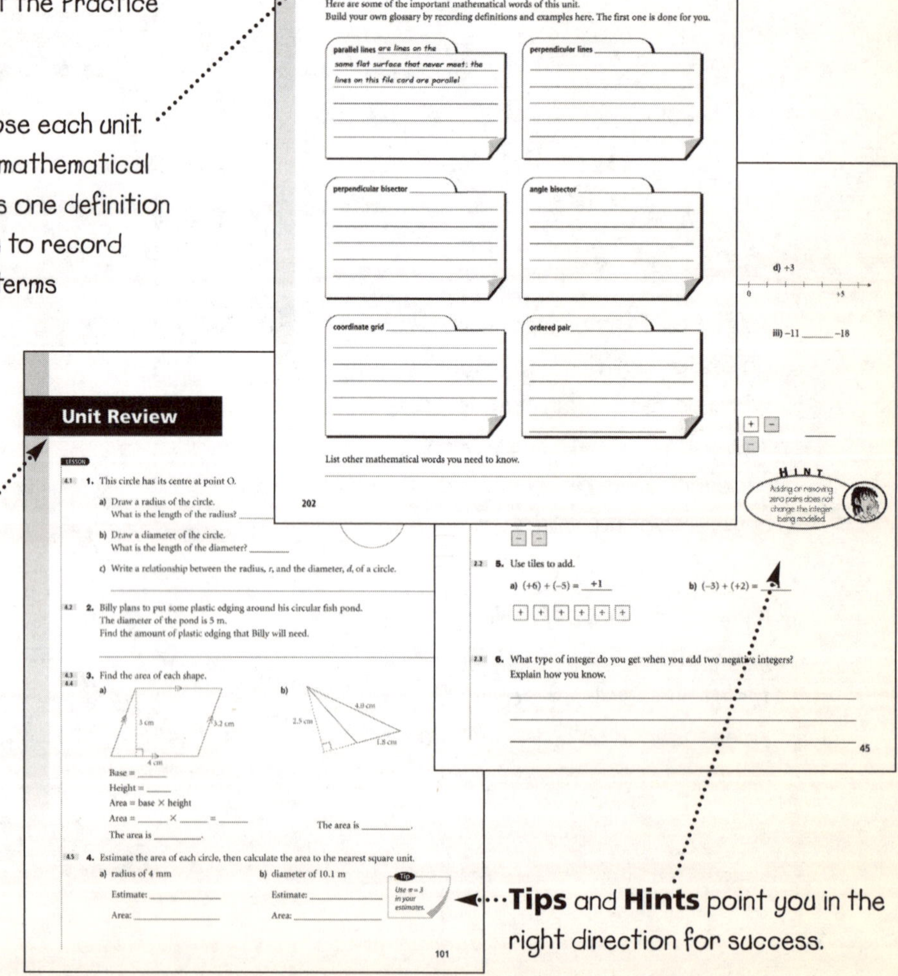

Unit Review pages provide the same level of support as lesson Practice. Each Unit Review question is referenced to the relevant lesson where related concepts are developed.

Tips and **Hints** point you in the right direction for success.

Just for Fun

Word Find

Find the following words
in the puzzle below.
You can move in any direction.

term
divisibility rule
unit
tile

d	i	v	i	s
e	t	e	l	i
l	m	r	i	b
u	n	i	t	i
r	y	t	i	l

Pattern Search

Choose a grid of any 4 squares in the calendar.
What patterns do you see in the numbers?

May						
1	2	3	4	5	6	7
8	9	10	11	12	13	14
15	16	17	18	19	20	21
22	23	24	25	26	27	28
29	30	31				

Variation: Choose a grid of any 9 squares
or pick a different month and try again.

A Game for **2 or more**

Express Yourself!

Make as many words as you can from the letters of the words "algebraic expression."
The person with the most words after 3 minutes wins!

Activating Prior Knowledge

Order of Operations

Perform operations inside the brackets first.
Next, divide and multiply in order from left to right.
Then add and subtract in order from left to right.

Example 1

Simplify.

a) $10 - 3 \times 2$ **b)** $12 \div (5 + 1)$ **c)** $6 \times 2 \div 3 + 1$

Solution

a) $10 - 3 \times 2 = 10 - 6$ Multiply first.
$ = 4$ Then subtract.

b) $12 \div (5 + 1) = 12 \div 6$ Add inside the brackets first.
$ = 2$ Then divide.

c) $6 \times 2 \div 3 + 1 = 12 \div 3 + 1$ Multiply first.
$ = 4 + 1$ Then divide.
$ = 5$ Then add.

✔ Check

1. Simplify.

a) $12 - 2 \times 4$

$= 12 - \underline{\hspace{2cm}}$

$= \underline{\hspace{2cm}}$

b) $20 \div (2 + 3)$

$= 20 \div \underline{\hspace{2cm}}$

$= \underline{\hspace{2cm}}$

c) $12 \div 6 \times 5 + 4$

$= \underline{\hspace{1.5cm}} \times 5 + 4$

$= \underline{\hspace{2cm}}$

d) $10 + 4 \div 2$

$= 10 + \underline{\hspace{2cm}}$

$= \underline{\hspace{2cm}}$

e) $(9 - 5) \times 6$

$= \underline{\hspace{1cm}} \times 6$

$= \underline{\hspace{2cm}}$

f) $5 + 2 \times 3 - 4$

$= 5 + \underline{\hspace{2cm}}$

$= \underline{\hspace{2cm}}$

Graphing on a Coordinate Grid

An ordered pair, such as (5, 3), tells you the position of a point on a grid.
The first number is the horizontal distance from the origin.
The second number is the vertical distance from the origin.
The numbers of an ordered pair are also called the **coordinates** of a point.

Example 2

Graph the points A(5, 3), B(2, 0), and C(0, 4) on a grid.

Solution

To plot point A, start at 5 on the
horizontal axis, then move up 3.

To plot point B, start at 2 on the
horizontal axis, then move up 0.
Point B is on the horizontal axis.

To plot point C, start at 0 on the
horizontal axis, then move up 4.
Point C is on the vertical axis.

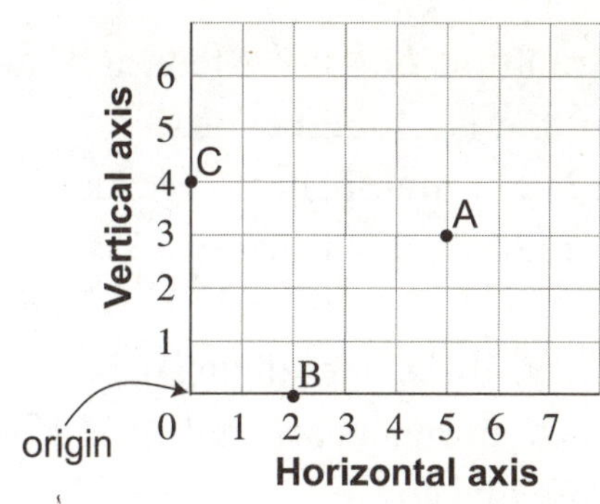

✓ Check

2. Write the ordered pair for
each point on the grid.

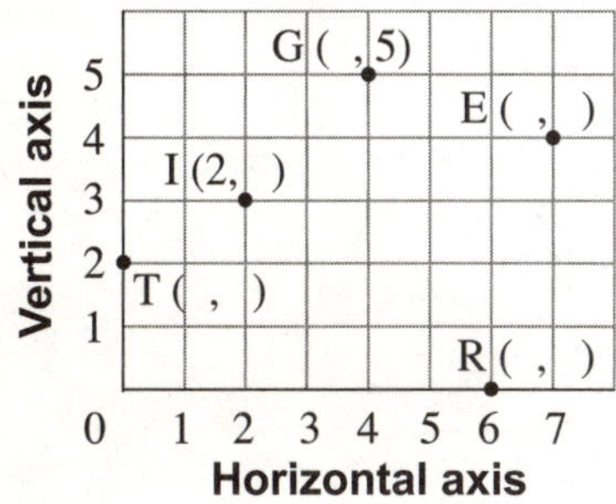

3. Plot and label these points:
A(0, 5), B(2, 4), E(4, 3), R(5, 0)

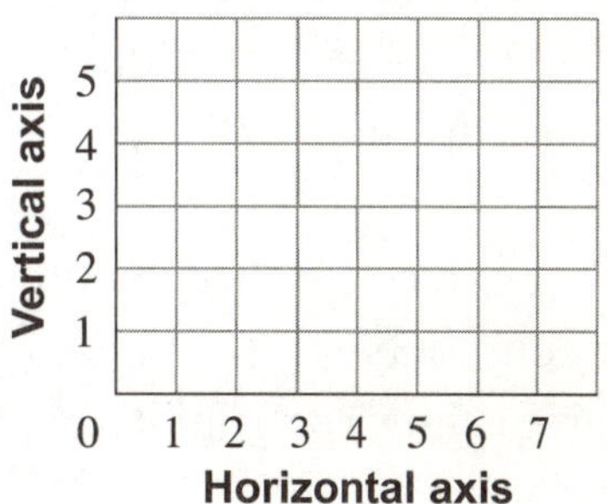

4. The graph shows the number
of bracelets Jan can make over time.
  a) How many bracelets can Jan make

   in 3 h? _______________

  b) How long will it take to make

   10 bracelets? _______________

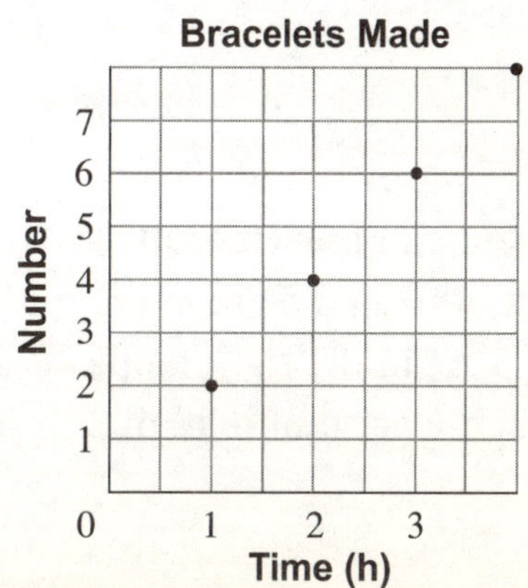

Quick Review

➤ Multiples of 2 are even numbers.
They have these ones digits: 0, 2, 4, 6, 8
For example, these are even numbers and multiples of 2: 32, 74, 88, 96, 100
All even numbers are divisible by 2.

➤ A number is a multiple of 4 if the tens and ones digits of the number
form a number that is a multiple of 4.
For example, 1**24** is a multiple of 4 because **24** is a multiple of 4.
And, 30**36** is a multiple of 4 because **36** is a multiple of 4.

➤ Multiples of 5 have these ones digits: 0, 5
For example, these numbers are multiples of 5: 5, 20, 45, 350
Multiples of 5 are divisible by 5.

➤ A number is a multiple of 8 if the hundreds, tens, and ones digits
of the number form a number that is a multiple of 8.
For example, 1**888** is a multiple of 8 because **888** is a multiple of 8.
And, 1**040** is a multiple of 8 because **040**, or **40** is a multiple of 8.

➤ Multiples of 10 have a ones digit that is 0.
For example, these numbers are multiples of 10: 20, 40, 130, 770
Multiples of 10 are divisible by 10.

➤ You can use a Venn diagram to show numbers that are divisible
by two or more numbers.
This Venn diagram shows divisibility by 2 and by 5.

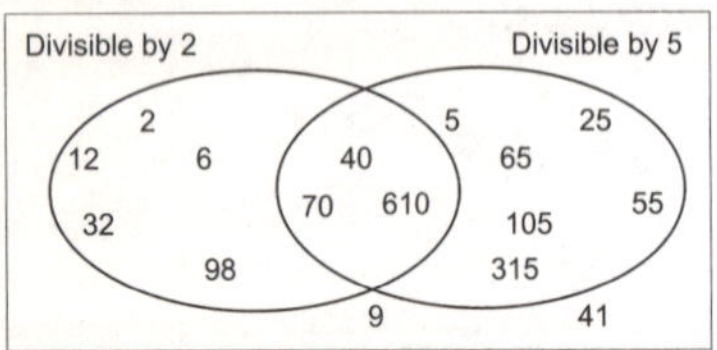

Multiples of 2 are in the left loop.
Multiples of both 2 and 5 are in the middle loop.
Multiples of 5 are in the right loop.
Numbers that are *not* multiples of 2 or of 5 are outside the loops.

1. Circle the numbers that are divisible by 2.

23   98   21   44   11   77   34

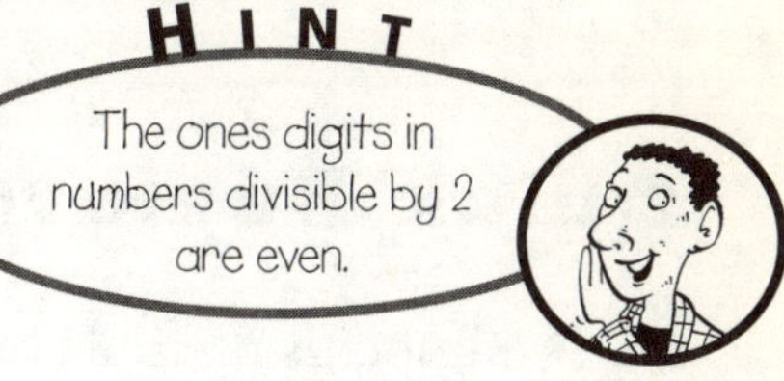

2. Circle the numbers that are divisible by 5.

55   10   7   59   105   775   1025

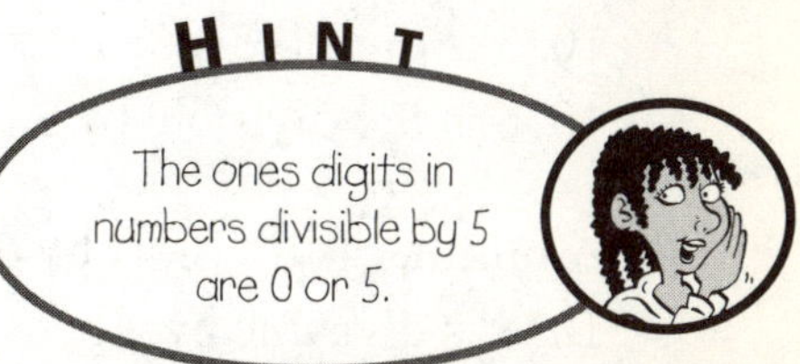

3. Circle the numbers that are divisible by 2 and by 5.

10   30   25   55   1000   52

4. Write each number in the correct place in the Venn diagram.

16, 20, 33, 64, 80, 95, 97, 105, 214, 216, 324, 405

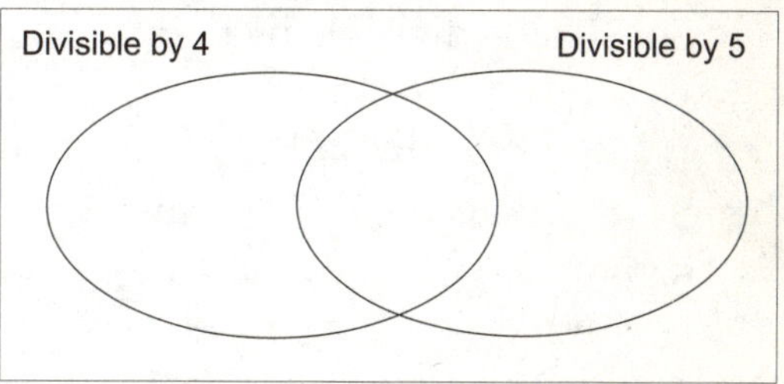

5. Write four 3-digit numbers that are divisible by 10.

____

6. Write three 4-digit numbers that are divisible by 8.

____

7. a) Write each number in the correct place in the Venn diagram.

115, 116, 120, 168, 450, 753, 800, 928, 1008, 1110

b) Write 4 more numbers in the Venn diagram – one in each loop and one outside the loops. How do you know you placed each number correctly?

____

____

Quick Review

➤ A number is divisible by 3 if the sum of its digits is divisible by 3. For example, 1035 is divisible by 3 because $1 + 0 + 3 + 5 = 9$, and 9 is divisible by 3.
1036 is *not* divisible by 3 because $1 + 0 + 3 + 6 = 10$, and 10 is *not* divisible by 3.

➤ A number is divisible by 6 if the number is divisible by 2 and by 3. For example, 1038 is divisible by 2 because the number is even.
1038 is divisible by 3 because $1 + 0 + 3 + 8 = 12$, which is divisible by 3.
So, 1038 is divisible by 6.

➤ A number is divisible by 9 if the sum of its digits is divisible by 9. For example, 5418 is divisible by 9 because $5 + 4 + 1 + 8 = 18$, and 18 is divisible by 9.
5428 is *not* divisible by 9 because $5 + 4 + 2 + 8 = 19$, and 19 is *not* divisible by 9.

➤ No number is divisible by 0.

➤ You can use a Carroll diagram to show numbers that are divisible by two numbers. This Carroll diagram shows divisibility by 6 and by 9.

	Divisible by 6	Not divisible by 6
Divisible by 9	18, 36, 126, 162	27, 45, 963, 711
Not divisible by 9	6, 12, 204, 402	10, 29, 325, 802

➤ You can use divisibility rules to help list the factors of a number.
To list the factors of 156:
Try each rule in turn.
Divide by 2: $156 \div 2 = 78$
Divide by 3: $156 \div 3 = 52$
Divide by 4: $156 \div 4 = 39$
156 is not divisible by 5.
Divide by 6: $156 \div 6 = 26$
156 is not divisible by 7, by 8, by 9, or by 10.
Use a calculator to check for divisibility by 11 and 12.
156 is not divisible by 11.
Divide by 12: $156 \div 12 = 13$
Since the factors 12 and 13 are close in value, you have found all the factors.
In order, the factors of 156 are: 1, 2, 3, 4, 6, 12, 13, 26, 39, 52, 78, 156

1. Match the number with the correct divisibility statement.
   Draw more than one line if it is needed.

54	Divisible by 10.
56	Divisible by 3.
50	Divisible by 9.
92	Divisible by 8.
75	Divisible by 5.
93	Divisible by 2.
30	Divisible by 6.

2. Cross out the numbers that are *not* divisible by 2.

   12   79   98   134   227   2469

   How do you know the numbers are not divisible by 2?

   ____

3. Circle the numbers that are divisible by 9.

   91   331   333   153   99   12 321

   How do you know you are correct?

   ____

   ____

4. Write four numbers that are divisible by 6: _______________________________
   How did you choose those numbers?

   ____

5. Solve each riddle.

   a) I am divisible by 2 and by 3.
   I am between 21 and 29.
   Which number am I? _________

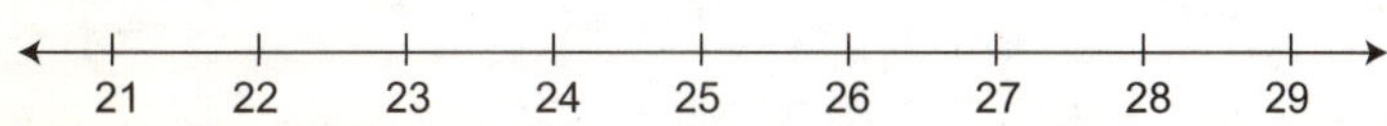

   b) I am divisible by 5 and by 10.   **c)** I am divisible by 2 and by 9.
   I am between 56 and 64.   I am between 424 and 449.
   Which number am I? _________   Which number am I? _________

6. Which numbers below are divisible by 3? By 6? By 9?
How do you know?

a) 124 ____

b) 215 ____

c) 330 ____

____

d) 450 ____

____

e) 150 ____

____

7. Use your answers to question 6 to help you list the factors of each number.

a) 124: ____

b) 215: ____

c) 150: ____

8. a) Sort these numbers in the Carroll diagram below.
16, 18, 27, 37, 120, 180, 281, 288, 352, 411, 432, 540

	Divisible by 9	Not divisible by 9
Divisible by 4		
Not divisible by 4		

b) Write one more number in each part of the Carroll diagram.
Explain how you knew where to place each number.

____

____

9. a) Sort these numbers in the Venn diagram.
12, 28, 36, 54, 72, 79, 135, 256, 270, 318, 371, 432

b) Which loop is empty? _________________________________
Explain why there is no number that belongs in that loop.

____

____

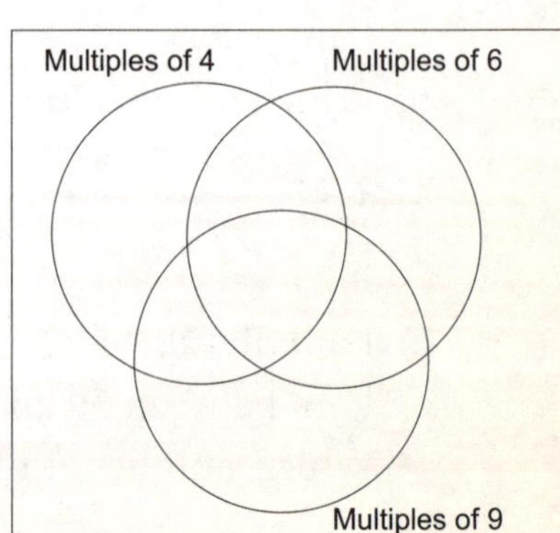

Quick Review

➤ **Algebraic expressions** contain **variables** such as *x* and *n*.
x and **n** can represent any numbers you choose.

Here are some examples of algebraic expressions and what they mean.

$x + 5$:	Five more than a number
$n - 3$:	Three less than a number
$3 - n$:	Three subtract a number
$5x$:	Five times a number
$5n + 3$:	Five times a number, then add 3; or three more than five times a number
$\dfrac{100}{n}$:	One hundred divided by a number
$\dfrac{n}{100}$:	A number divided by one hundred

➤ In the algebraic expression $7t + 2$

7 is the **numerical coefficient** of the variable.
2 is the **constant term**.
t is the variable.

➤ An algebraic expression can help you solve
similar problems more efficiently. Once you
know the algebraic expression, you can use
it again, even if the numbers change.

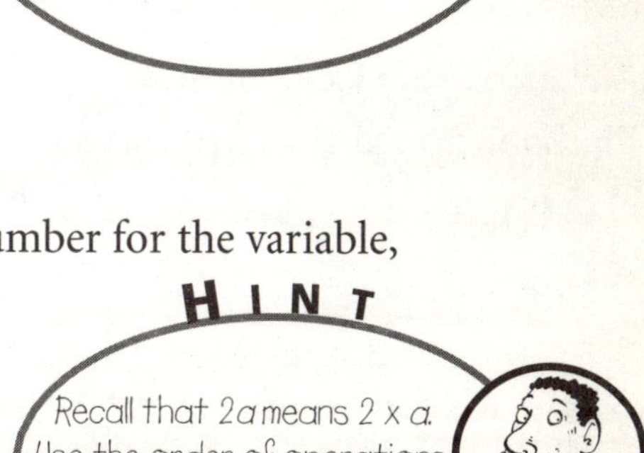

Suppose you earn \$8 per hour.

For 3 hours, you earn: $3 \times \$8 = \$24$

For *t* hours, you earn: $t \times \$8 = 8t$ dollars

➤ To evaluate an expression means to substitute a number for the variable,
then calculate the answer.
To evaluate $2a - 5$ for $a = 7$:
Replace *a* with 7 in the expression $2a - 5$.
$2a - 5 = 2(7) - 5$

$$= 14 - 5$$
$$= 9$$

1. Match each algebraic expression with its meaning.

$6 + x$ Five less than a number

$4n$ One more than double a number

$1 + 2t$ Five subtract a number

$5 - p$ Four times a number

$s - 5$ Three times a number subtract four

$3g - 4$ Six more than a number

2. Identify the numerical coefficient, the variable, and the constant term in each expression.

a) $4 + 5s$

Numerical coefficient: _________   Variable: _________   Constant term: _________

b) $x + 7$

Numerical coefficient: _________   Variable: _________   Constant term: _________

c) $9m$

Numerical coefficient: _________   Variable: _________   Constant term: _________

3. An algebraic expression has constant term 12, variable t, and numerical coefficient 8.
What might the expression be? _______________________________

4. Write an algebraic expression for each phrase.
Use the variable n.

a) Ten times a number _____________________   **b)** Double a number _____________________

c) A number divided by four _____________   **d)** Six less than a number _____________

e) Three more than ten times a number ____

f) Six less than ten times a number ____

5. A clerk earns $12 an hour.
Find how much the clerk earns for each time.

a) 5 h work   **b)** 8 h work   **c)** p hours work

$5 \times$ _____ = _____   _______ = _____   _______ = _________

6. A car travels at an average speed of 60 km/h.
Find how far it travels in each time.

a) 3 h   **b)** 5 h   **c)** x hours

$3 \times$ _______ = _______   _________ = _______   _________ = _______

7. Evaluate each expression by replacing z with 10.

   a) $z + 5 = 10 + 5$
            $= \underline{\hspace{2cm}}$

   b) $8 + z = \underline{\hspace{2cm}}$
            $= \underline{\hspace{2cm}}$

   c) $z - 6 = \underline{\hspace{2cm}}$
            $= \underline{\hspace{2cm}}$

   d) $15 - z = \underline{\hspace{2cm}}$
            $= \underline{\hspace{2cm}}$

   e) $3z = \underline{\hspace{2cm}}$
            $= \underline{\hspace{2cm}}$

   f) $5z = \underline{\hspace{2cm}}$
            $= \underline{\hspace{2cm}}$

8. Evaluate each expression by replacing n with 2.

   a) $2n + 3$
     $= 2 \times \underline{\hspace{2cm}} + 3$
     $= \underline{\hspace{2cm}} + 3$
     $= \underline{\hspace{2cm}}$

   b) $20 - 5n$
     $= \underline{\hspace{2cm}} - 5 \times 2$
     $= \underline{\hspace{2cm}}$
     $= \underline{\hspace{2cm}}$

   c) $\dfrac{n}{2} + 8$
     $= \underline{\hspace{2cm}}$
     $= \underline{\hspace{2cm}}$
     $= \underline{\hspace{2cm}}$

   d) $14 - \dfrac{n}{2}$
     $= \underline{\hspace{2cm}}$
     $= \underline{\hspace{2cm}}$
     $= \underline{\hspace{2cm}}$

9. Sofia works part-time in a convenience store.
She earns \$6/h during the day, and \$8/h during the evening.

   a) In one week, Sofia worked 10 h in the day and 9 h in the evening.
      Write an expression for her earnings in dollars.

      $\underline{\hspace{12cm}}$

   b) Suppose Sofia works n hours in the day and 7 h in the evening.
      i) Write an expression for her earnings in dollars.

        $\underline{\hspace{10cm}}$

      ii) How much does Sofia earn when $n = 5$?

        $\underline{\hspace{10cm}}$

   c) Suppose Sofia works 9 h in the day and
      m hours in the evening.
      i) Write an expression for her earnings in dollars.

        $\underline{\hspace{8cm}}$

      ii) How much does Sofia earn when $m = 11$?

        $\underline{\hspace{8cm}}$

Quick Review

➤ You can describe a number pattern using the term number.

Term number	1	2	3	4	5	6
Term	8	16	24	32	40	48

We can write an algebraic expression for the term when we know the term number.
Each term is 8 times the term number.
Let n represent any term number.
Then the term is represented by $8 \times n$, or $8n$.

When you compare or *relate* a variable to an expression that contains the variable, you have a *relation*.
The variable is n.
The expression is $8n$.
The relation is: $8n$ is related to n

➤ The table and relation above can represent the total number of beats in a music score when there are 8 beats in each bar.

Number of bars of music	1	2	3	4	5	6
Total number of beats	8	16	24	32	40	48

You can use the relation to find the number of beats in 17 bars of music.
Substitute $n = 17$ in the expression $8n$.
$8n = 8(17)$
$\quad = 136$
There are 136 beats in 17 bars of music.

Practice

1. Complete each chart.

a)

Term number	1	2	3	4	5	6
Term	5		15		25	

b)

Term number	1	2	3	4	5	6
Term	5		7		9	

c)

Term number	1	2	3	4	5	6
Term	3		9		15	

2. Every day, Ray rides his bike 12 km around Stanley Park.
Complete the chart to show the total distance Ray travelled.

Number of days	1	2	3	4	5	6
Distance (km)	12					72

3. Write a relation for the pattern rule for each pattern.
Use the relation to find the 12th term.
Let n represent any term number.

a) 6, 12, 18, 24, ... ________________________________

b) 10, 11, 12, 13, ... ________________________________

4. a) Write a relation for the perimeter of a regular pentagon

with side length n centimetres. ________________________

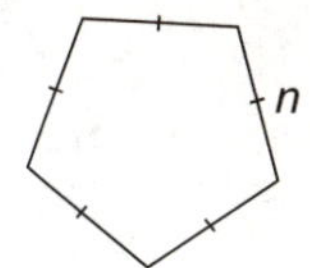

b) What is the perimeter of a regular pentagon with side length 9 cm?

____

5. Ally is organizing an end-of-term party.
The cost to rent the hall is $100. The cost of food is $8 per person.
a) Write a relation for the total cost of the party, in dollars, for n people.

____

b) How much will the party cost if:

i) 20 people attend? ________________________________

ii) 50 people attend? ________________________________

c) How does the relation in part a change in each case?
i) The cost of food doubles.

____

ii) The cost of the food increases by $2 per person.

____

d) For each scenario in part c, find the cost when 40 people attend.

i) ____

ii) ____

Quick Review

➤ You can make a table of values for a relation such as: $2n + 5$ is related to n

Choose values for n. These are Input numbers.

Substitute each value of n in $2n + 5$ to get the Output numbers.

When $n = 1$, $2n + 5 = 2(1) + 5$
$$= 7$$

When $n = 2$, $2n + 5 = 2(2) + 5$
$$= 9$$

When $n = 3$, $2n + 5 = 2(3) + 5$
$$= 11$$

When $n = 4$, $2n + 5 = 2(4) + 5$
$$= 13$$

Here is the table:

Input n	Output $2n + 5$
1	7
2	9
3	11
4	13

➤ You can find a relation given its table of values.

Input	Output
1	2
2	6
3	10
4	14
5	18

$+1$ ↷ (Input) $+4$ ↷ (Output)

Let n represent any Input number.

When n increases by 1, the Output number increases by 4.

This means that the expression for the Output numbers contains $4n$.

So, compare the Output numbers to multiples of 4: 4, 8, 12, 16, 20, . . .

Each Output number is 2 less than a multiple of 4.

So, the output is $4n - 2$.

The table shows how $4n - 2$ relates to n.

1. a) Evaluate the expression $3n + 1$.

When $n = 1$, $3n + 1 = 3(1) + 1$

$$= \underline{\qquad}$$

When $n = 2$, $3n + 1 = 3(2) + 1$

$$= \underline{\qquad}$$

When $n = 3$, $3n + 1 = 3(3) + \underline{\qquad}$

$$= \underline{\qquad}$$

When $n = 4$, $3n + 1 = 3(\underline{\qquad}) + \underline{\qquad}$

$$= \underline{\qquad}$$

When $n = 5$, $3n + 1 = 3(\underline{\qquad}) + \underline{\qquad}$

$$= \underline{\qquad}$$

b) Complete the table. Use your results from part a.

Input n	Output $3n + 1$
1	
2	
3	
4	
5	

2. Complete each table.
Explain how the Output number is related to the Input number.

a)

Input n	Output $n + 5$
1	
2	
3	
4	
5	

b)

Input b	Output $8 - b$
1	
2	
3	
4	
5	

c)

Input a	Output $6 + a$
1	
2	
3	
4	
5	

____

____

3. Complete each table.

a)

Input d	Output $2d + 3$
1	
2	
3	
4	
5	

b)

Input f	Output $3f - 2$
1	
2	
3	
4	
5	

c)

Input h	Output $5h + 1$
1	
2	
3	
4	
5	

4. Use algebra. Write a relation for each table.

a)

Input n	Output
1	2
2	3
3	4
4	5
5	6

____

b)

Input p	Output
1	0
2	1
3	2
4	3
5	4

____

c)

Input m	Output
1	8
2	16
3	24
4	32
5	40

____

5. Use algebra. Write a relation for each table.
Then extend each table 3 more rows.

a)

Input r	Output
1	4
2	6
3	8
4	10
5	12

____

b)

Input s	Output
1	2
2	5
3	8
4	11
5	14

____

c)

Input n	Output
1	9
2	14
3	19
4	24
5	29

____

Quick Review

➤ You can use a graph to show a relation.
This table and graph show how $5n - 4$ relates to n.

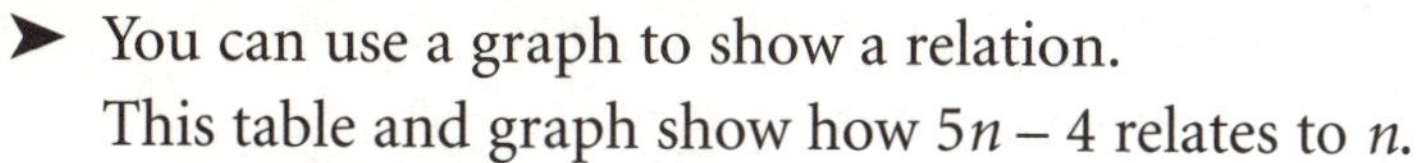

Input n	Output $5n - 4$
1	1
2	6
3	11
4	16
5	21

+1 ↷ ↶ +5
+1 ↷ ↶ +5
+1 ↷ ↶ +5
+1 ↷ ↶ +5

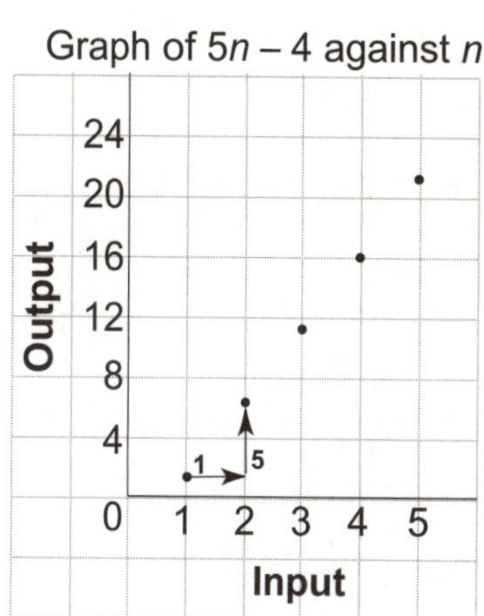

The scale on the *Output* axis is 1 square to 4 units.
The points lie on a straight line, so the relation is linear.
Both the table and the graph show that when the input increases by 1,
the output increases by 5.

Practice

1. Complete each table.

a)

Input n	Output $2n + 8$
1	10
2	12
3	14
4	16
5	
6	
7	

b)

Input n	Output $5n + 1$
1	6
2	11
3	16
4	21
5	
6	
7	

c)

Input n	Output $9 - n$
1	8
2	7
3	6
4	5
5	
6	
7	

2. Choose a suitable scale.

Graph each relation in question 1.

a)

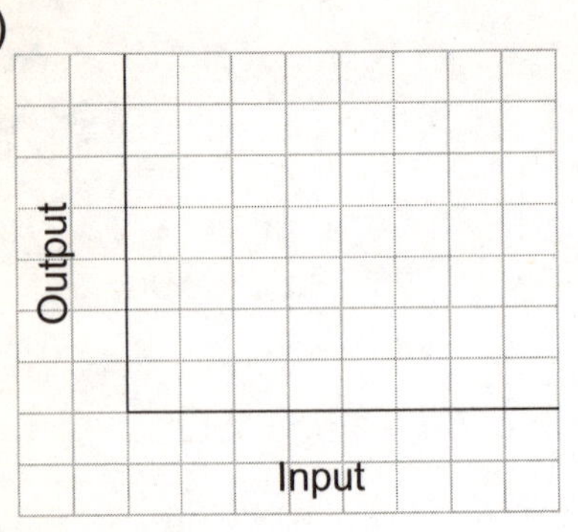

b)

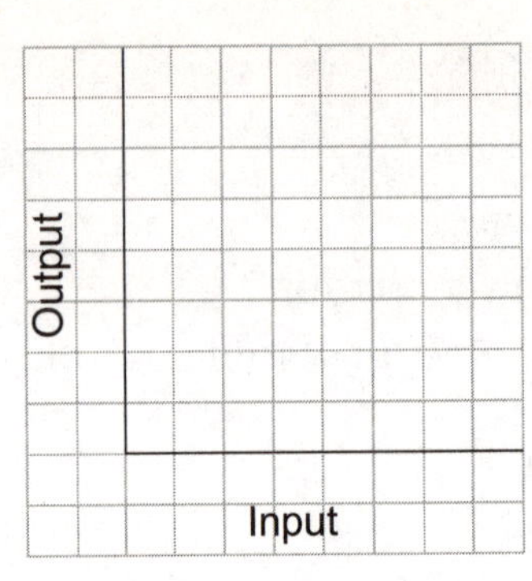

c)

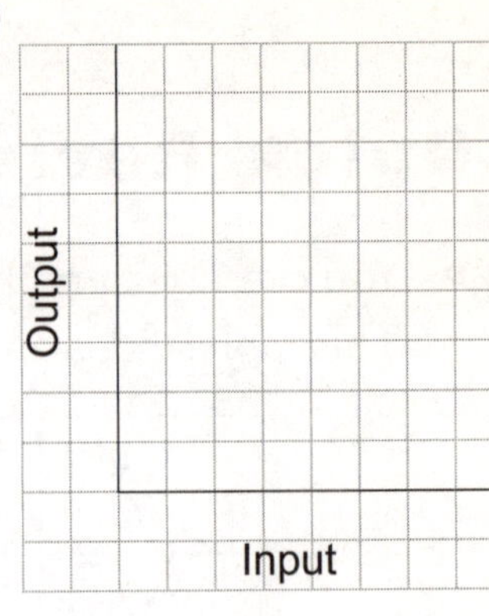

3. Look at the graph at the right.

a) What is the output when the input is 1? _________

b) Which input gives an output of 13? _________

c) Extend the graph.

   i) What is the output when the input is 8? _________

   ii) What is the input when the output is 21? _________

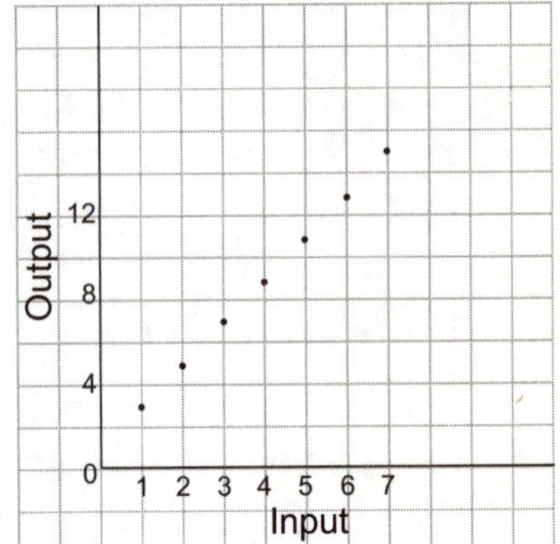

4. a) Complete this table.

b) Graph the relation in part a.

Input a	Output $5a + 3$
2	
4	
6	
8	
10	

c) How does the graph illustrate the relation?

____

____

18

5. The members of the student council wash cars to raise money for charity.
The students charge $3.00 per car.

a) Let c represent the number of cars washed.

Write a relation to show how the money collected, in dollars, is related to the number

of cars washed. ____

b) Complete this table to show the relation.   **c)** Graph the data.

Number of cars	Money collected ($)
10	
20	
30	
40	
50	

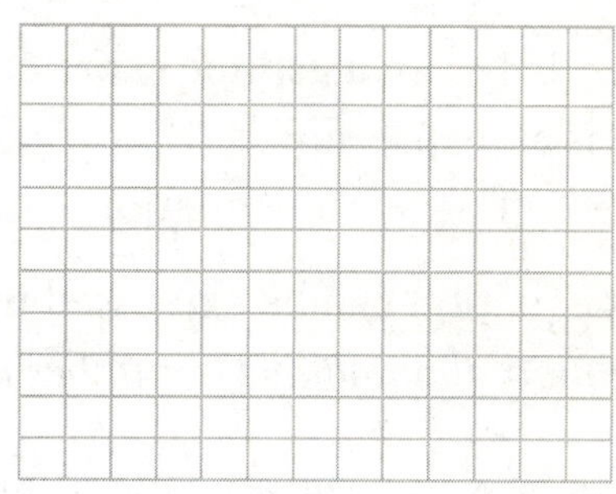

d) Describe the graph.

____

____

e) Use the relation, the graph, or the table to answer these questions.
Explain your choice.

i) Suppose the students wash 33 cars.

How much money will they collect? ________

I used the: ____

ii) Suppose the students wash 60 cars.

How much money will they collect? ________

I used the: ____

____

6. Match each graph to its relation.

a)

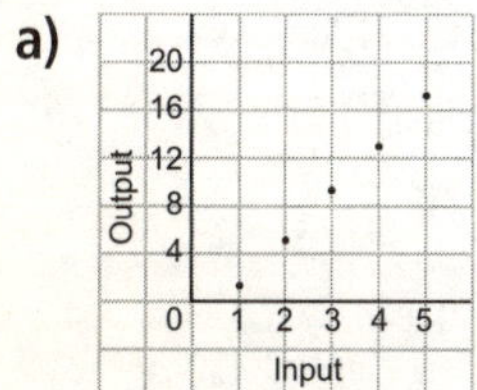

b)

c)

A. $10 - n$ relates to n **B.** $3n + 5$ relates to n **C.** $4n - 3$ relates to n

________________   ________________   ________________

Quick Review

➤ An equation is a statement that two expressions are equal.

$2x + 1$ is an algebraic expression.

7 is an expression.

$2x + 1 = 7$ is an equation.

This equation can be expressed in words as:
One more than double a number is seven.

➤ Here's how to write an equation from a statement.

1. Choose a letter for the variable.
2. Write an algebraic expression to represent the relationship described.
3. Write an equals sign between the expression and the constant term.

Five more than a number is 20.
Let p represent the number.
Five more than p: $p + 5$
The equation is: $p + 5 = 20$

A number subtracted from ten is 4.
Let x represent the number.
x subtracted from ten: $10 - x$
The equation is: $10 - x = 4$

A number divided by two is 8.
Let n represent the number.

n divided by two: $\frac{n}{2}$

The equation is: $\frac{n}{2} = 8$

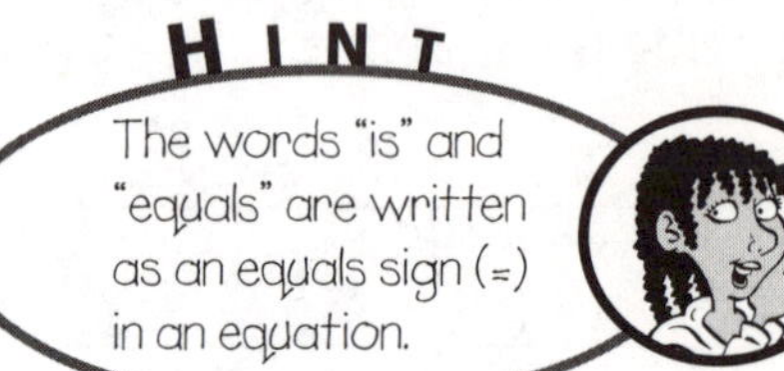

Practice

1. Match each sentence with an equation. The first one is done for you.

A number divided by three is 4.	$20 - n = 6$
Twenty subtract a number equals 6.	$2n + 3 = 11$
Nine subtract one-half a number is 6.	$\frac{n}{3} = 4$
Three added to double a number is 11.	$9 - \frac{n}{2} = 6$

2. Write an equation for each sentence.
Let n represent the number.

  a) Eight less than a number is 2. $n -$ _____ $=$ _____

  b) One-half a number equals 5. ______________________

  c) Four more than double a number is 20. _________________

  d) Six plus three times a number is 9. ____________________

3. Write a sentence for each equation.

  a) $n - 6 = 12$

____

  b) $\dfrac{x}{2} = 10$

____

  c) $2p + 10 = 14$

____

4. Write an equation for each sentence.
Let x represent the number.

  a) Three more than a number is 12. _____________________

  b) Three less than a number is 12. _____________________

  c) Three times a number equals 12. _____________________

  d) Three more than three times a number is 12. ____________

  e) Three subtracted from three times a number equals 12. _______

5. Write an equation for each sentence.

  a) The cost of 2 adult tickets at \$5 each and n child tickets at \$3 each is \$25.

____

  b) William's age 4 years ago was 12. Let a years represent William's age now.

____

  c) The perimeter of a square with side length s is 28.

____

Quick Review

➤ You can use tiles to represent an expression.

This **unit tile** represents +1.

This **variable tile** or ***x*-tile** represents *x*.

➤ You can use tiles to solve an equation. For example, to solve: $x + 3 = 14$:
Draw a vertical line in the centre of the page.
It represents the equals sign in the equation.
Arrange the tiles on each side of the line to represent the
expression or number on each side of the equation.
On the left side, place tiles to represent $x + 3$.
On the right side, place tiles to represent 14.

To isolate the *x*-tile, remove 3 unit tiles from each side.

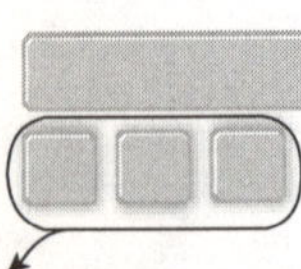
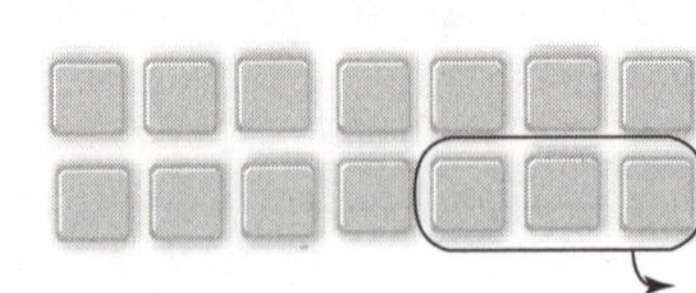

The tiles show the solution is $x = 11$.

To *verify* the solution, replace *x* with 11 tiles.

Left side:

+

14 unit tiles

Right side:

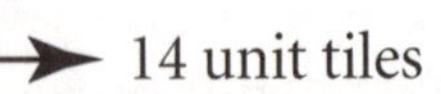
14 unit tiles

Since both sides have equal numbers of tiles, the solution $x = 11$ is correct.

1. Complete each algebraic expression.

   a) A number increased by 3: $x +$ ________

   b) Two times a number: ________ x

   c) Three more than 4 times a number: $4x +$ ________

   d) Twelve less than a number: ________ $- 12$

2. Match each picture to its equation.

   a) $x + 1 = 3$

   b) $x + 2 = 4$

   c) $x + 20 = 12$

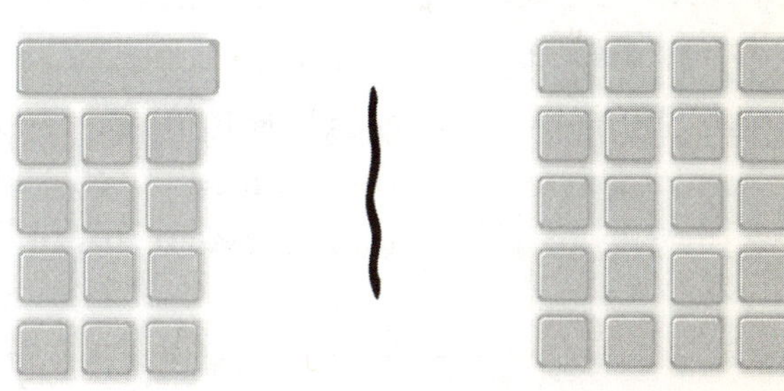

   d) $x + 12 = 20$

3. Zephyr had songs in his music player folder.
   He bought 7 more. Zephyr then had 10 songs.
   How many did he start with?
   Complete the solution for the equation: $x + 7 = 10$

Step 1

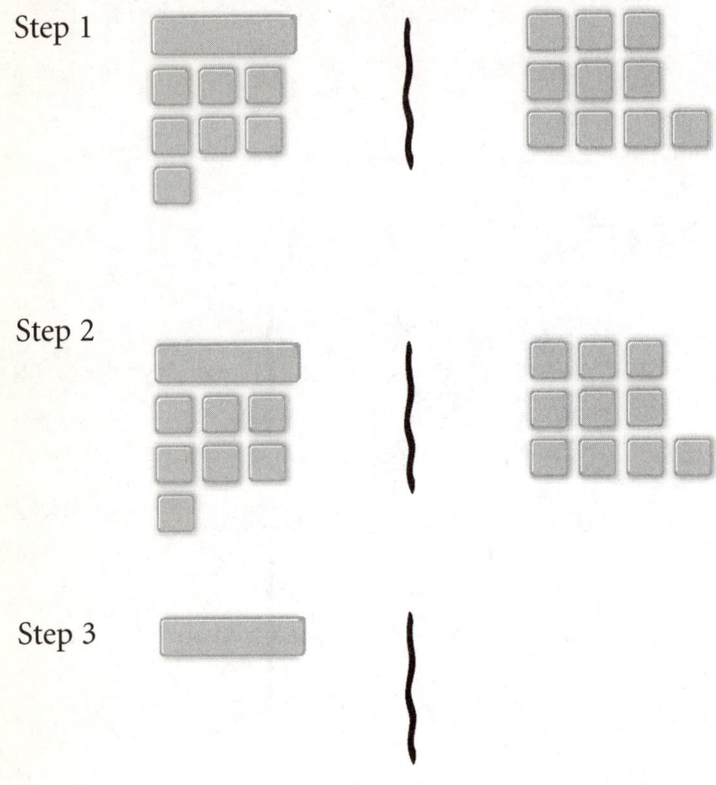

Step 2

Step 3

The solution is: _______________________________

4. An online book costs $15.00 to upload to a computer.
   How many online books can be purchased for $75.00?
   a) Write an equation to represent this problem.

   ____

   b) Solve the equation to find how many online books can be purchased.

   ____

5. Erica is thinking of a number. She multiplies it by 2, then adds 5.
   The result is 19. Which number did Erica begin with?
   a) Write an equation to represent this problem.

   ____

   b) Solve the equation to find the number.

   ____

In Your Words

Here are some of the important mathematical words of this unit.
Build your own glossary by recording definitions and examples here. The first one is done for you.

divisibility rules *rules I can use to find out multiples of numbers and factors of numbers. For example, to find out if a certain number is a multiple of 3, I add the digits of the number; if the sum is a multiple of 3, then the number is also a multiple of 3.*

algebraic expression _______________

variable _______________

evaluate _______________

equation _______________

solve an equation _______________

List other mathematical words you need to know.

1.1

1. **a)** Circle the numbers that are divisible by 4.

312   1407   204   3441   640   763

b) How do you know if a number is divisible by 4?

____

2. **a)** Circle the numbers that are divisible by 2 and by 3.

606   330   501   2466   492   9342

b) What other number are the circled numbers in part a divisible by? _________

How do you know?

____

1.2

3. Which numbers below are divisible by 8? Divisible by 5?
How do you know?

a) 244: ____

____

b) 160: ____

____

c) 315: ____

____

d) 608: ____

____

4. Use your answers from question 3 to help you list all the factors of each number.

a) 244: ____

b) 160: ____

c) 315: ____

d) 608: ____

1.3 **5.** Write an algebraic expression for each phrase. Use the variable n.

    a) Three times a number: ____

    b) Five less than a number: ____

    c) Twenty divided by a number: ____

    d) Seven more than four times a number: ____________________________________

6. Evaluate each expression for $n = 5$.

    a) $n + 7 =$ _________   **b)** $10 - n =$ _______   **c)** $2n + 3 =$ _______

1.4 **7. a)** Zadie climbed four sets of stairs every minute for the Charity Stair Climb Fundraiser. Complete this table. The pattern continues.

Time (minutes)	1	2	3	4	5	6	7	8
Sets of stairs climbed								

    b) How many sets of stairs will Zadie have climbed after 15 minutes? ________

8. Write a relation for the pattern rule for each number pattern.

    a) 3, 6, 9, 12, 15, . . . ____

    b) 8, 9, 10, 11, 12, . . . ____

1.5 **9.** Complete each table.

How is each Output number related to its Input number?

a)

Input n	Output $3n + 5$
1	
2	
3	
4	
5	

b)

Input n	Output $5n + 3$
1	
2	
3	
4	
5	

c)

Input n	Output $5n - 3$
1	
2	
3	
4	
5	

10. Use algebra. Write a relation for each table.

a)

Input *m*	Output
1	9
2	11
3	13
4	15
5	17

b)

Input *m*	Output
1	9
2	16
3	23
4	30
5	37

c)

Input *m*	Output
1	5
2	12
3	19
4	26
5	33

_______________________   _______________________   _______________________

1.6   **11.** Graph each relation in question 10.

a) 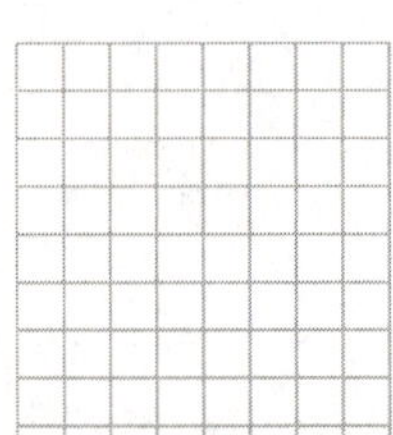

b) 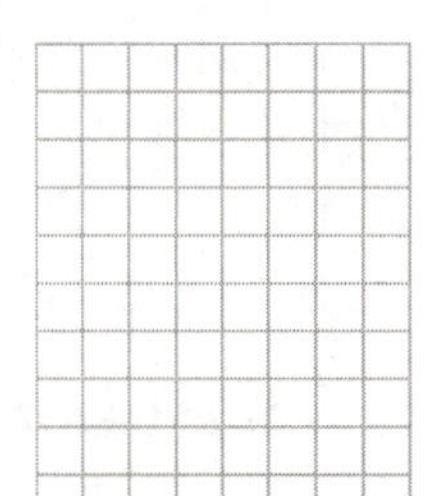

c) 

1.7   **12.** Write an equation for each sentence.
Let *n* represent the number.

a) Four times a number is sixteen. _______________________

b) Eight subtracted from four times a number is sixteen. _______________________

c) Twelve more than four times a number is sixteen. _______________________

d) Thirty-two minus four times a number is sixteen. _______________________

13. Write an equation for each sentence. Let *n* represent the number.

a) Four less than a number is sixteen. _______________

b) A number divided by five is ten. _____________

c) Five more than three times a number is eleven. _______________

1.8   **14.** Robin walked twice around a lake, plus an extra 3 km.
Her pedometer showed that she had walked a total of 19 km.
Write then solve an equation to find how far it is around the lake.

____

Integers

Just for Fun

Magic Square

In this magic square, each row, column, and diagonal has a sum of 15.
Use each number from 1 to 9 once.
Complete the magic square.

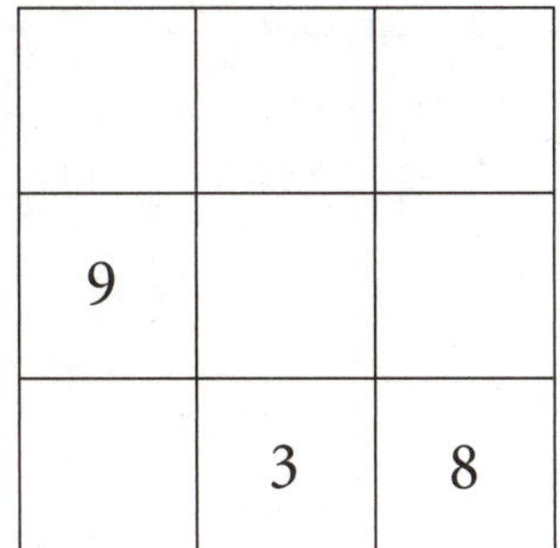

The Square Route

Go from Start to Finish by adding and subtracting.
Do not pass through the same point twice.
Which route has the greatest total?

What is the total? ___________

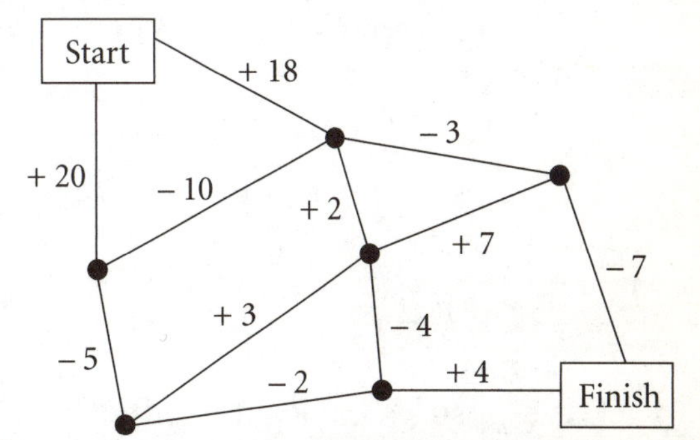

The Three Towers

A Game for 2 to 4

Use counters or coins to build three towers: one of 8, one of 9, and one of 10.

On a turn, a player can either
- take 1 counter from each tower, or
- take 2 counters from one tower

Score 1 point for every counter you collect.
Score 5 points every time you take the last counter from a tower.

Continue until the towers have gone.
If you have the most points, you win!

Variation: Use towers of different heights or a different number of towers.

Activating Prior Knowledge

What Is an Integer?

➤ A **positive number** is greater than 0.
A **negative number** is less than 0.
0 is neither positive nor negative.

➤ The **integers** are the numbers
... −3, −2, −1, 0, +1, +2, +3, ...

You can show integers on a number line.

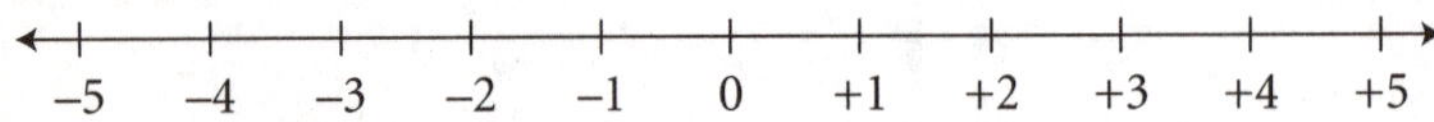

➤ **Opposite integers** are the same distance from 0 on a number line
but are on opposite sides of 0.

For example, −3 and +3 are opposite integers.

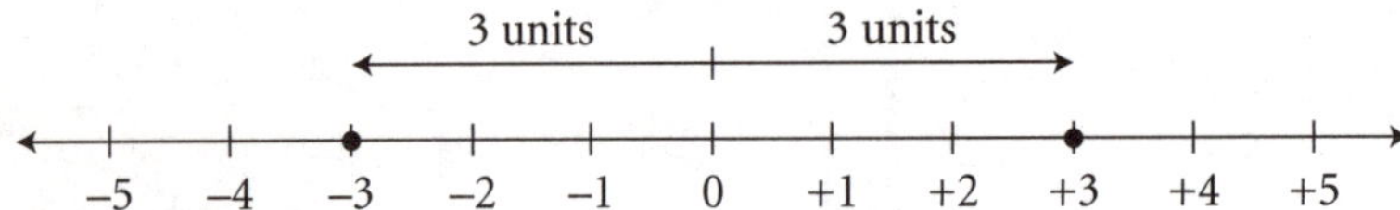

✓ Check

1. Use a positive or negative integer to represent each situation.

    a) losing $15: _________

    b) throwing a ball 9 m straight up: _________

    c) seventeen days from now: _________

    d) an elevator descending 8 floors: _________

2. Mark each integer on the number line.

    a) +2   **b)** −7   **c)** +8   **d)** −3

3. Write the opposite of each integer.
Show the pairs of opposite integers on the number line.

    a) +1: ____________   **b)** −5: ____________   **c)** −7: ____________

Comparing and Ordering Integers

➤ You can use a number line to compare integers.

Compare +2 and –3.

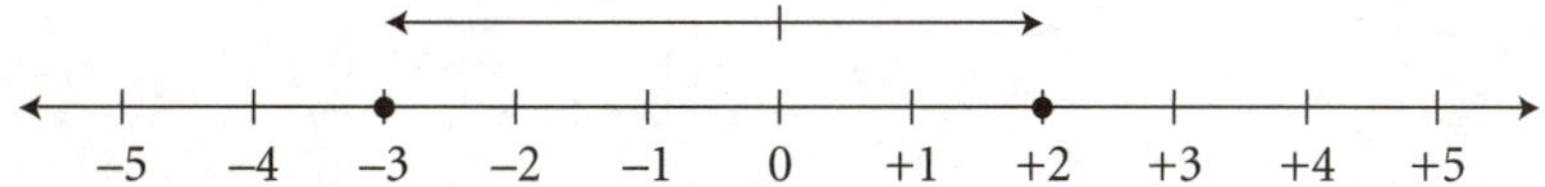

+2 is to the right of –3 on a number line.
+2 is greater than –3, so you write: +2 > –3
–3 is less than +2, so you write: –3 < +2
–3 < +2 or +2 > –3

➤ To order integers from least to greatest,
write them as they appear from left to right on a number line.

➤ To order integers from greatest to least,
write them as they appear from right to left on a number line.

Order +2, –3, 0, and +5 from least to greatest.

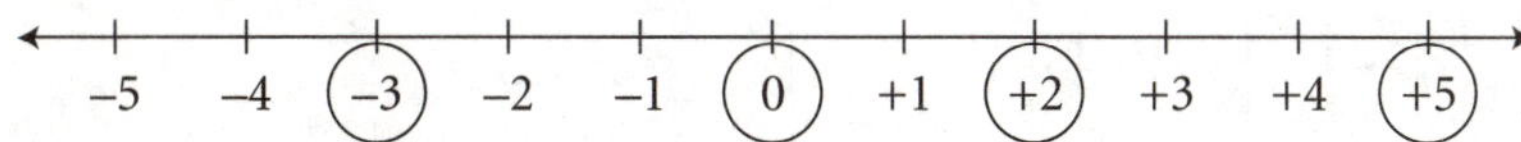

From left to right, or from least to greatest: –3, 0, +2, +5

4. Place either > or < between the integers. Use a number line if it helps.

a) +9 _______ 0

b) +7 _______ +2

c) +4 _______ +8

d) –10 _______ –1

e) –2 _______ +10

f) +2 _______ –10

5. Order the integers in each set from greatest to least.

a) +2, +4, –3

b) –3, +1, –4

c) +2, –7, –18

_______________   _______________   _______________

Quick Review

➤ You can use tiles to represent integers.

| + | represents +1. | | − | represents −1. | | + − = 0   This is a zero pair.

Here are 3 ways to model −3.

- − − −

- Each set models −3.

- Each set models −3.

➤ Write the integer modelled by these tiles.

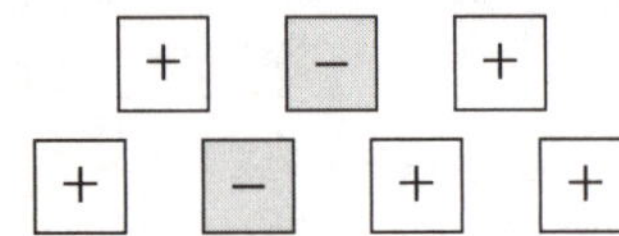

Arrange the tiles in rows.   Circle the zero pairs.

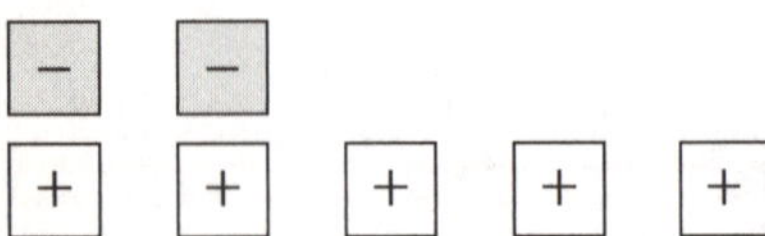 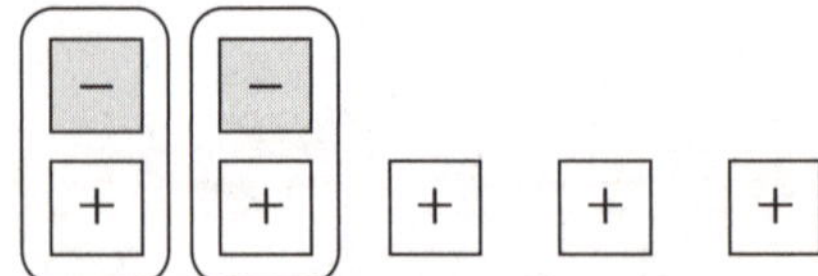

There are 3 + tiles left. They model +3.

1. Write the integer modelled by each set of tiles.

a) ______ 

b) ______ 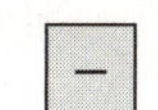

c) ______ 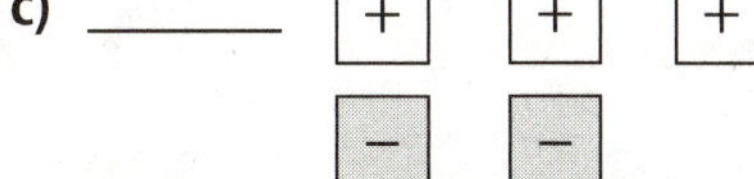

d) ______ 
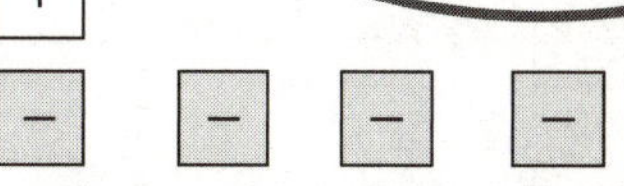

e) ______ 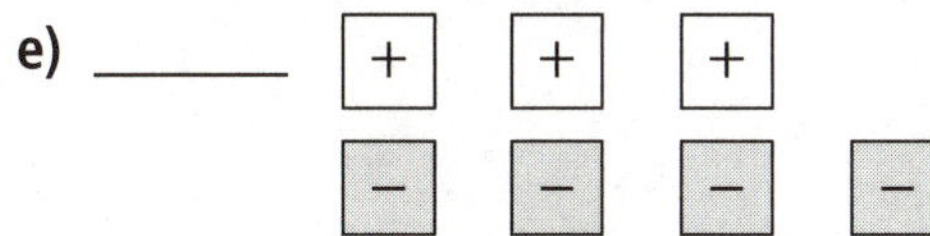

f) ______ 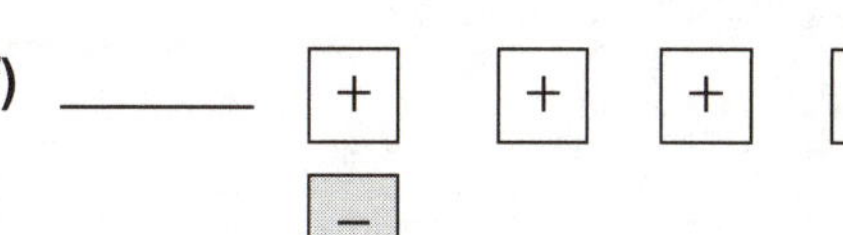

2. Draw tiles to model each integer.

a) +2

b) +5

c) −1

d) −3

e) +8

f) −7

3. Use tiles representing +1 and tiles representing −1.
Draw tiles to model +2 two more ways.

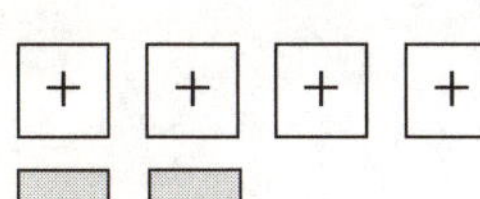

4. Explain why you cannot model +2 using three tiles.

____

____

____

____

Quick Review

You can add integers by modelling with tiles.

- Add: (−2) + (−4)

−2:   [−] [−]

−4:   [−] [−] [−] [−]

There are 6 [−] tiles.

They model −6.

So, (−2) + (−4) = −6

- Add: (+3) + (−4)

+3:   [+] [+] [+]

−4:   [−] [−] [−] [−]

Circle the zero pairs. Count the tiles that are left.

[+] [+] [+]
[−] [−] [−] [−]

There are 3 zero pairs.

There is 1 [−] tile left.

It models −1.

So, (+3) + (−4) = −1

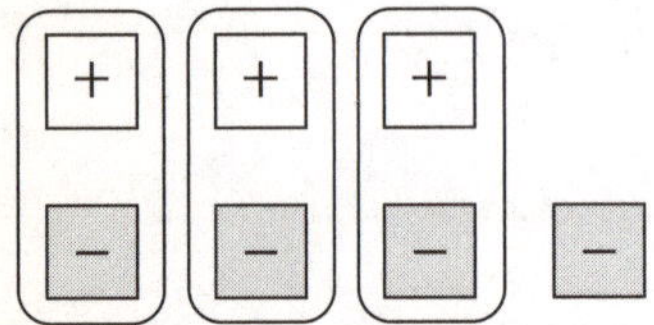

1. Use tiles representing +1 and tiles representing −1 to add (+4) + (−6).

Circle zero pairs.

What tiles are left? _______________

So, (+4) + (−6) = _______

2. Use tiles to add (−5) + (+3).

Circle zero pairs.

What tiles are left? ______________

(−5) + (+3) = _______

3. What sum does each set of tiles model?

a)

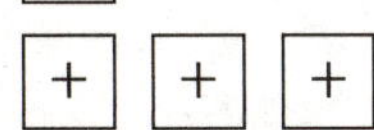

(+1) + (+3) = _______

b)

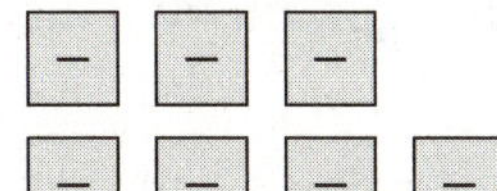

(−3) + _______ = _______

c)

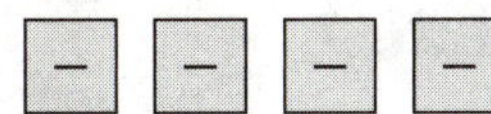

_______ + _______ = _______

d)

_______ + _______ = _______

4. Draw tiles to represent each sum. Complete the addition equation.

a) (+3) + (+4) = _______

b) (−2) + (+5) = _______

c) (−7) + (+2) = _______

d) (−3) + (+4) = _______

5. A mine elevator was at level −5 (5 levels below ground).
It went up 3 levels.
What level is it at now? _______

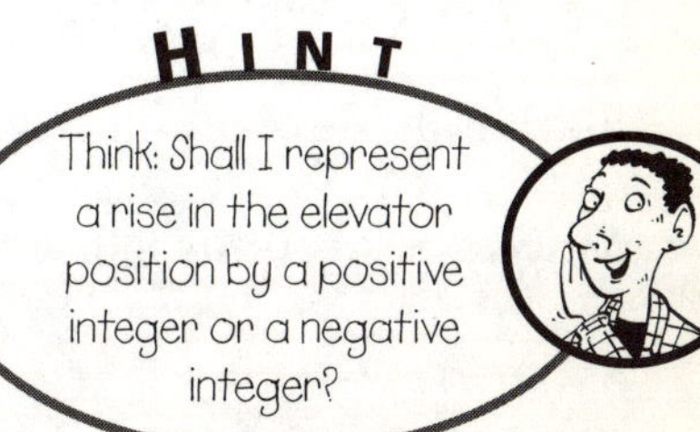

Quick Review

➤ You can add integers using a number line.

To add a positive integer, move right.
To add a negative integer, move left.

To add: $(-7) + (+13)$
Start at -7.
This is 7 units to the left of 0.

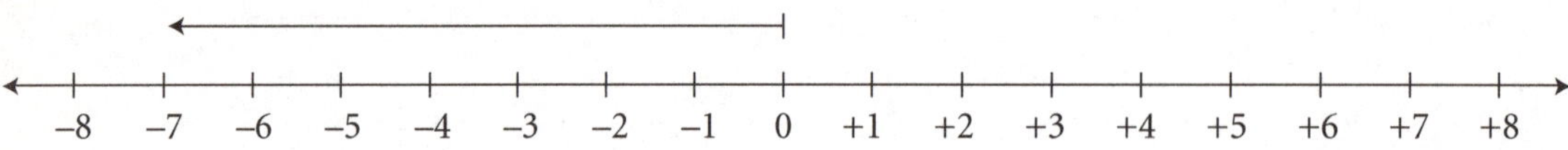

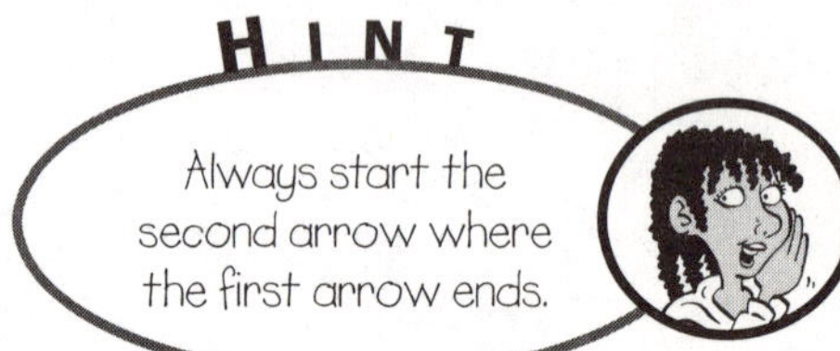

Then, add $+13$.
Move 13 units to the right.

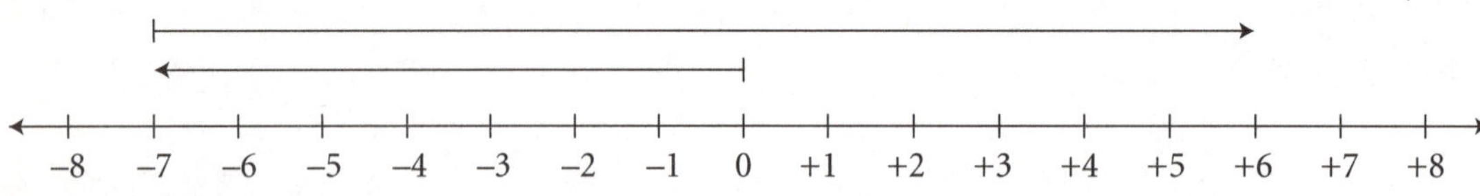

$(-7) + (+13) = +6$

Practice

1. Use the number line to add $(+3) + (-7)$.

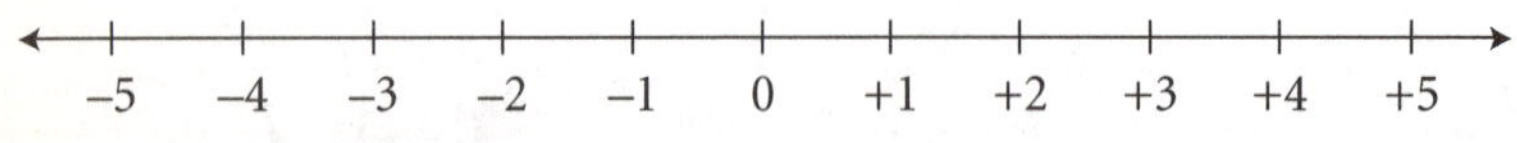

Start at 0. Move 3 units right.

Move _______ units left.

So, $(+3) + (-7) =$ _______

KEY TO SUCCESS

If you know different methods,
you can solve a problem in
one way, and check the answer
in another way.

2. Use the number line to add.

a) $(+4) + (-5) =$ _______

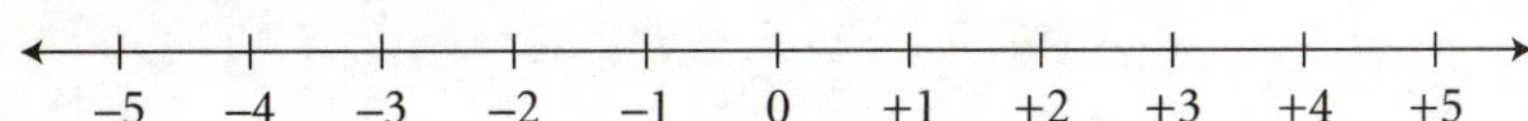

b) $(-2) + (-2) =$ _______

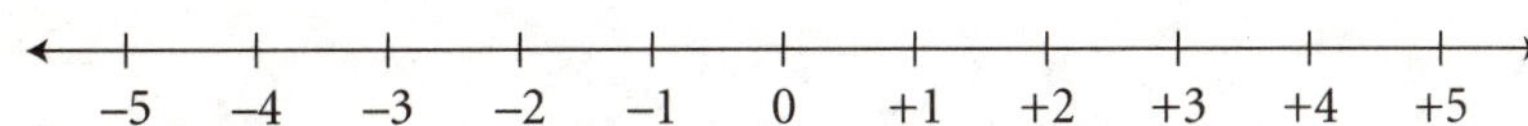

c) $(-4) + (+8) =$ _______

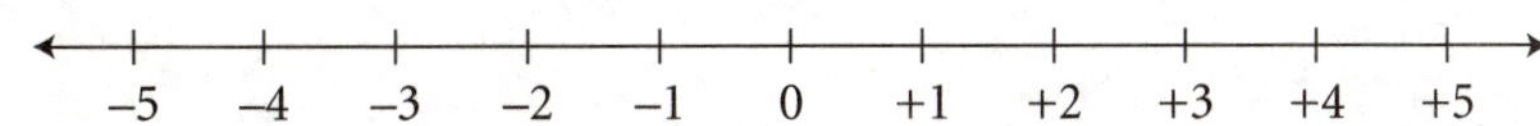

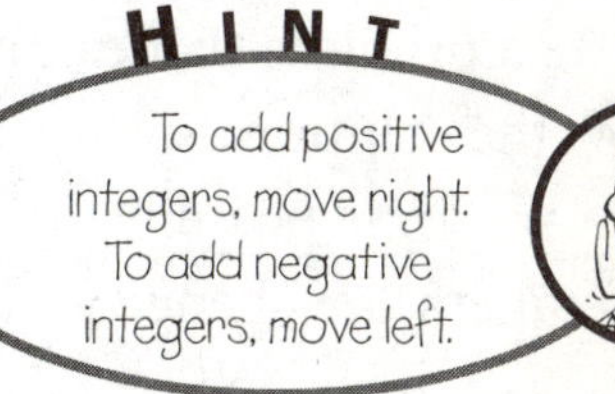

d) $(-1) + (+2) =$ _______

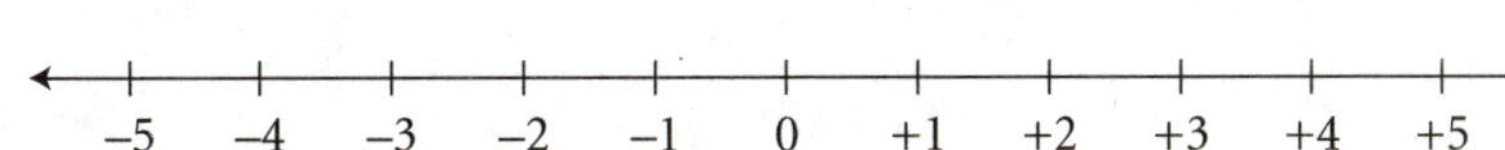

3. Add.

a) $(+4) + (+7) =$ _______   **b)** $(-2) + 0 =$ _______

c) $(+9) + (-5) =$ _______   **d)** $(-10) + (+3) =$ _______

4. Match each addition statement with its sum. The first one is done for you.

$(-6) + (-5)$	$+11$
$(-6) + (+5)$	-11
$(+6) + (-5)$	$+1$
$(+6) + (+5)$	-1

5. Add, using a method of your choice.
   Use a different method to check your work.

   a) $(-1) + (+5) = $ _______

   b) $(-8) + (+2) = $ _______

   c) $(-8) + (-6) = $ _______

   d) $(+2) + (-5) = $ _______

6. Kim earned $24 baby-sitting.
   He spent $7 buying lunch at school.

   How much does Kim have left? ___________

7. Create a problem that can be solved using integer addition.
   Show the solution.
   Here are some possible ideas.
   - temperature change
   - elevation change
   - bank balance

   ____

   ____

   ____

   ____

8. Play this game with 2 to 4 people.
   You will need a deck of cards with face cards removed, paper, and pencil.

   Red cards are negative. Black cards are positive.

   Deal 2 cards to each player.
   ➤ Players find the sum of their 2 numbers.
   ➤ If a player has a sum of 0, he or she is "out."
   ➤ Each remaining player takes 1 card from the deck.
     Add this number to the previous sum.
   ➤ Any player with a total of 0 is "out."
   ➤ Play continues until 1 player remains.
   ➤ The last player in the game wins.

Quick Review

➤ To model subtraction using tiles, begin by modelling the first number.
Then, take away tiles that model the number to be subtracted.
If there are not enough tiles to take away, add zero pairs.

Use tiles to subtract. $(-2) - (-4)$
Model -2.  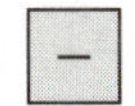

There are not enough tiles to take away -4.

You need more $-$ tiles.

Add 2 zero pairs.

 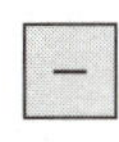 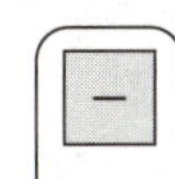 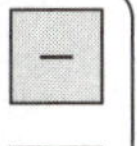
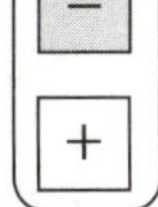

Now take away 4 $-$ tiles. 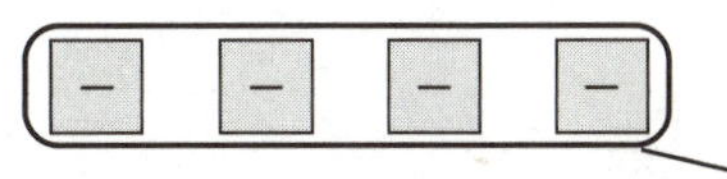
There are 2 $+$ tiles left.
These model $+2$, so we write: 

$(-2) - (-4) = +2$

Practice

1. Use tiles to subtract $(+2) - (+5)$.
Start with 2 $+$ tiles.   

Can you take away $+5$ from $+2$? ______

Add zero pairs until you can take away 5 $+$ tiles.

So, $(+2) - (+5) =$ ______

2. Use tiles to subtract $(-3) - (+4)$.

Model -3 with $\boxed{-}$ tiles.

Can you take away $+4$ from -3? ______

Add zero pairs until you can take away 4 $\boxed{+}$ tiles.

So, $(-3) - (+4) =$ ______

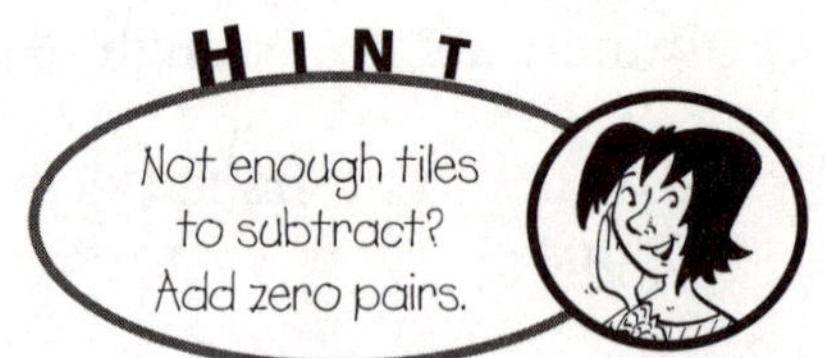

3. Draw tiles to represent each difference.
Then complete the subtraction equation.

a) $(+4) - (+3) =$ ______

$\boxed{+}$ $\boxed{+}$ $\boxed{+}$ $\boxed{+}$

b) $(-2) - (-5) =$ ______

$\boxed{-}$ $\boxed{-}$

c) $(+1) - (+6) =$ ______

d) $(+5) - (+3) =$ ______

4. Subtract.

a) $(-7) - (-5) =$ ______

b) $(+3) - (+8) =$ ______

c) $(+6) - (-4) =$ ______

d) $(+3) - (-2) =$ ______

5. Subtract. Then complete the subtraction equation.

C. $(+3) - (+5) =$ ______ E. $(-2) - (-1) =$ ______ L. $(+3) - (-1) =$ ______

I. $(+3) - (+3) =$ ______ H. $(-2) - (+1) =$ ______ T. $(+3) - (-3) =$ ______

O. $(+3) - (+1) =$ ______ N. $(-2) - (+3) =$ ______ R. $(+3) - (-5) =$ ______

Why is it always warm in Brazil and Peru? Fill in the corresponding letters to find out.

They are ____ ____ ____   ____ ____ ____ ____ ____ !
       -5 $+2$ $+6$ -2 -3 0 $+4$ -1

Quick Review

➤ You can subtract integers using a number line.

When you subtract, you move in the opposite direction of addition.
Subtraction is the opposite of addition.

To subtract: $(-1) - (-3)$
Start at -1.
This is 1 unit to the left of 0.

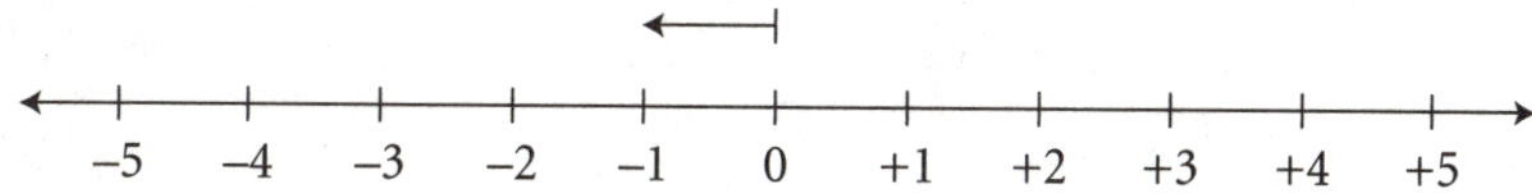

Then, move in the opposite direction of adding (-3).

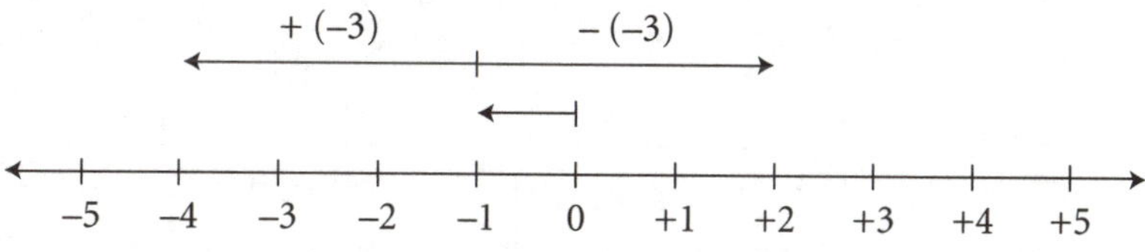

So, $(-1) - (-3) = +2$

➤ The result is the same as adding the opposite integer.
$(-1) - (-3)$ is the same as $(-1) + (+3)$. Both equal $+2$.

Practice

1. Use the number line to subtract $(+3) - (+5)$.

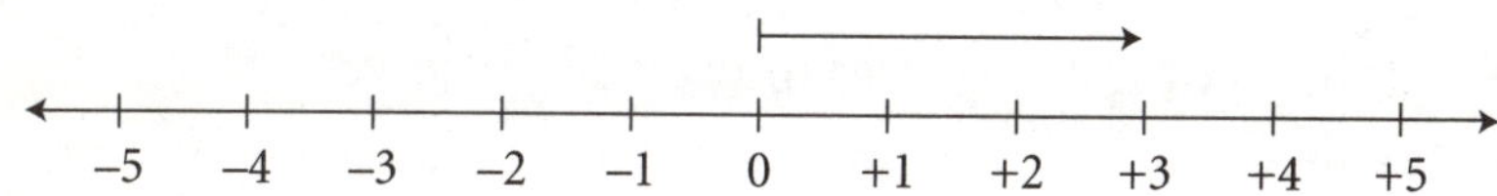

Start at 0. Move 3 units to the __________.

Then move _______ units left.

So, $(+3) - (+5) =$ _______

2. Use a number line to subtract.

a) $(+3) - (+4) = $ _______

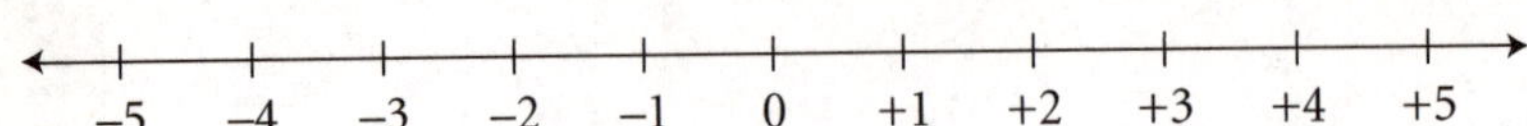

b) $(-2) - (+3) = $ _______

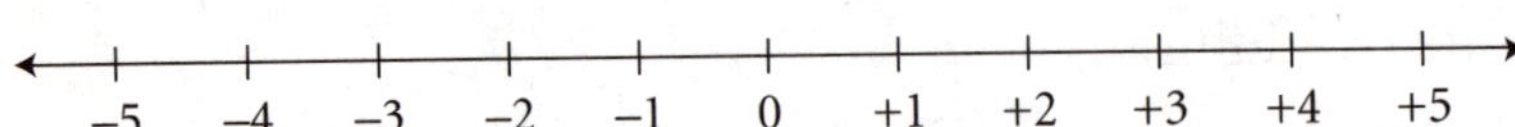

c) $(-1) - (-6) = $ _______

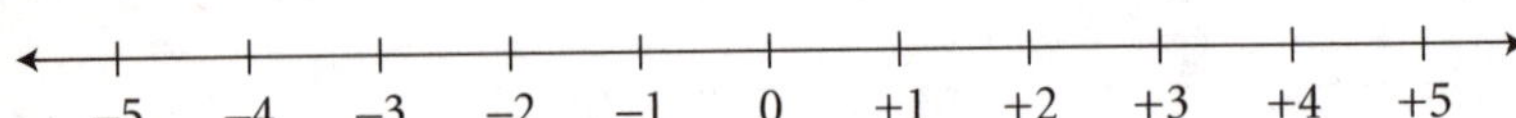

3. Rewrite each subtraction as an addition statement. Then use a number line to solve.

a) $(+4) - (+7) = (+4) + $ _______

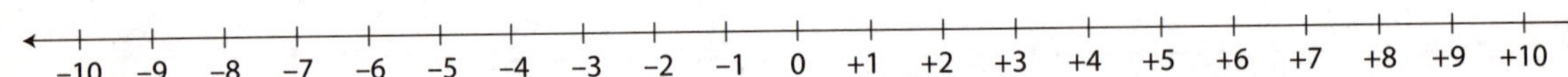

$(+4) - (+7) = $ _______

b) $(-3) - (-5) = (-3) + $ _______

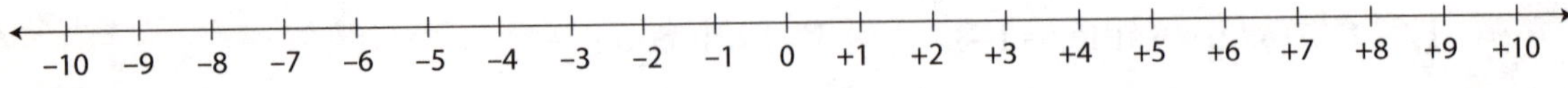

$(-3) - (-5) = $ _______

c) $(-1) - (+4) = $ _______ $+$ _______

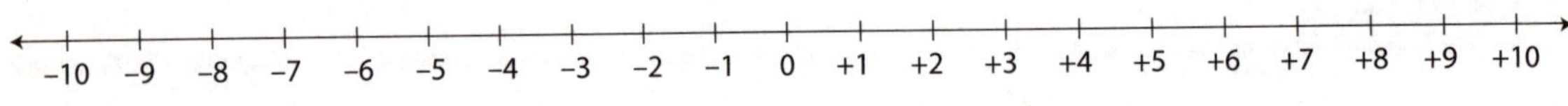

$(-1) - (+4) = $ _______

4. Rewrite each subtraction as the addition of the opposite integer. Then solve.

a) $(+2) - (-6) = (+2) + (+6)$

$= $ _______

b) $(-2) - (-4) = (-2) + $ _______

$= $ _______

c) $(+1) - (+5) = $ _______ $+$ _______

$= $ _______

d) $(-12) - (+9) = $ _______ $+$ _______

$= $ _______

5. Subtract.

a) $(+4) - (+7) = $ ______

b) $(+6) - (-5) = $ ______

c) $0 - (-4) = $ ______

d) $(-10) - (-2) = $ ______

e) $(+2) - (+12) = $ ______

f) $(-1) - (-10) = $ _____

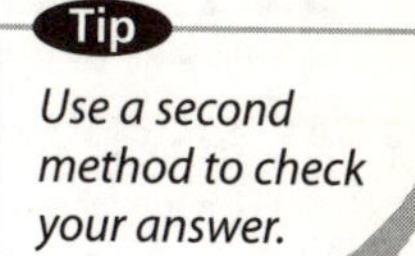

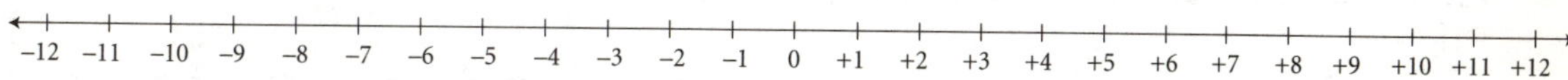

6. a) Ava's golf score changed from 2 above par to 3 below par.
How did her score change?

$(-3) - (+2) = $ ______   It decreased by ______.

b) Murphy's golf score changed from 1 below par to 5 above par.
How did his score change?

It _______________ by ______.

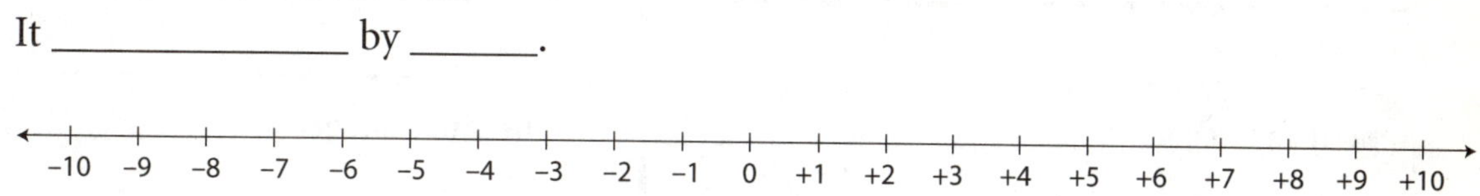

7. Play this game with a partner.
You will need a deck of cards with the face cards removed.
Use red cards to represent positive integers and black cards to represent negative integers.

➤ Shuffle the cards. Each player draws one card.
The player with the greater number takes the first turn.
➤ Shuffle the cards again and place them in a pile, face down.
➤ The player turns over the top 4 cards. She chooses 2 cards to play.
She uses the integers represented by these cards to make a subtraction statement.
The player records the difference.
➤ The partner checks the difference. This is the player's score for the round.
If the result is incorrect, it is erased.
The 4 cards are placed at the bottom of the pile.
➤ The play passes to the partner.
Each player records her or his own differences.
➤ After 4 rounds, the player with the lesser total score wins.

In Your Words

Here are some of the important mathematical words of this unit.
Build your own glossary by recording definitions and examples here. The first one is done for you.

negative number *any number less than zero*

A negative number appears to the left of zero on a number line.

For example, -2, -18, and -4000 are negative numbers.

integer

positive integer

negative integer

opposite integers

zero pair

List other mathematical words you need to know.

APK **1.** Show each integer on the number line.

    a) +1   **b)** −4   **c)** −11   **d)** +3

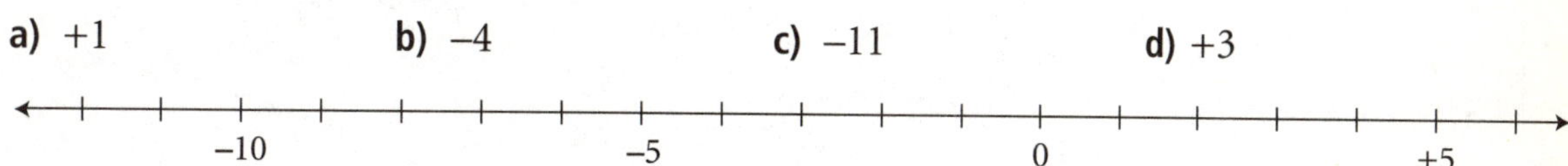

2. a) Place either < or > between the integers.

    i) +1 _______ −2   **ii)** −8 _______ 0   **iii)** −11 _______ −18

    b) Order all the integers in part a from least to greatest.

    _______, _______, _______, _______, _______, _______

2.1 **3.** Write the integer modelled by each set of tiles.

    a) 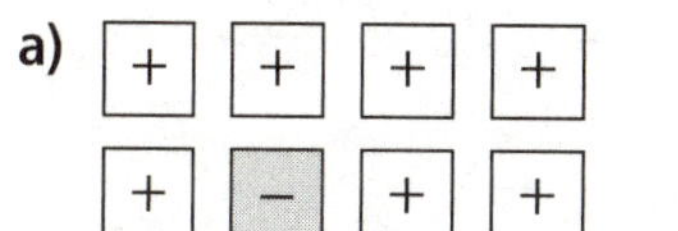   _______   **b)** 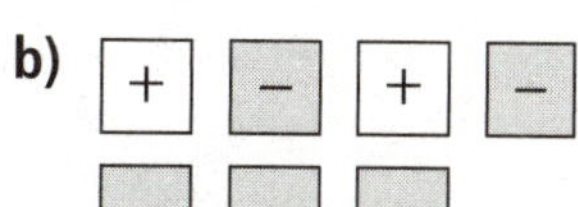   _______

4. One way to model −2 is shown.
Draw tiles to model −2 three more ways.

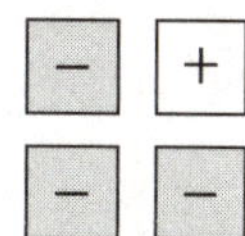

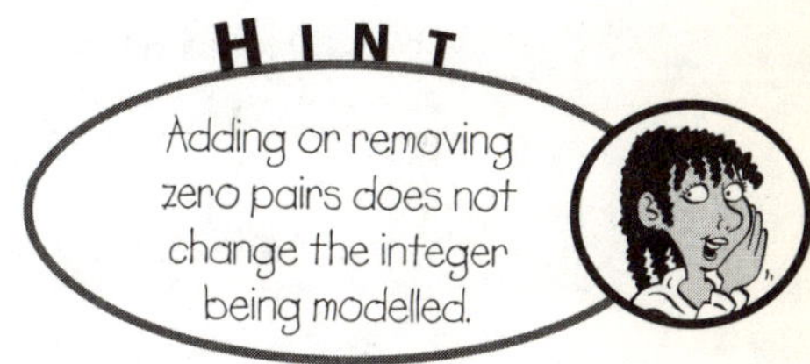

2.2 **5.** Use tiles to add.

    a) (+6) + (−5) = _______   **b)** (−3) + (+2) = _______

2.3 **6.** What type of integer do you get when you add two negative integers?
Explain how you know.

____

____

____

2.4 **7.** Use tiles to add or subtract.

a) $(+3) - (-2) = $ _______

b) $(+5) + (-4) = $ _______

2.5 **8.** Use a number line to add or subtract.

a) $(+5) + (-8) = $ _______

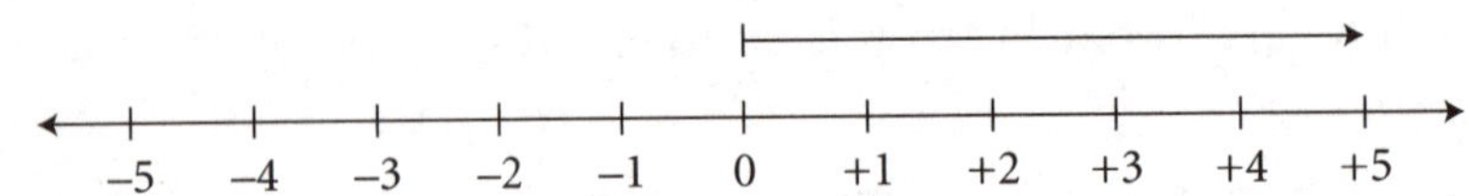

b) $(-4) - (-7) = $ _______

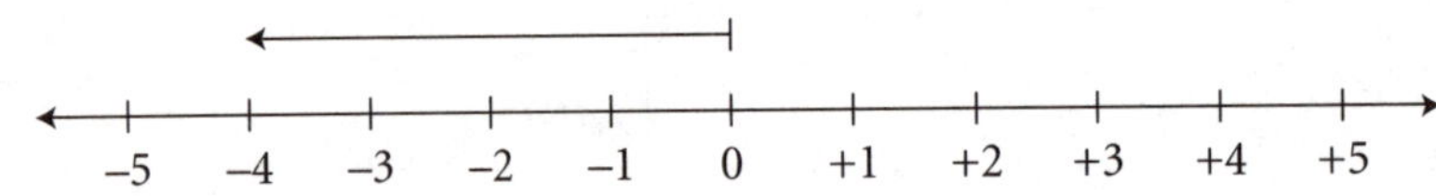

c) $(-4) + (+6) = $ _______

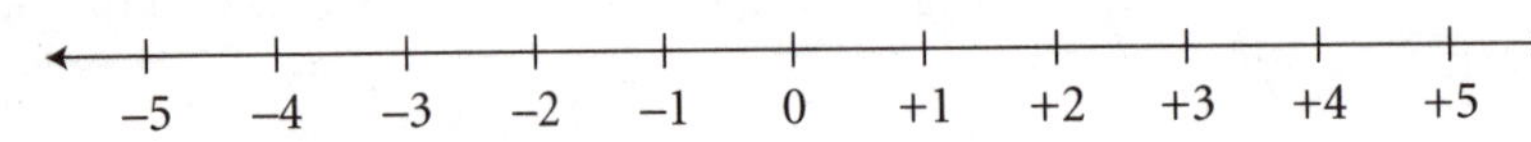

d) $(-3) - (-7) = $ _______

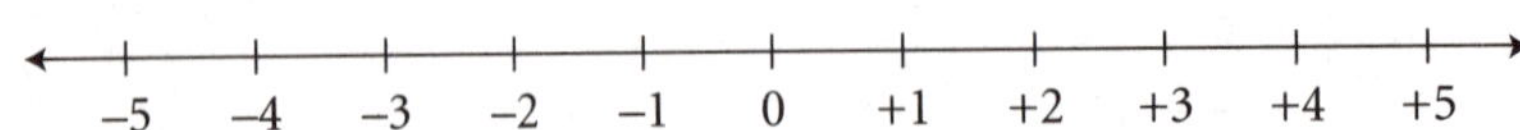

9. Calculate each difference.

a) The temperature went from $-7°C$ to $+8°C$.

____

b) The temperature went from $+20°C$ to $+3°C$.

____

Fractions, Decimals, and Percents

Just for Fun

Magic Square

In a Magic Square, the numbers in each row, column, and diagonal have the same sum, which is called the Magic Sum.
Complete this Magic Square.

Magic Sum: _____

9.3	3.6	
	6.0	
		2.7

What Tree Is It?

What tree does a math teacher climb?

______ ______ ______ ______ ______ ______ ______ ______ ______ ______ ______

To solve the riddle:

- unscramble the letters in each row to form a math word
- for each word, circle the letter indicated in brackets

The circled letters will solve the riddle.

gaptinree   ___ ___ ___ ___ ___ ___ ___ ___ ___   (last letter)

tvaeilnuqe   ___ ___ ___ ___ ___ ___ ___ ___ ___ ___   (1st letter)

mnoocm   ___ ___ ___ ___ ___ ___   (2nd letter)

ledcima   ___ ___ ___ ___ ___ ___ ___   (5th letter)

rotaremun   ___ ___ ___ ___ ___ ___ ___ ___ ___   (4th letter)

ncafrtio   ___ ___ ___ ___ ___ ___ ___ ___   (5th letter)

dnmortaeino   ___ ___ ___ ___ ___ ___ ___ ___ ___ ___ ___   (last letter)

umltipyl   ___ ___ ___ ___ ___ ___ ___ ___   (last letter)

Mental Math

There are many ways to calculate mentally.

- Look for 10s, or the nearest 10.
- Add or subtract in a different order.
- Separate a number into smaller parts to obtain friendly numbers.

Example 1

Use mental math.

a) 36×4 **b)** $403 + 55 - 4$ **c)** $305 + 498$

Solution

a) Separate 36 into 30 and 6:

$30 \times 4 + 6 \times 4$

$= 120 + 24$

$= 144$

b) Subtract first: **c)** $498 = 500 - 2$

$55 - 4 = 51$ Then: $305 + 500 - 2 = 803$

Then: $403 + 51 = 454$

 **Check**

1. Use mental math.

a) $289 + 171 = 289 + \underline{\quad} + 170$ **b)** 51×2

$\quad\quad = \underline{\quad\quad} + 170$ $50 \times 2 = \underline{\quad\quad}$ $1 \times 2 = \underline{\quad\quad}$

$\quad\quad = \underline{\quad\quad}$ $\underline{\quad\quad\quad\quad}$

2. Use mental math. Explain your strategy.

a) $65 \times 3 = \underline{\quad\quad\quad\quad}$ **b)** $158 + 86 = \underline{\quad\quad\quad}$ **c)** $34 \times 25 \times 4 = \underline{\quad\quad\quad}$

Percent

Percent means "per hundred" or "out of 100."
One whole, or 1, is 100%.

So: 25% is $\frac{25}{100}$ 4% is $\frac{4}{100}$ 100% is $\frac{100}{100}$ or 1

Example 2

This is a hundredths grid.

a) What percent of the hundredths grid is shaded?
b) What percent of the hundredths grid is not shaded?

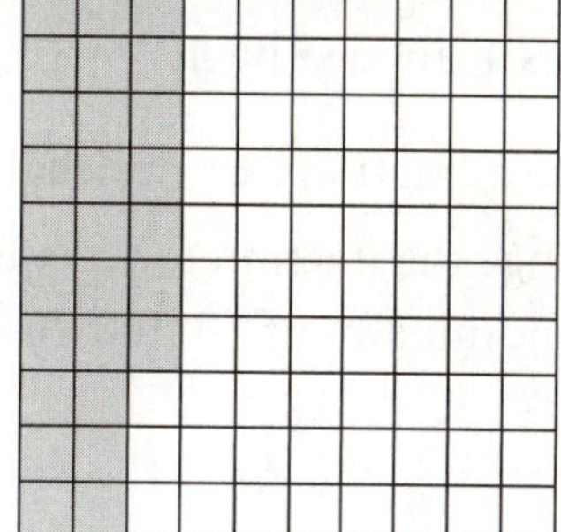

Solution

a) 27 out of 100 squares are shaded.

$$\frac{27}{100} = 27\%$$

27% of the grid is shaded.

b) 73 out of 100 squares are not shaded.

$$\frac{73}{100} = 73\%$$

73% of the grid is not shaded.

✓ Check

3. Write a fraction with denominator 100 for the shaded part of each hundredths grid.
Then write each fraction as a percent.

a)

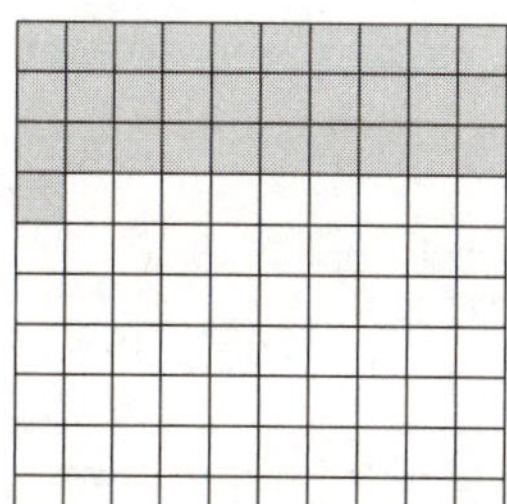

__________ = __________

b)

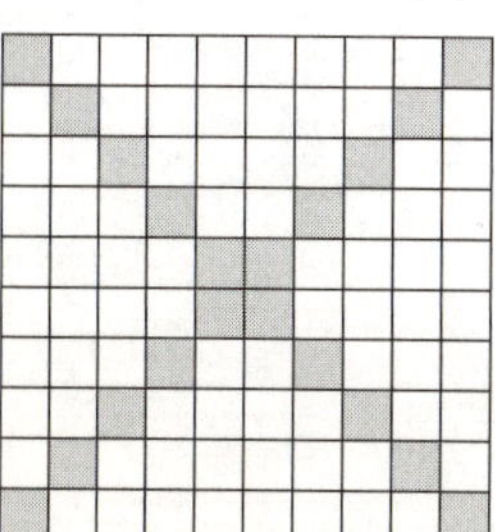

__________ = __________

Quick Review

➤ $\frac{1}{4}$ is read as one-fourth, or one-quarter.

$\frac{1}{4}$ means 1 divided by 4.

➤ To write a fraction as a decimal:

- Change the fraction to an equivalent fraction with a denominator of 10, 100, or 1000.

$$\frac{1}{4} \;\overset{\times 25}{\underset{\times 25}{=}}\; \frac{25}{100} = 0.25$$

- Or, divide the numerator by the denominator.
  1 divided by 4

$$
\begin{array}{r}
0.25 \\
4\overline{)1.00} \\
\underline{8} \\
20 \\
\underline{20} \\
00
\end{array}
$$

0.25 is a terminating decimal.
It has a definite number of decimal places.

➤ Look at this fraction:
$\frac{25}{99} = 0.252525\ldots = 0.\overline{25}$

$0.\overline{25}$ is a repeating decimal.
You draw a bar over the repeating digits.

➤ You can use patterns to change some decimals to fraction form.
Since $\frac{4}{9} = 0.\overline{4}$ $\qquad \frac{5}{9} = 0.\overline{5}$ $\quad \frac{8}{9} = 0.\overline{8}$,

you can use the pattern to predict that the fraction for $0.\overline{2}$ is $\frac{2}{9}$.

1. Identify each decimal as terminating or repeating.

a) 2.5______________________   b) 9.0______________________

c) $22.\overline{2}$______________________   d) 0.37______________________

e) $2.\overline{152}$______________________   f) 3.125______________________

2. Match each fraction with its corresponding decimal.

$\frac{5}{9}$ $0.1\overline{6}$ Which fractions form terminating decimals?

$\frac{16}{99}$ $0.\overline{5}$ _______________________________________

$\frac{1}{6}$ 0.5 Which fractions form repeating decimals?

$\frac{5}{10}$ $0.\overline{16}$ _______________________________________

3. Complete this table.

Fraction in simplest form				$\frac{12}{25}$		$\frac{9}{50}$
Fraction with denominator 10, 100, or 1000	$\frac{6}{10}$		$\frac{125}{1000}$			
Decimal		0.35			0.256	

4. Use a calculator to write each fraction as a decimal.

a) $\frac{2}{9}$ _______   b) $\frac{5}{8}$ _______   c) $\frac{5}{24}$ _________

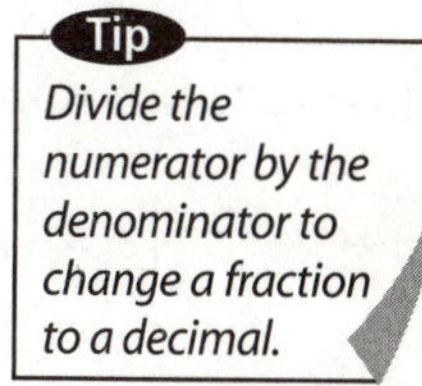

5. a) Express the fractions $\frac{8}{99}$, $\frac{9}{99}$, $\frac{10}{99}$, $\frac{11}{99}$, as decimals.

____

b) Describe the pattern in the decimals in part a.

____

____

c) Use the pattern to predict the decimal forms of $\frac{5}{99}$ and $\frac{21}{99}$. __________________

Quick Review

To order 3.25, $3\frac{1}{8}$, and $\frac{11}{3}$ from least to greatest:

➤ Use benchmarks on a number line.
Compare the fraction parts of the numbers.
3.25 is halfway between 3 and 3.5. $3\frac{1}{8}$ is close to 3.

$$\frac{11}{3} = \frac{9}{3} + \frac{2}{3} = 3\frac{2}{3}$$

$3\frac{2}{3}$ is greater than $3\frac{1}{2}$.

$$3 \qquad 3\tfrac{1}{8} \quad 3.25 \qquad\qquad 3\tfrac{1}{2}=3.5 \quad \tfrac{11}{3} \qquad\qquad 4$$

So, from least to greatest: $3\frac{1}{8}$, 3.25, $\frac{11}{3}$

➤ Use place value.
Express each number as a decimal. Use a calculator.

$$3.25 \qquad 3\frac{1}{8} = 3.125 \qquad \frac{11}{3} = 3.\overline{6}$$

Compare the digits, beginning with the greatest place value.
In the ones place: 3.25, 3.125, and $3.\overline{6}$ have the same value, which is 3.
In the tenths place: 1 tenth < 2 tenths < 6 tenths
So, $3.125 < 3.25 < 3.\overline{6}$

So, from least to greatest: $3\frac{1}{8}$, 3.25, $\frac{11}{3}$

To write a fraction between $3\frac{1}{8}$ and $3\frac{1}{4}$:

Since $3\frac{1}{4} = 3\frac{2}{8}$, find a fraction between $3\frac{1}{8}$ and $3\frac{2}{8}$.

Write equivalent fractions with common denominator 16.

$$3\frac{1}{8} = 3\frac{2}{16} \qquad 3\frac{2}{8} = 3\frac{4}{16}$$

Look at the numerators: 3 is between 2 and 4

So, $3\frac{3}{16}$ is between $3\frac{1}{8}$ and $3\frac{1}{4}$.

Practice

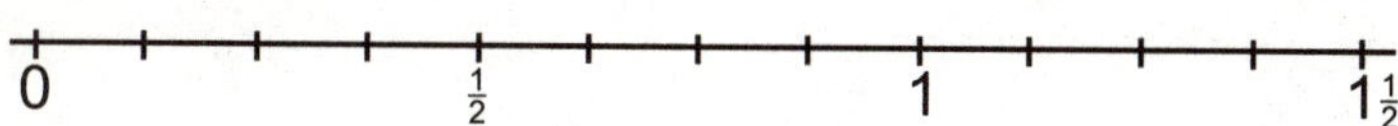

1. Use the number line to order each set of numbers from least to greatest.

a) $\frac{7}{8}, \frac{5}{8}, \frac{3}{8}, \frac{10}{8}$

From least to greatest: ______________________________

b) $\frac{4}{10}, \frac{12}{10}, \frac{9}{10}, 1\frac{4}{10}$

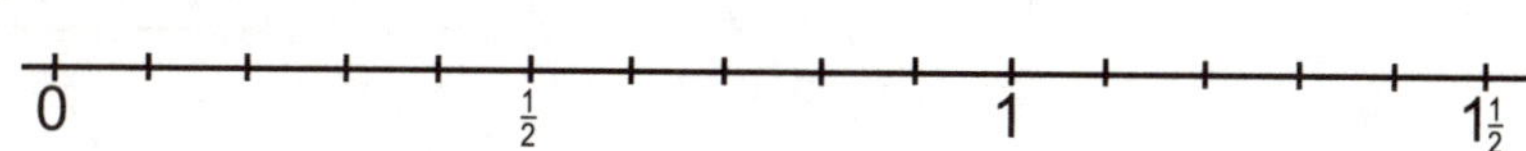

From least to greatest: ______________________________

2. Write >, <, or =.

a) $\frac{11}{7}$ ___ $\frac{10}{9}$ **b)** $\frac{21}{8}$ ___ $\frac{31}{12}$ **c)** $\frac{17}{7}$ ___ $2\frac{3}{4}$

d) $1\frac{1}{2}$ ___ $\frac{24}{16}$ **e)** $\frac{24}{5}$ ___ $\frac{48}{10}$ **f)** $3\frac{4}{5}$ ___ $\frac{78}{25}$

Tip
Find equivalent fractions.

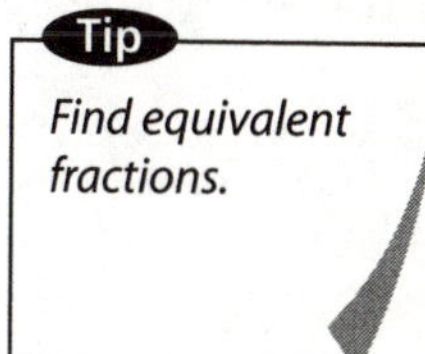

3. Use benchmarks and a number line to order this set of numbers from greatest to least.

$\frac{7}{12}, \frac{5}{6}, \frac{3}{4}, \frac{2}{3}$

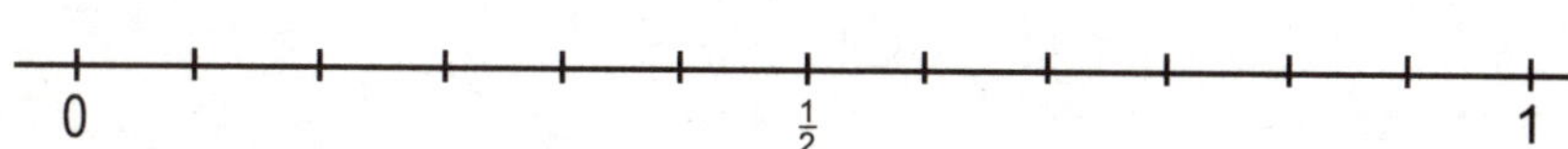

From greatest to least: ______________

4. Use benchmarks and a number line to order each set of numbers from least to greatest.

a) $\frac{11}{12}, \frac{1}{3}, \frac{7}{6}, \frac{5}{4}$

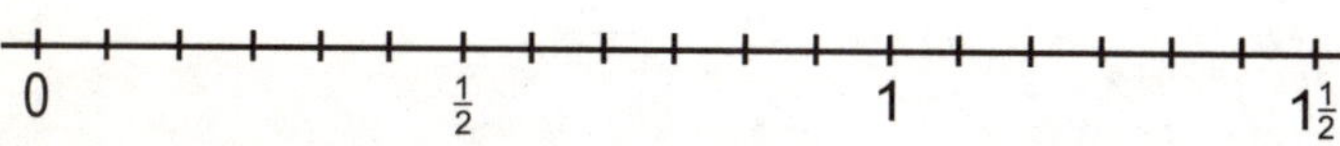

From least to greatest: ______________

b) $2\frac{1}{12}, \frac{15}{8}, \frac{17}{6}, 2\frac{3}{4}$

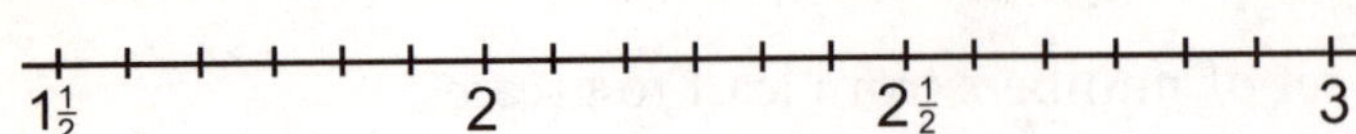

From least to greatest: _________________________

5. Write each fraction as a decimal. Then insert <, >, or =.

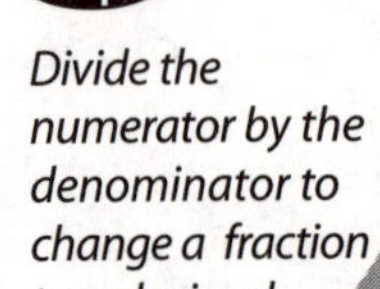

a) $\frac{1}{2}$ ____ 0.43: _____________

b) $\frac{1}{12}$ ____ $0.\overline{3}$: _____________

c) 0.675 ____ $\frac{7}{8}$: _____________

d) 0.575 ____ $\frac{7}{12}$: _____________

6. Use place value to order each set of numbers from least to greatest.

a) $0.97, \frac{7}{8}, \frac{19}{20}, 0.8, \frac{9}{10}$: _____________________

From least to greatest: _________________________

b) $1\frac{5}{12}, 1.\overline{552}, 1\frac{9}{16}, 1.89, 1.0\overline{12}$: _____________________

From least to greatest: _________________________

7. Determine a number between the two given numbers. Answers may vary.

a) $\frac{4}{3}$ ___ $\frac{7}{6}$ **b)** $2\frac{1}{10}$ ___ $\frac{11}{5}$ **c)** $5\frac{1}{5}$ ____ 5.3   **d)** $1.\overline{3}$ ___ $\frac{10}{6}$

8. Jeremiah thinks that $3\frac{5}{8}, \frac{35}{8}$, and 3.58 are equivalent. Is he correct? ______

Explain how you know. ____

____

Quick Review

➤ Add: 5.763 + 3.94

Step 1 Use front-end estimation to estimate the sum: $5 + 3 = 8$
Step 2 Add. Write each number with the same number of decimal places,
using zeros as place holders. Record the numbers without the decimal points.

```
  5763
+ 3940
  9703
```

Since the estimate is 8, place the decimal point after the 9.
The sum is 9.703.

➤ Subtract: 5.763 − 3.94

Step 1 Use front-end estimation to estimate the difference: $5 - 3 = 2$
Step 2 Subtract. Write each number with the same number of decimal places,
using zeros as place holders. Record the numbers without the decimal points.

```
  5763
− 3940
  1823
```

Since the estimate is 2, place the decimal point after the 1.
The difference is 1.823.

Practice

1. Use front-end estimation to estimate each sum or difference.

a) 13.1 + 2.4 ___________   b) 4.52 + 3.09 __________

c) 87.6 − 73.5 ___________   d) 8.47 − 7.16 __________

2. Add. Use front-end estimation to place the decimal point.

a) 3.51 + 9.73   b) 2.168 + 0.948   c) 7.169 + 8.47   d) 6.7 + 0.491

_________   _________   _________   _________

> **Tip**
> *Rewrite the question to make the calculation easier.*

3. Subtract. Use front-end estimation to place the decimal point.

a) 9.73 − 0.41   b) 6.371 − 1.09   c) 4.152 − 4.097   d) 3.6 − 1.981

_________   _________   _________   _________

4. The difference in the masses of 2 objects is 0.479 kg.

    a) What might the mass of each object be? _______________________________________

    b) What might the objects be? ____

5. Salvatore ran 2.457 km on Saturday and 3.169 km on Sunday.

    a) Estimate to find out about how far he ran on both days. ____________________

    b) Calculate how far Salvatore ran on both days. ________________________________

    c) Estimate how much farther he ran on Sunday than on Saturday. ______________

    d) Calculate how much farther Salvatore ran on Sunday than on Saturday. ________

6. When the Andisons left on a trip, the trip meter on their car showed 63589.2 km.
When they returned home, the trip meter showed 67178.4 km.

    a) Estimate to find the distance the Andisons drove on their trip. ______________

    b) Calculate the distance the Andisons drove. ___________________________________

7. Silvia purchased these groceries: peanut butter for $3.18, smoked turkey for $5.43,
bread for $2.29, milk for $1.89, and fish for $6.79.

    a) Estimate to find the total cost of the groceries without tax.

    ____

    b) Calculate the total cost of Silvia's purchases. ________

    c) What is the difference in prices of the peanut butter and the fish? ____________

    d) Silvia gave the clerk $20.00. How much change should she receive? ____________

8. Paul packages boxes of apples for an orchard.
In one hour, Paul lifted, weighed, and stored five boxes of apples with these masses:
9.71 kg, 9.39 kg, 8.97 kg, 8.72 kg, 8.98 kg

    a) Estimate to find the total mass. ____

    b) Calculate the total mass. __________

Quick Review

➤ You can use Base Ten Blocks to multiply decimals.
To multiply 2.4×1.8, display the Base Ten Blocks as shown.
The flat represents 1.
The rod represents 0.1.
The small cube represents 0.01.
This picture shows the product
$$2.4 \times 1.8 = 1 + 1 + 0.8 + 0.8 + 0.4 + 0.32$$
$$= 4.32$$

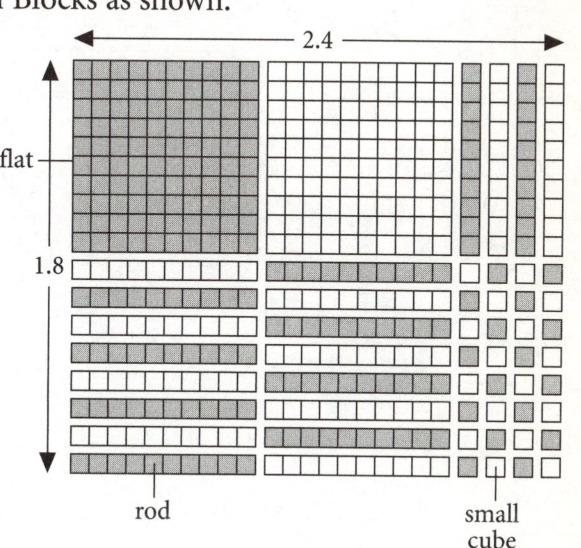

➤ You can multiply decimals the same
way you multiply whole numbers.
To multiply 2.4×1.8, multiply 24×18.

$$\begin{array}{r} 24 \\ \times\ 18 \\ \hline 432 \end{array}$$

Use front-end estimation to place the decimal point: $2 \times 1 = 2$
So, 2.4×1.8 is about 2.
Place the decimal point between the 4 and the 3.
So, the product is 4.32.

Practice

1. Write a multiplication equation for each picture.
Each small square represents 0.01.

a)

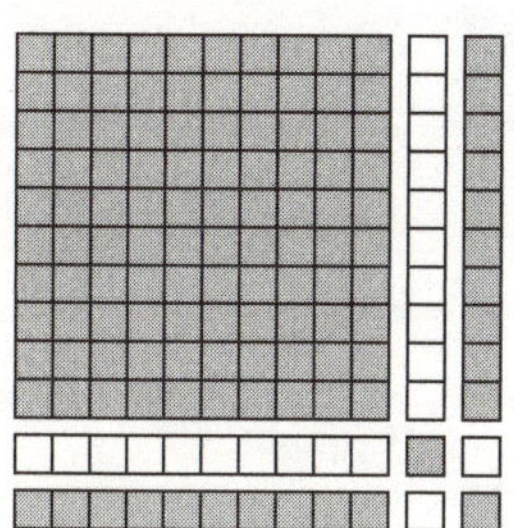

b)

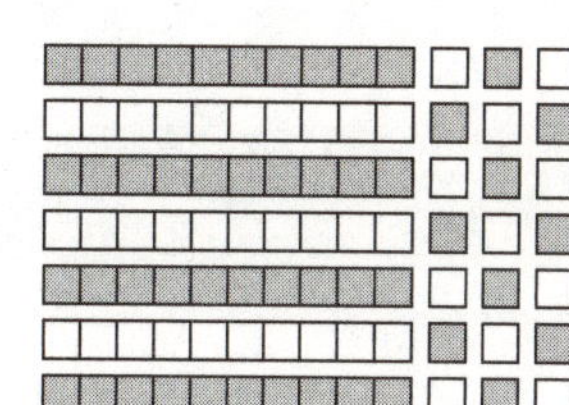

___________________   ___________________

2. Use Base Ten Blocks to find each product.
Record your work on the grid.

a) 2.6 × 1.3

__________ flats × 1 = __________

__________ rods × 0.1 = __________

__________ small cubes = __________

The product is __________ + __________ + __________ = __________

b) 2.1 × 0.8

The product is __________.

c) 0.7 × 0.3

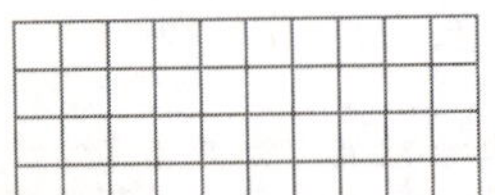

The product is __________.

3. Multiply. Use front-end estimation to place the decimal point in the answer.

a) 6.3×0.7

Multiply: 63×7

$$\begin{array}{r} 63 \\ \times\ 7 \\ \hline \end{array}$$

Estimate to place the decimal point.

$6.3 \times 0.7 = $ _____

b) 1.8×1.4

Multiply: 18×14

$1.8 \times 1.4 = $ _____

c) 4.8×6

d) 3.4×2.1

e) 0.4×1.4

$4.8 \times 6 = $ _____　　　　$3.4 \times 2.1 = $ _____　　　　$0.4 \times 1.4 = $ _____

4. A rectangular room measures 2.3 m by 3.2 m.
Find the area of the room.

____

5. The product of 2 decimals is 0.24.
Write 3 pairs of decimals that give this product.

_____________　　_____________　　_____________

6. Chiang has a part-time job as a playground leader supervising children.
Her hourly wage is \$9.25. She works 17.5 h per week.

a) Find Chiang's weekly wage.

Estimate: _______________　Calculation: _________________________

b) How much money would Chiang earn in 5 weeks? _________________________

Quick Review

➤ You can use Base Ten Blocks to divide decimals,
similar to the way you multiplied decimals.
For example, to divide 3.6 ÷ 0.8:
Make a rectangle with an area of 3.6 and a width of 0.8:

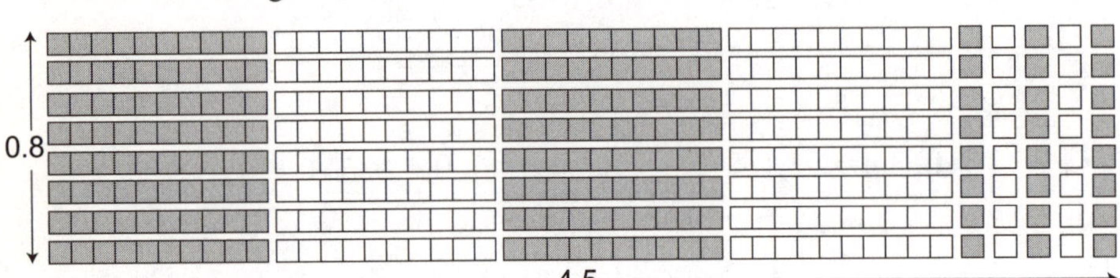

The length of the rectangle is 4.5.
So, 3.6 ÷ 0.8 = 4.5

➤ You can also divide decimals the same way as you divide whole numbers.
Use front-end estimation to place the decimal point.
For example, to divide 24.3 ÷ 0.6:
Estimate first: 24 ÷ 1 = 24
So, 24.3 ÷ 0.6 is about 24.

Divide as you would whole numbers.

$$
\begin{array}{r}
405 \\
6\overline{)2430} \\
24 \\
\hline
03 \\
00 \\
\hline
30 \\
30 \\
\hline
00
\end{array}
$$

Divide until the quotient terminates.

Since the estimate was 24, place the decimal point after the zero: 24.3 ÷ 0.6 = 40.5

Practice

1. Write a division equation for this picture. Each small square represents 0.01.

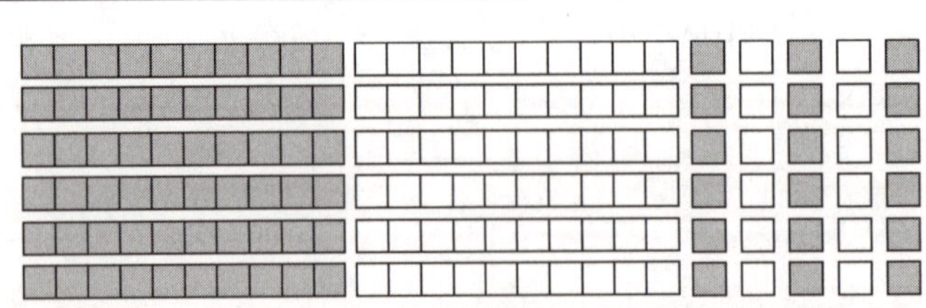

2. Use Base Ten Blocks to find each quotient.
Record your work on the grid.

a) $0.8 \div 0.5$

The quotient is:______

b) $0.98 \div 0.7$

The quotient is:______

3. Divide.
a) $17.4 \div 2.4$

b) $34.2 \div 3.6$

$17.4 \div 2.4$ is about

_______ $\div$ _______ = _______

So, $17.4 \div 2.4 =$ _________

So, $34.2 \div 3.6 =$ ______

c) $89.9 \div 3.1 =$ ___________

d) $15.3 \div 6.8 =$ _________

4. Divide.

a) $452 \div 10 =$ _________

    $452 \div 100 =$ _______

    $452 \div 1000 =$ ______

b) $89.12 \div 10 =$ _________

    $89.12 \div 100 =$ _________

    $89.12 \div 1000 =$ ________

Describe any patterns you see.

____

____

____

5. Divide.

a) $452 \div 0.1 =$ ___________

    $452 \div 0.01 =$ __________

    $452 \div 0.001 =$ ________

b) $89.12 \div 0.1 =$ __________

    $89.12 \div 0.01 =$ ________

    $89.12 \div 0.001 =$ _______

Describe any patterns you see.

____

____

____

6. Divide. Estimate to place the decimal point.

a) $3.9 \div 0.6$

    $3.9 \div 0.6$ is about:____________

b) $6.2 \div 0.8$

    $6.2 \div 0.8$ is about: ____________

So, $3.9 \div 0.6 =$ ______

So, $6.2 \div 0.8 =$ ______

c) $8.51 \div 0.2$

    $8.51 \div 0.2$ is about: ____________

d) $6.7 \div 0.5$

    $6.7 \div 0.5$ is about: ____________

So, $8.51 \div 0.2 =$ ____________

$6.7 \div 0.5 =$ ____________

7. A case of soup is on sale for $18.63.
There are 27 cans in a case.

What is the cost of each can of soup? _________

8. Divide. Write each quotient to the nearest tenth if necessary.

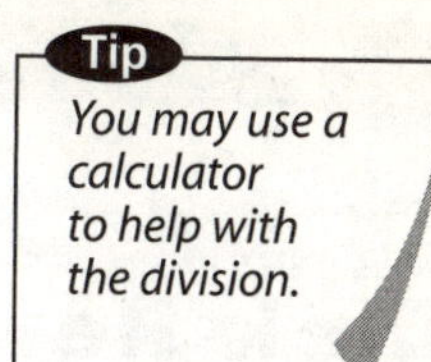

   a) $5.14 \div 1.07 =$ _________   b) $95 \div 5.4 =$ _________

   c) $80.96 \div 41.8 =$ _______   d) $381.5 \div 2.4 =$ _______

9. Sheldon rode his bicycle 53.4 km in 3 days.
   He rode the same distance each day.
   How far did Sheldon ride in 1 day?

10. Nadine has a part-time job after school.
    She earns $91.98 for working 12.6 h.
    How much does Nadine earn per hour? Use a calculator to find out.

11. The possible quotients for $72.09 \div 8.1$ are: 0.89, 89, 890, and 8.9.
    Which number is correct? Explain how you know.

12. The area of a rectangular room is approximately 47.3 m^2.
    The width of the room is 5.4 m.
    Find the length of the room.
    Write your answer to the nearest tenth.

Quick Review

You can use the same order of operations for decimals as you can
for whole numbers.

Here is the order of operations.
- Do the operations in brackets first.
- Then divide and multiply, in order, from left to right.
- Then add and subtract, in order, from left to right.

Practice

1. Evaluate.

a) $1.2 + 3.1 \times 2 - (2.7 + 0.6) \div 3$ Calculate in brackets.

   = _________________________   Multiply and divide from left to right.

   = _________________________   Add and subtract from left to right.

   = _________________________

b) $9.9 + 5 \times 4.6$ **c)** $(6.2 - 2.6) \div 2 =$ _______________

   = _____________________

   = _____________________

2. Evaluate.

a) $7 \times (6 + 7.1) =$ _______________   **b)** $16 - 9.6 \div 3.2 =$ _______________

c) $5.8 + 12.3 \times 3 =$ _______________   **d)** $4.9 + 17.6 \div 8 =$ _______________

3. a) Evaluate each expression.

$(5.3 + 7.5) \times (3 - 1) =$ _________________ $5.3 + 7.5 \times 3 - 1 =$ _________________

b) The numbers and operations are the same in the two expressions in part a. Explain why the results are different.

_________________________________   _________________________________

_________________________________   _________________________________

_________________________________   _________________________________

____

____

4. a) Evaluate each expression.

$7.2 \times 4.2 + 3.4 =$ _________________ $(7.2 \times 4.2) + 3.4 =$ _________________

b) Explain the results.

____

____

____

5. Evaluate.

a) $3.6 \times 5 - 4.8 \div 4 + 10.2 =$ _______   **b)** $(8.4 + 3.6) \div 6 \times 10 - 9.5 \times 2 =$ _______

6. A radio station contest used this skill-testing question: $4 + 6 \times 1.3 - 2.4 \div 2$
Grace said the answer was 10.6. Rob said the answer was 5.3.
Who was correct? How do you know?

____

____

____

Quick Review

You can describe part of a whole in 3 ways:

- as a fraction
- as a decimal
- as a percent

The hundredths grid has $\frac{3}{4}$ of the squares shaded.

➤ To write a fraction as a percent, first write the fraction with denominator 100.
75 out of 100 squares are shaded.

So, $\frac{3}{4} = 75\%$

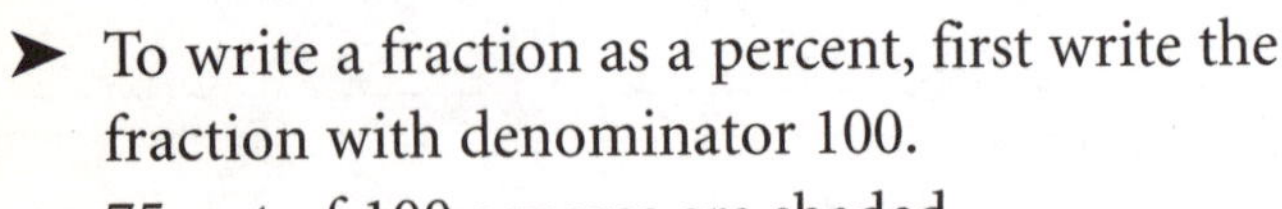

$$\frac{3}{4} = \frac{75}{100}$$

(× 25, × 25)

Since percent means per hundred, $\frac{75}{100} = 75\%$

If you divide 75 by 100, $\frac{75}{100} = 0.75$

So, $75\% = 0.75$

➤ You can use number lines to show the relationships among fractions, decimals, and percents. For example:

$$55\% = 0.55 = \frac{55}{100} = \frac{11}{20}$$

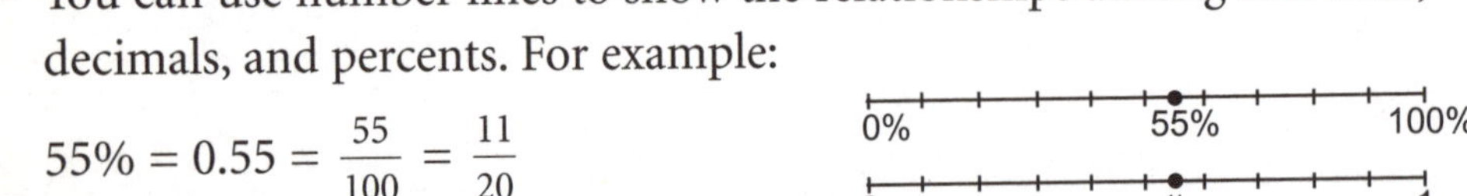

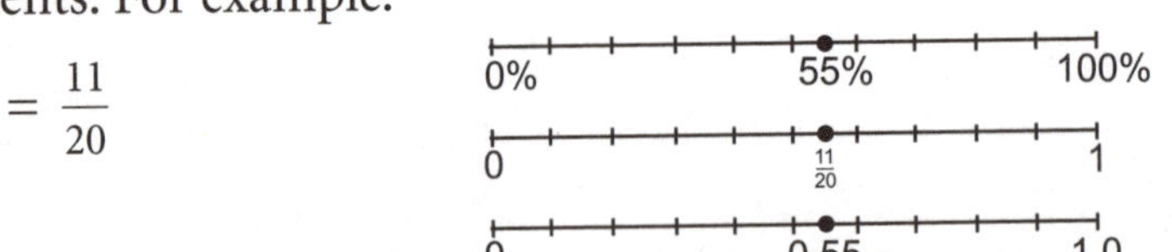

Practice

1. Use a fraction, decimal, and percent to describe the shaded part of each grid.

a)
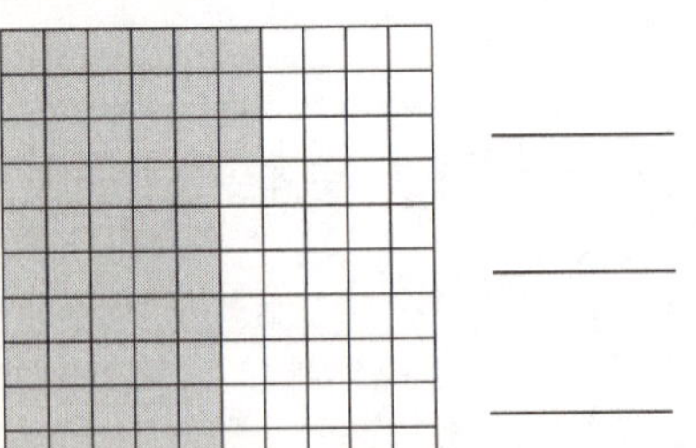

b)
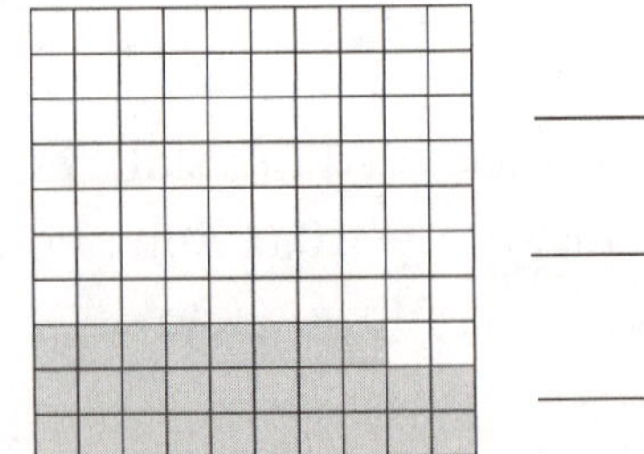

2. Complete the chart.

Shape	Shaded region as a fraction	Shaded region as a decimal	Shaded region as a percent
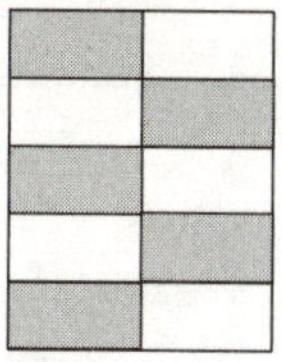			
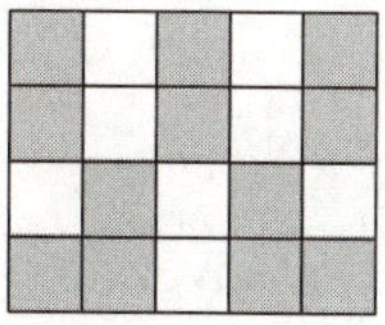			
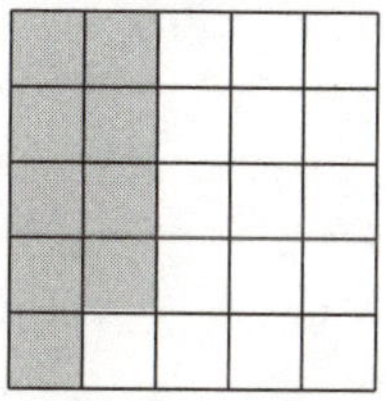			
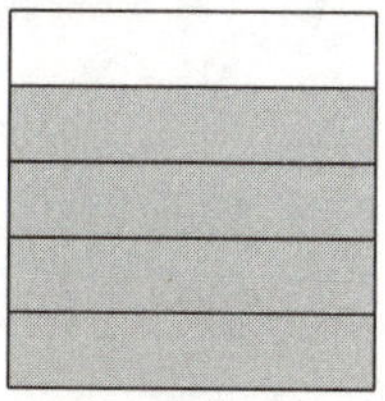			
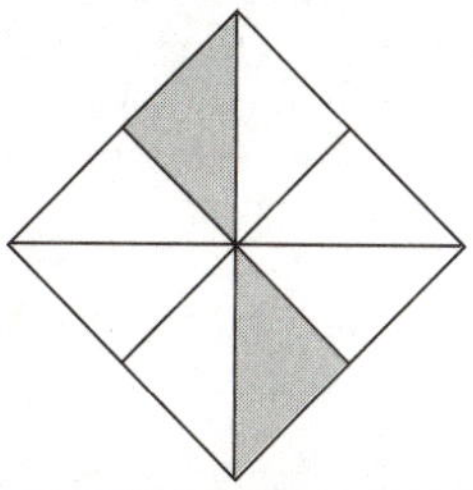			

3. Write each fraction as a decimal, and then as a percent.
Use a calculator if necessary.

a) $\frac{3}{10} =$ _______ = _______   **b)** $\frac{9}{10} =$ _______ = _______   **c)** $\frac{8}{50} =$ _______ = _______

d) $\frac{9}{20} =$ _______ = _______   **e)** $\frac{2}{5} =$ _______ = _______   **f)** $\frac{12}{40} =$ _______ = _______

g) $\frac{1}{5} =$ _______ = _______   **h)** $\frac{6}{30} =$ _______ = _______   **i)** $\frac{3}{25} =$ _______ = _______

4. Bennett had 19 out of 20 on a spelling test.

Write Bennett's mark as a percent.

---

5. In Ms. Khan's class, 22 out of 25 students hand in their projects on time.

What percent of the students hand in their projects on time?

---

6. Use 4 different colours to shade the squares on the hundredths grid below, as given in
the table.

Describe each coloured part as a fraction, a decimal, and a percent.

Colour	Fraction	Decimal	Percent
Red	$\frac{6}{25}$		
Yellow			35%
Green		0.20	
Purple			18%
White			

7. Lucy and Victor are sharing pens.

Lucy has $\frac{1}{4}$ of the pens, and Victor has 20% of the pens.

Who has more pens? Explain.

Since _______% > _______%, ____

8. Raymond surveyed 10 classmates to find out which shoe, left or right,
each person puts on first.

His results are shown in this table.

Left Shoe First	Right Shoe First
⦀⦀	⦀⦀

a) What percent of the students surveyed put on their left shoe first?

____

b) What percent of the students surveyed put on their right shoe first?

____

9. The Fashion Depot is having a big sale this week.

Everything is $\frac{1}{5}$ off the regular price.

What percent of the regular price do you pay? Explain.

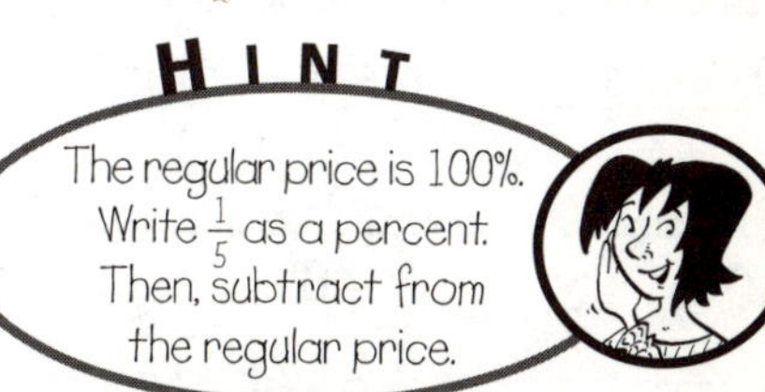

Quick Review

A scooter originally cost $90.00.
It is on sale at 40% off.
To find how much you save on the scooter,
find 40% of $90.00.

$$40\% = \frac{40}{100} = 0.40$$

So, 40% of $90.00 = 0.4 \times 90$
To multiply $0.4 \times \$90$, multiply
without the decimal point.

$$\begin{array}{r} 90 \\ \times\ \ 4 \\ \hline 360 \end{array}$$

Estimate to place the decimal point.
$90 is about $100.
1% of $100 is $1.
So, 40% of $100 is $40.

Insert the decimal point between the 6 and the 0.
So, 40% of $90 is $36.00.
You save $36 on the scooter.
You can show this on a number line.

```
$0              $36             $90
 +--+--+--+--+--+--+--+--+--+--+
0%              40%            100%
```

HINT

To calculate a percent
of a number, write the
percent as a decimal.

Practice

1. Find 10% of each number.

a) 60

10% of 60 = 0.1 × 60 = __________

b) 85

10% of 85 = _____ × _____ = _____

c) 150

d) 55

2. Find 30% of each number in question 1.

a) 3 × _________ = _____________

    30% of 60 = _____________

b) 3 × _________ = _____________

    30% of 85 = _____________

c) _________________________

    30% of 150 = _____________

d) _________________________

    30% of 55 = _____________

3. Find each percent.

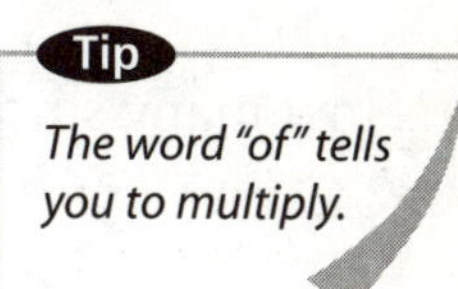

a) 7% of 80

$7\% = \dfrac{7}{100} =$ _______

_______ × 80 = _______

b) 1% of 25.5

____

____

c) 20% of 60.5

____

____

d) 37% of 182

____

____

4. Asher's new backpack costs $29.95, plus 14% sales tax.

a) How much sales tax does Asher pay? _________

b) How much does Asher pay in total for the backpack? _________

5. Here is a diagram of Sanjay's patio.
What percent of the patio does the hot tub take up?
Show your work.

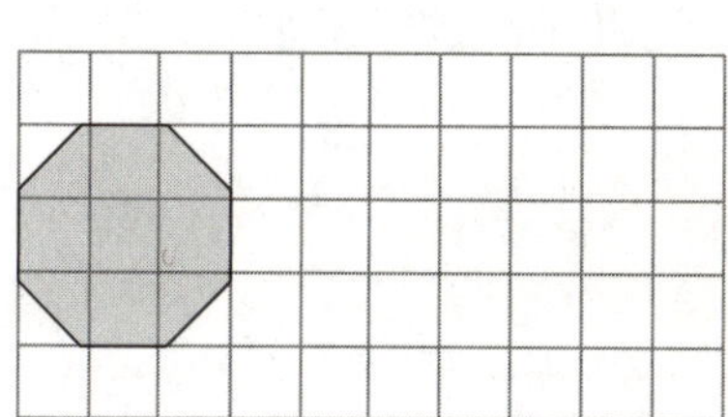

The hot tub takes up about _________ of Sanjay's patio.

6. Marco's dinner bill is $14.80.

He leaves the server a 15% tip.

How much does Marco pay for his dinner, including the tip?

Show your work.

So, Marco paid ____________ for his dinner.

7. There are 620 students at Irena's school.

Of these students, 45% have attended at least one other school.

a) How many students have attended more than 1 school?

So, ____________ students have attended more than 1 school.

b) How many students have attended just 1 school?

So, ____________ students have attended just 1 school.

8. Hraa has 120 baseball cards.

She gives 25% of them away.

How many cards does Hraa have left?

Hraa has ____________ cards left.

9. Which would you rather have? Explain.

90% of $70 or 15% of $500

In Your Words

Here are some of the important mathematical words of this unit.
Build your own glossary by recording definitions and examples here. The first one is done for you.

fraction

a way to show part of a whole; for example, $\frac{3}{4}$ shows 3 parts of a whole that has been divided into 4 equal parts

A fraction also shows division: $3 \div 4$

benchmark

equivalent fractions

repeating decimal

terminating decimal

percent

List other mathematical words you need to know.

Unit Review

3.1 **1.** Write each fraction as a decimal.
Identify each decimal as terminating or repeating.

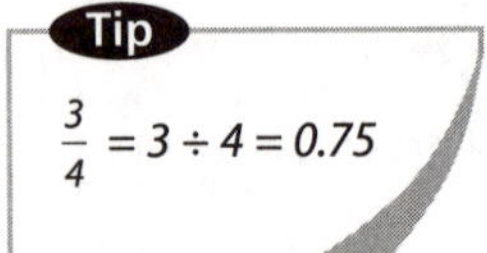

a) $\frac{3}{10}$ _______________

b) $\frac{1}{3}$ _______________

c) $\frac{7}{8}$ _______________

d) $\frac{1}{5}$ _______________

2. Write each decimal as a fraction or mixed number.

a) 0.6 ____   b) 0.75 ____   c) 2.5 ____   d) $0.\overline{7}$ ____

3.2 **3.** Order the numbers from least to greatest. Use the number line.

$0.9, \frac{11}{10}, \frac{4}{5}, 1.4, 1\frac{7}{20}$ 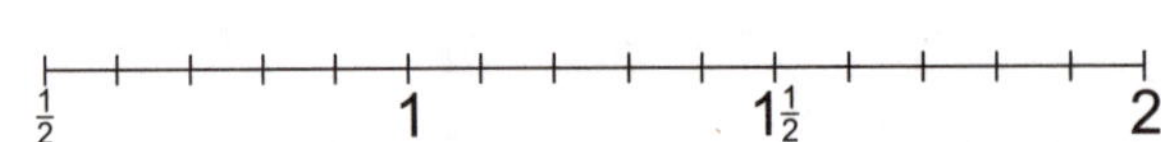

From least to greatest: _______________________

4. Use equivalent fractions to order these numbers from greatest to least:

$2\frac{1}{2}, 1\frac{3}{8}, 2\frac{3}{5}, 1\frac{7}{10}$

From greatest to least: _______________________

5. Use place value to order these numbers from least to greatest:

$1.3825, 1\frac{4}{5}, 1.236, 1\frac{1}{3}, 1.333, 1.810$

From least to greatest: _______________________

3.3   **6.**   Matthew bought a shirt for \$21.99, pants for \$36.78, and a belt for \$10.50.

What is the total amount for the purchases without sales tax? ________

7.   Kerry has grown 2.1 cm since last September.
She is now 165 cm tall.

How tall was Kerry last September?_________

3.4   **8.**   Multiply. Use front-end estimation to place the decimal point in the answer.

a) $0.5 \times 0.7 =$ ________   **b)** $2.9 \times 0.8 =$ ________

c) $3.5 \times 3.2 =$ ________   **d)** $1.4 \times 2.9 =$ ________

9.   Anne cycles 15.5 km each hour.
She cycles for 3.25 h.

How far does Ann cycle? __________

3.5   **10.**   Divide. Write each quotient to the nearest tenth where necessary.

a) $8.7 \div 0.6 =$ ____   **b)** $5.7 \div 1.5 =$ ____

c) $43.1 \div 2.1 =$ ____   **d)** $23.5 \div 4.8 =$ ____

11.   Amal bought 3.5 kg of bananas for \$2.42.

What was the cost of 1 kg of bananas? ______

3.6 **12.** Evaluate.

a) $5.3 - 2.3 \times 2 = $ _______   b) $(67.2 + 12) \div 2.4 - 1.2 = $ _______

3.7 **13.** Write each fraction as a decimal and a percent.

a) $\dfrac{1}{2} = $ ___ $= $ _____   b) $\dfrac{17}{25} = $ _____ $= $ _____

c) $\dfrac{19}{20} = $ _____ $= $ _____   d) $\dfrac{3}{5} = $ ___ $= $ _____

3.8 **14.** Ivana got $\dfrac{21}{25}$ on her science test.

She got 86% on her math test.

Which of her test marks is greater? Explain.

Ivana's _______________ test mark is greater.

15. Find each percent.

a) 3% of 25   b) 24% of $9.00   c) 40% of 95

$3\% = \dfrac{3}{100} = 0.03$ $24\% = $

$0.03 \times 25 = $ _____   _______________   _______________

16. Sylvia is going to buy a new jacket.
The regular price is $68.00.
The jacket is on sale for 25% off.
There is 14% sales tax on the jacket.
How much will Sylvia pay for the jacket?

Sylvia will pay _________ for the jacket.

Circles and Area

Just for Fun

Counting Rectangles

Challenge a classmate to see who can find the greatest number of rectangles in the room.

Set a time limit of 1 minute. Write down all the rectangles you can see.

At the end of 1 minute, exchange papers with your classmate.

Check each other's list.

Geometric Designer

Use only circles, triangles, rectangles, and parallelograms.

Draw any 3 of the following items:
- car, bus, truck, motorcycle
- person
- building
- animal
- landscape

Trade drawings with a classmate. Identify your classmate's drawings.

Products and Factors

A Game for 2

Work with a partner.

You will need two number cubes labelled 1 to 6 and 7 to 12, a pencil, and paper.

Take turns to roll the two cubes.
Record the two numbers and find their product.
In 10 seconds, write all the factors of that product that you can.
Score 1 point for each factor you find.
For which products did you score the fewest points? Why?

Activating Prior Knowledge

Perimeter and Area of a Rectangle

Perimeter is the distance around a shape.
Area is the amount of surface a shape covers.

Example 1

a) Find the perimeter and area of the square.

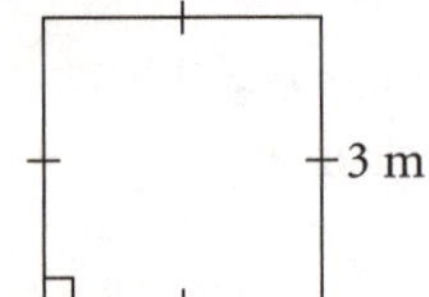

b) Find the perimeter and area of the rectangle.

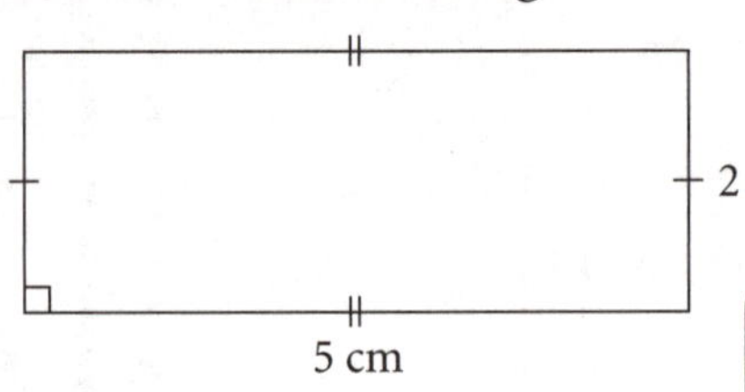

Solution

a) Perimeter, $P = 4s$
Substitute $s = 3$.
$P = 4 \times 3 = 12$
The perimeter is 12 m.

Area, $A = s^2$
Substitute $s = 3$.
$A = 3^2 = 9$
The area is 9 m².

b) Perimeter, $P = 2(b + h)$
Substitute $b = 5$ and $h = 2$.
$P = 2(5 + 2) = 14$
The perimeter is 14 cm.

Area, $A = bh$
Substitute $b = 5$ and $h = 2$.
$A = 5 \times 2 = 10$
The area is 10 cm².

✓ Check

1. Find the perimeter and area of each shape.

a)

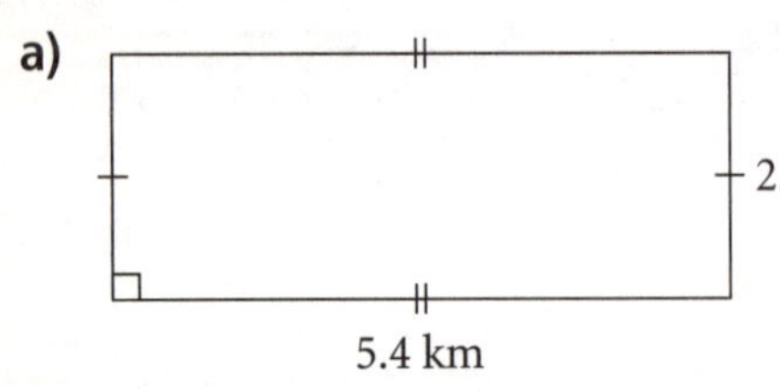

$P = 2(b + h)$

$= 2(\underline{\ 2\ } + \underline{\ 5.4\ })$

$= \underline{2(7.4)}$

Perimeter = $\underline{14.8\ km}$

$A = bh$

$= \underline{5.4} \times \underline{2.0}$

$= \underline{10.8}$

Area = $\underline{10.8\ km^2}$

b)

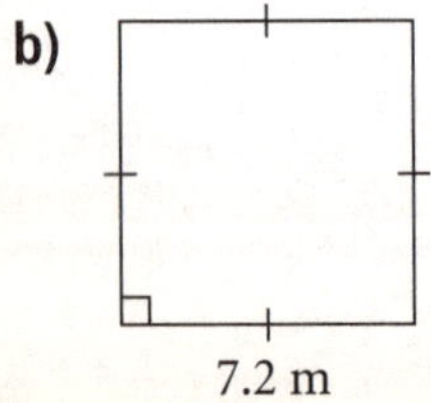

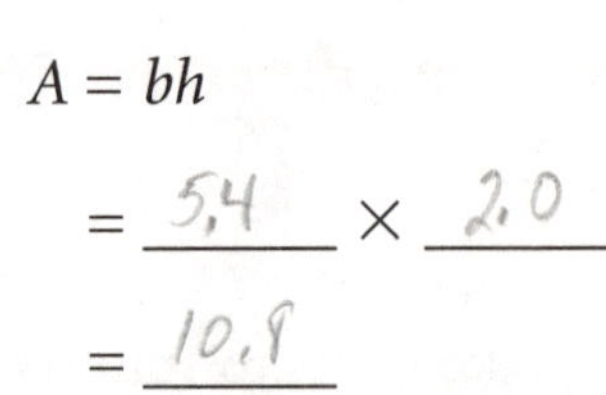

Perimeter = $\underline{28.8\ Km}$ Area = $\underline{51.84\ m^2}$

Using a Protractor to Measure Angles

To measure an angle, place the base line of a protractor along one arm of the angle, with the centre of the protractor on the vertex of the angle.

Read the angle measure from the scale that has its 0 on the arm of the angle.

Example 2

Find the measure of this angle.

Solution

The measure of the angle is 35°.

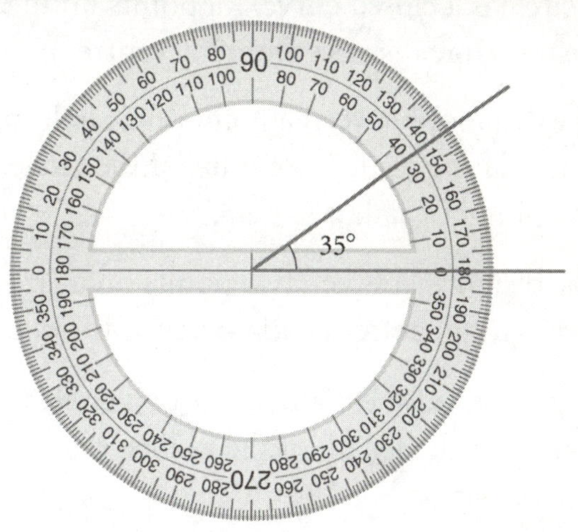

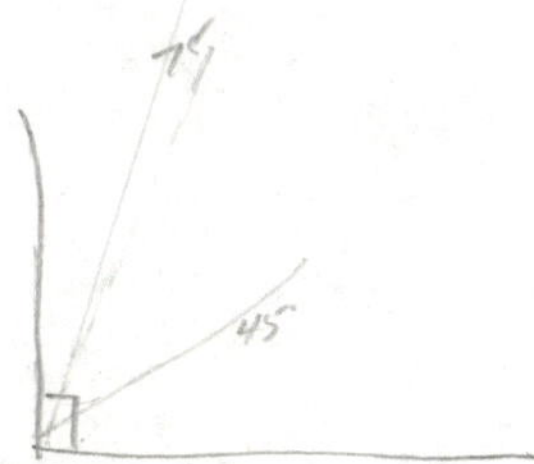

✓ Check

2. Measure each angle in polygon ABCDE.

$\angle A = 90°$ $\angle B = \underline{135}°$ $\angle C = \underline{112}°$

$\angle D = \underline{120}°$ $\angle E = \underline{62}°$

Find the sum of the angles.

$\angle A + \angle B + \angle C + \angle D + \angle E = \underline{}°$

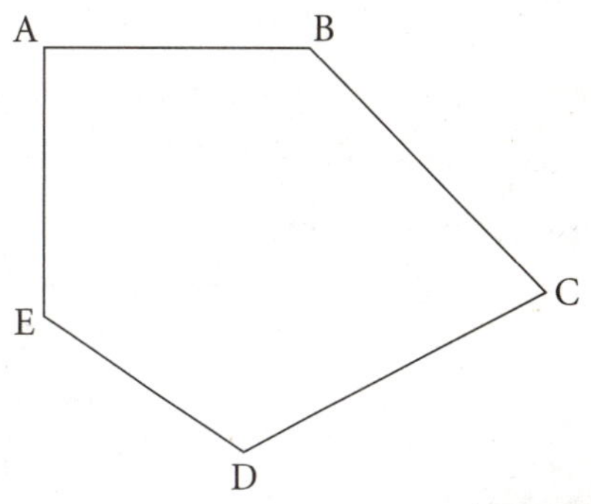

3. a) Use a ruler but not a protractor.
Draw an angle that you think measures 75°.

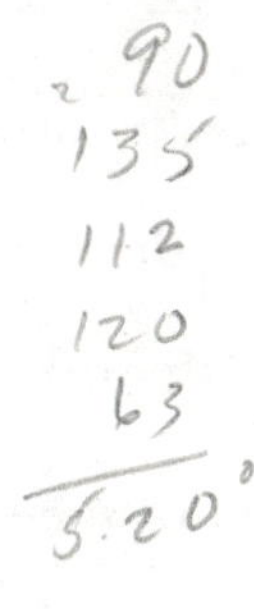

b) Measure the angle with a protractor.
How close was your angle to 75°?

Quick Review

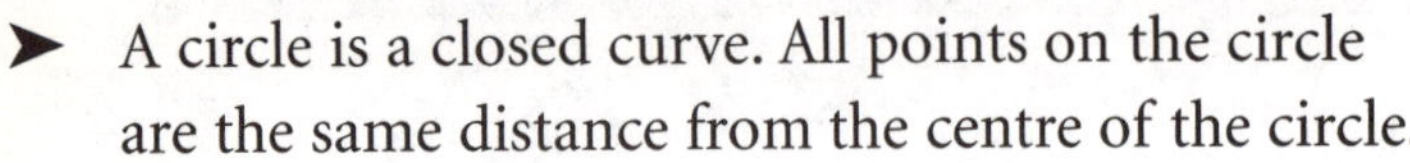

➤ A circle is a closed curve. All points on the circle are the same distance from the centre of the circle.

The distance between a point on a circle and the centre of the circle is a **radius** of the circle. The plural of radius is *radii*.

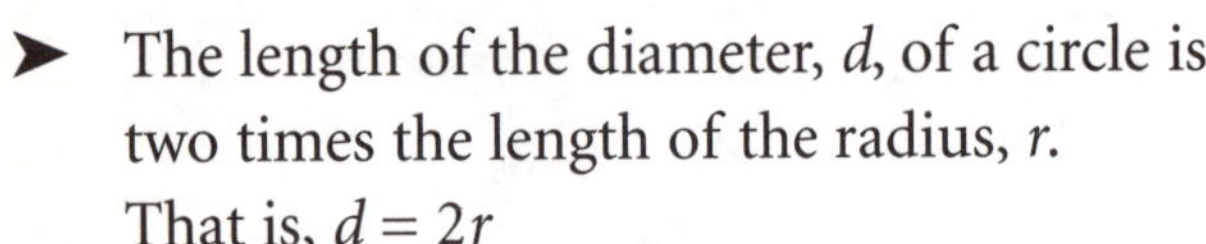

The distance between two points on a circle through its centre is a **diameter** of the circle.

➤ The length of the diameter, d, of a circle is two times the length of the radius, r.
That is, $d = 2r$

Also, the radius, r, of a circle is one-half the diameter, d.
That is, $r = \frac{1}{2}d$, or $\frac{d}{2}$

You can find the radius of a circle, given the diameter.

For example, in a circle, d is 10 cm.
Since $r = \frac{1}{2}d$, $r = \frac{1}{2} \times 10 = 5$
The radius is 5 cm.

You can find the diameter of a circle, given the radius.

For example, in a circle, r is 4 cm.
Since $d = 2r$, then $d = 2 \times 4 = 8$.
The diameter is 8 cm.

Practice

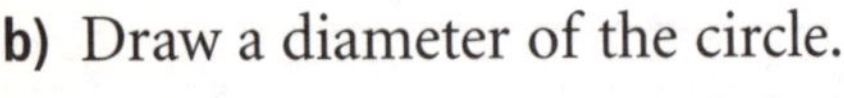

1. This circle has its centre at point O.

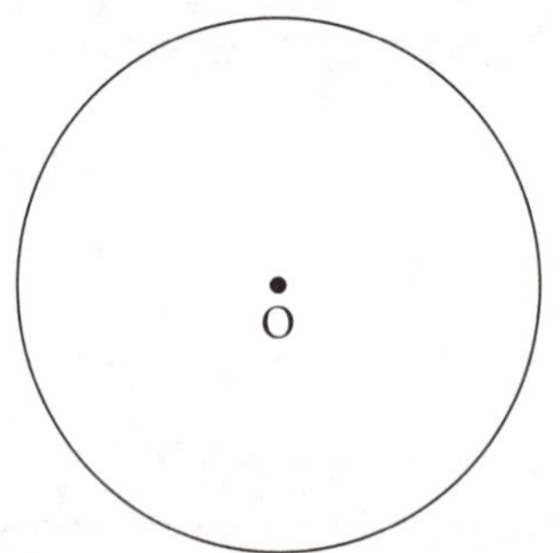

a) Draw a radius of the circle.

What is the length of the radius? _______________

b) Draw a diameter of the circle.

What is the length of the diameter? _______________

2. From your results in question 1, write a relationship between the radius and the diameter of a circle.

____

3. Find the diameter of the circle with each radius.

    a) 12 cm _____________   **b)** 27 cm _____________   **c)** 3.4 cm _____________

4. Find the radius of the circle with each diameter.

    a) 12 cm _____________   **b)** 28 cm _____________   **c)** 3.4 cm _____________

5. Write the steps you would take to draw a circle with radius 1 cm.
Draw the circle.

____

____

____

____

6. Draw 4 radii in the circle you drew in question 5.
What is the sum of the central angles of the circle? _____

7. Write the steps you would take to draw a circle with diameter 4 cm.

____

____

____

____

8. Circular plates with diameter 20 cm are placed side by side on a table.
The table measures 2.4 m by 1.2 m.

    a) What is the length of the table in centimetres? _____________

    b) How many plates can fit side by side along the length of the table?

____

    c) What is the width of the table in centimetres? _____________

    d) How many plates can fit side by side along the width of the table? _____________

    e) How many plates can fit on the table? _______

    f) How many plates can fit around the perimeter of the table? _____

Quick Review

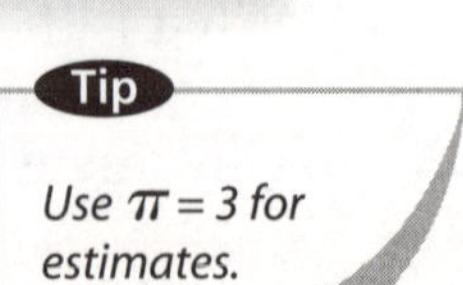

➤ The distance around a circle is its **circumference**.

The ratio of the circumference, C, to the diameter, d, of a circle, $\frac{C}{d}$, is a number close to 3.

That is, the circumference is approximately 3 times the diameter, or 6 times the radius.

➤ The Greek letter π is used to represent the constant for $\frac{C}{d}$.

In symbols: $\frac{C}{d} = \pi$
π is an **irrational number** equal to about 3.14.

HINT

An irrational number is a decimal that never repeats and never terminates.

So, the circumference, C, is π multiplied by d.

$C = \pi d$

Since $d = 2r$, $C = \pi \times 2r$, or $C = 2\pi r$

➤ You can use one of the formulas above to find the circumference of a circle given the diameter or radius.

The radius of a circle is 5 cm.

To estimate the circumference,
use: $C = 6r$
Substitute: $r = 5$
$C = 6(5)$
$\quad = 30$
The circumference is about 30 cm.

To calculate the circumference,
use: $C = 2\pi r$
Substitute: $r = 5$
$C = 2 \times \pi \times 5$ Use a calculator.
$\quad \doteq 31.4$
The circumference is 31.4 cm to one decimal place.

Practice

1. Estimate the circumference of each circle with the given diameter.

Tip

Use $\pi = 3$ for estimates.

a) 2 cm

b) 24 cm

c) 4.2 m

_______________   _______________   _______________

2. Estimate the circumference of each circle with the given radius.

a) 2 cm

b) 24 cm

c) 4.2 m

____

____

____

3. Calculate the circumference of each circle in question 2.
Give the answers to one decimal place.

a) $r = 2$ cm

b) $r = 24$ cm

c) $r = 4.2$ m

____

____

____

4. The circumference of each circle is given.
Calculate the diameter and radius. Give the answers to one decimal place.

a) $d =$ _______________

$r =$ _______________

b) $d =$ _______________

$r =$ _______________

c) $d =$ _______________

$r =$ _______________

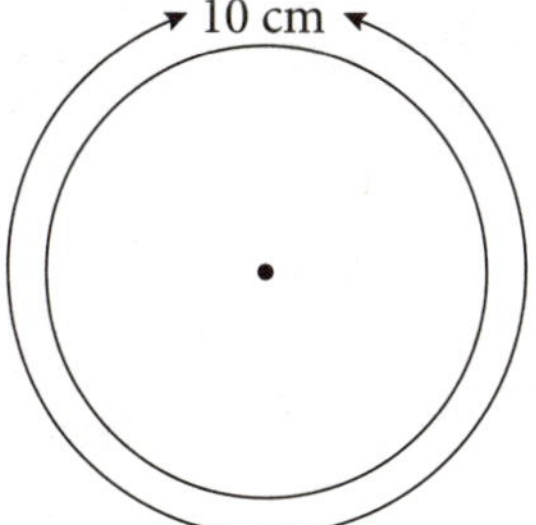

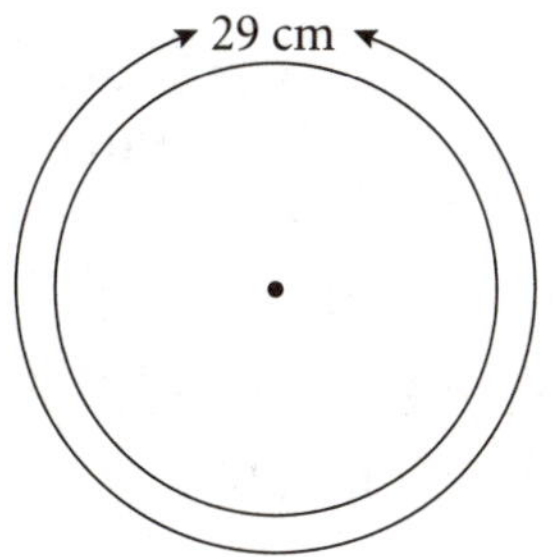

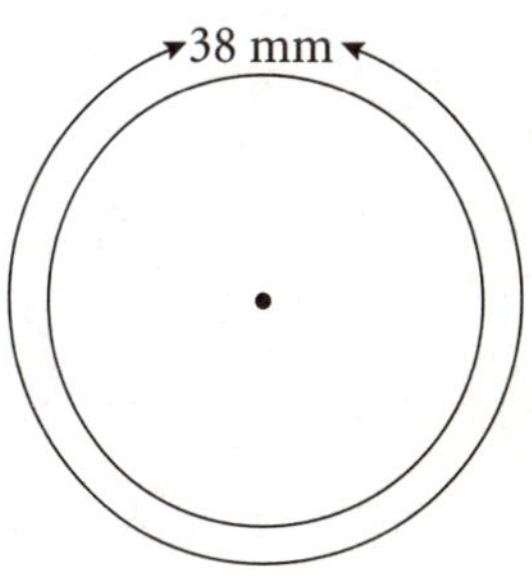

5. A drinking glass has a circular base with a circumference of 21.4 cm.

a) Calculate the diameter of the circular base. _______________

b) Circular coasters are made to extend beyond the edge of the glass base by 1 cm.

What is the diameter of the coaster? _______________

c) Calculate the circumference of the coaster. _______________

6. A car tire has a radius of 36 cm. A stone gets stuck in the tire. How many times will the stone hit the ground when the car travels 1 km? Show your work.

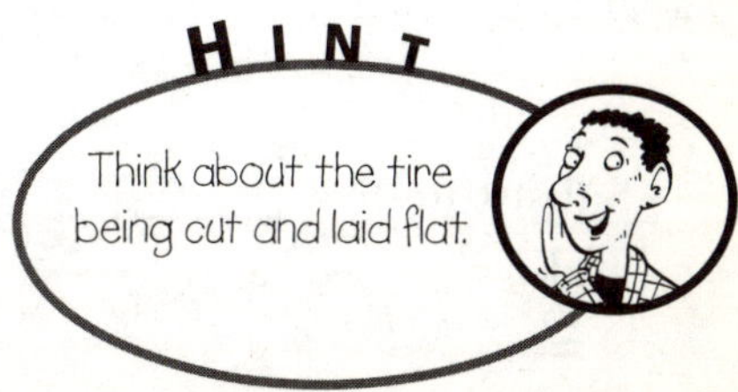

The stone will hit the ground _______________ times.

Quick Review

➤ You can rearrange a parallelogram to form a rectangle.
They have the same area.

➤ The formula for the area of a parallelogram is the same as for the area of a rectangle:
Area = base × height or $A = bh$

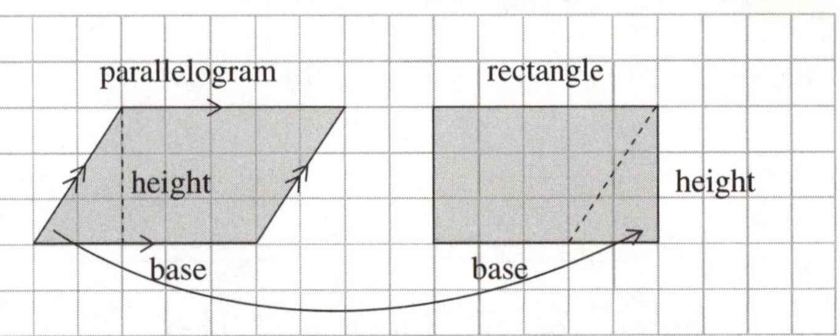

For the parallelogram at the left:
$A = bh$
Substitute $b = 6$ and $h = 4$.
$$A = 6 \times 4$$
$$= 24$$
The area is 24 m².

HINT
The height of a parallelogram must be perpendicular to the base.

For the parallelogram at the left:
$A = bh$
Substitute $b = 3.6$ and $h = 2.0$.
$$A = 3.6 \times 2.0$$
$$= 7.2$$
The area is 7.2 cm².

Practice

1. Find the area of each parallelogram.

a)
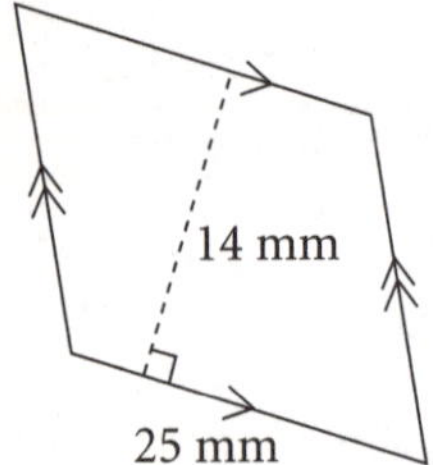

$A = bh$
Substitute $b =$ _______
and $h =$ _______.
$A =$
   $=$
The area is _________.

b)
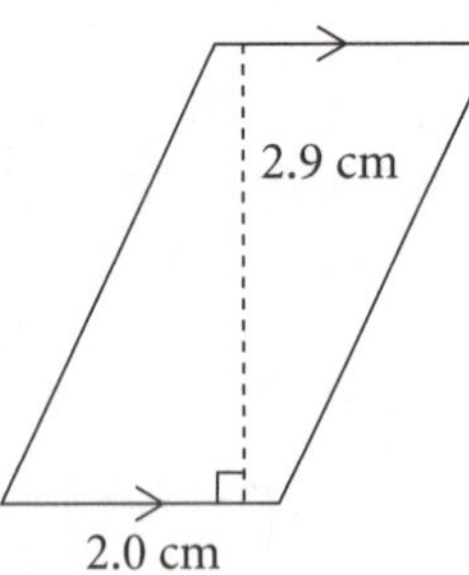

The area is _________.

Key to success

• Record formulas in your journal so that they can be found easily.
• Write an example of how to use each formula.

2. Find the area of each parallelogram.

a)

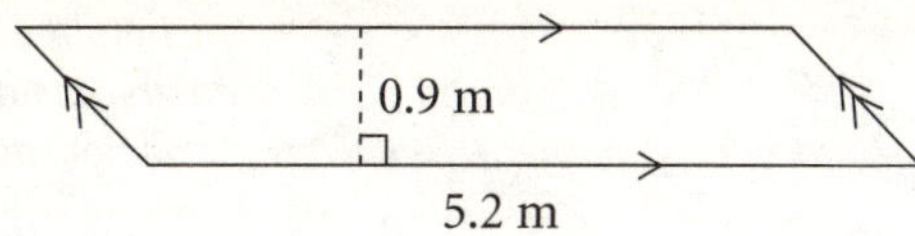

b)

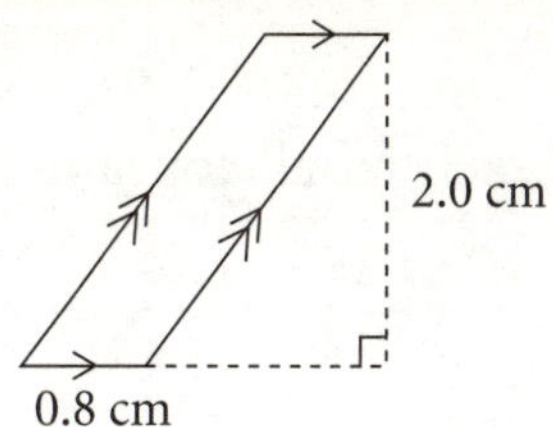

The area is _____________________.   The area is _____________________.

3. Draw the height of each parallelogram.
Measure the height and the corresponding base.
Then find the area.

a)

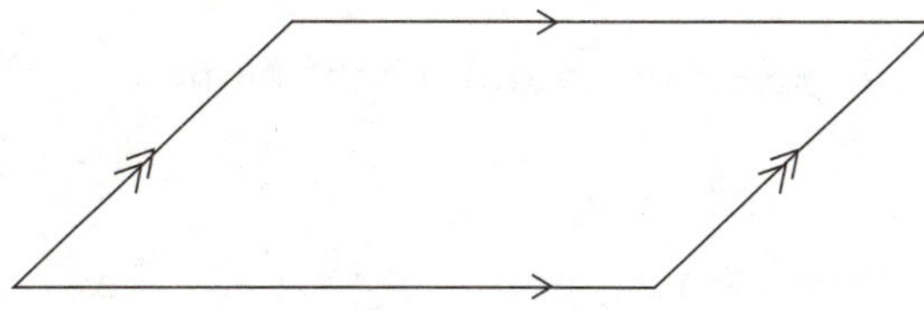

Height = _______ cm

Base = _______ cm

Area = _______ cm^2

b)

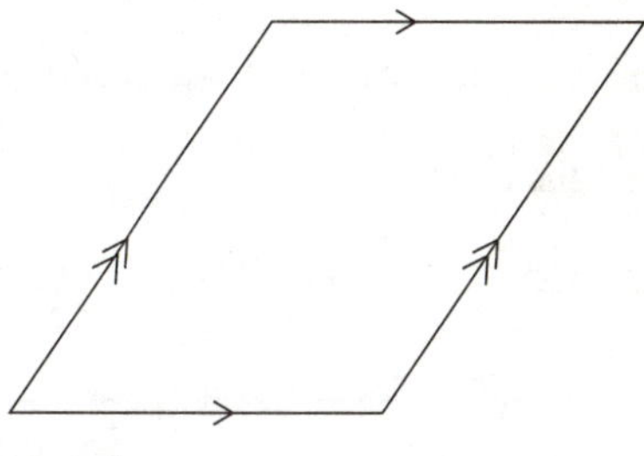

Height = _______________

Base = _______________

Area = _______________

4. The area and height of each parallelogram are given.
Find the measure of the base in each parallelogram.

a)

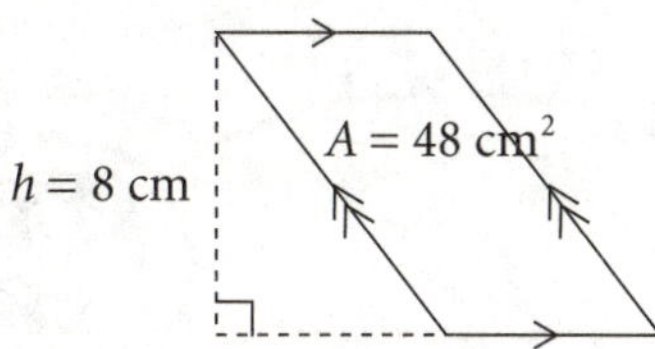

b)

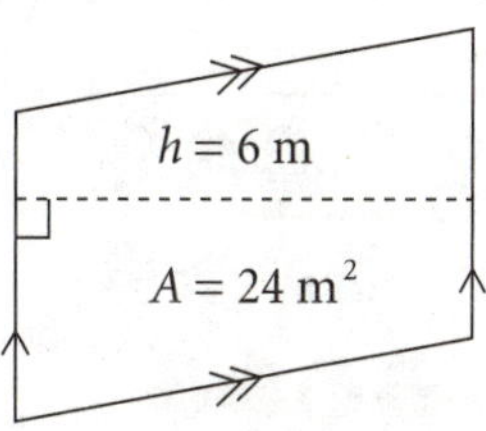

Area = base × height

48 = _______ × 8

Base = _______ cm   Base = _____________

5. a) On the grid below, draw 3 different parallelograms with base 6 units and height 2 units.

Find the area of each parallelogram.

____

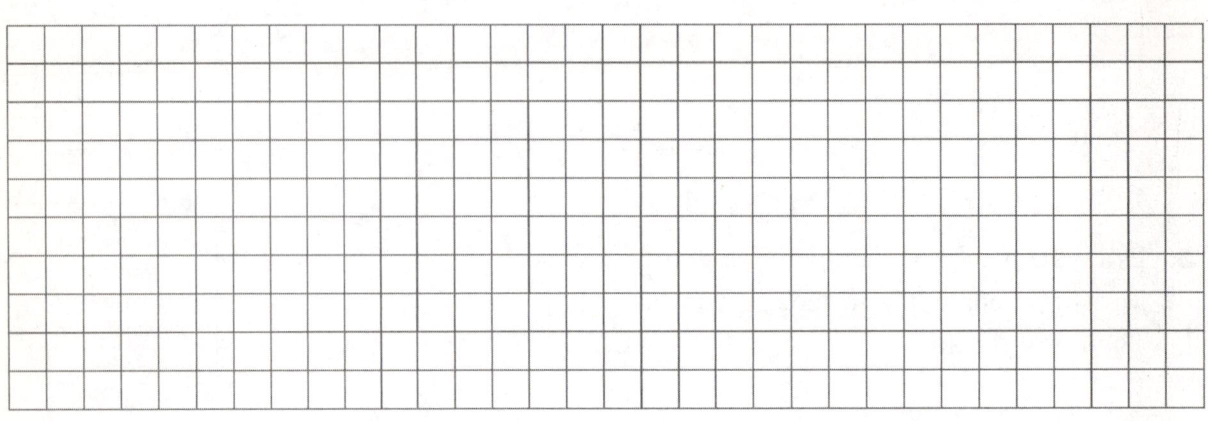

b) On the grid above, draw a parallelogram with base 3 units and height 2 units.

Find its area. _________________

How does the area compare with the area of the parallelograms in part a?

____

c) On the grid above, draw a parallelogram with base 6 units and height 4 units.

Find its area. _________________

How does the area compare with the area of the parallelograms in part a?

____

6. Jamie makes a road through his wooded lot.
What is the area of the part of the lot that has trees? Show your work.

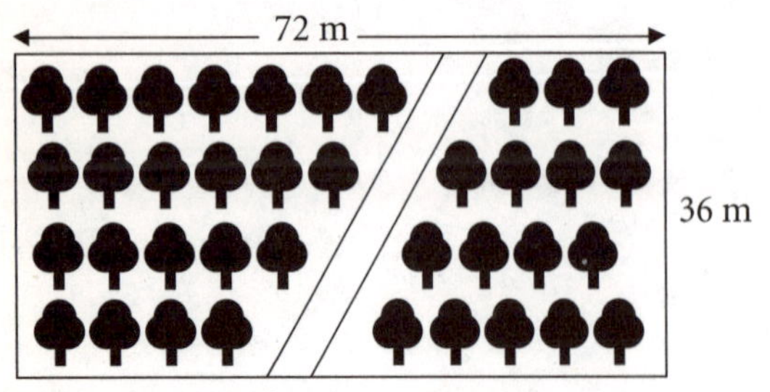

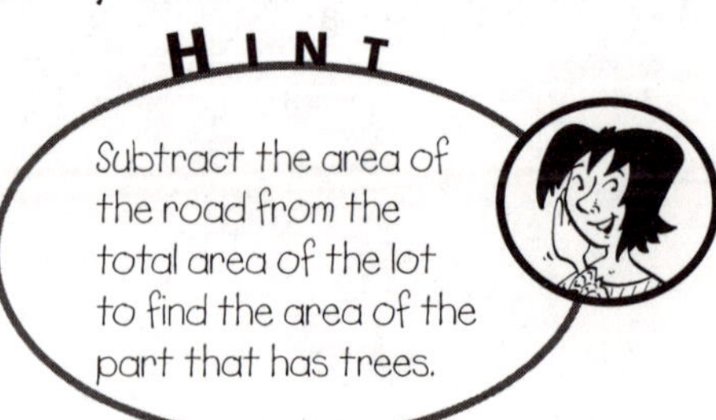

____

86

Quick Review

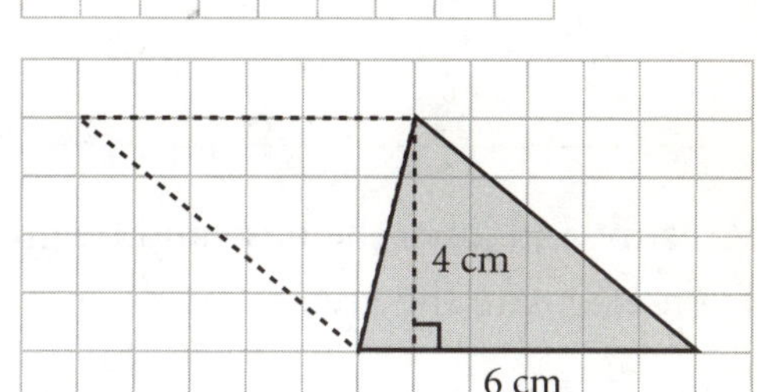

➤ This parallelogram has been divided
  into 2 congruent triangles.
  So, the area of one triangle is $\frac{1}{2}$ the area of
  the parallelogram.

➤ To find the area of a triangle with base 6 cm
  and height 4 cm, complete a parallelogram
  on one side of the triangle.

➤ The area of the parallelogram is:
  $A = \text{base} \times \text{height}$
  $A = 6 \times 4 = 24$
  The area of the parallelogram is 24 cm².
  So, the area of the triangle is: $\frac{1}{2}$ of 24 cm² = 12 cm²

➤ You can use this formula for the area of a triangle.
  $\text{Area} = \frac{1}{2} \text{base} \times \text{height}$
  $A = \frac{1}{2} bh$
  or $A = bh \div 2$
  or $A = \dfrac{bh}{2}$

Practice

1. Find the area of each triangle.

a)

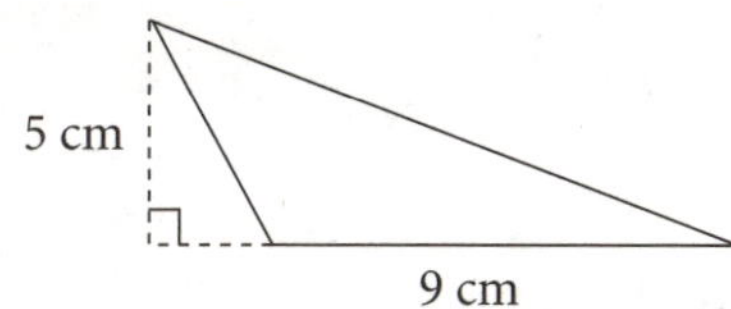

$A = \dfrac{bh}{2}$

$A = $ __________

$= $ __________

The area is __________ cm².

b)

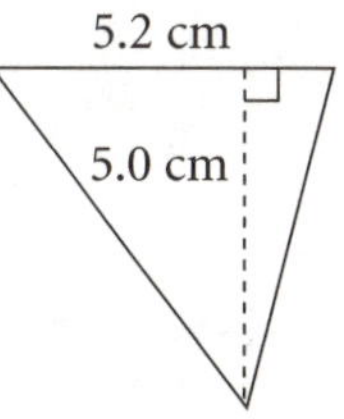

HINT

Write the formula first.
Then substitute for each
variable.

$A = \frac{1}{2} bh$

$A = $ __________

$= $ __________

The area is __________ cm².

2. Find the area of each triangle.

a)

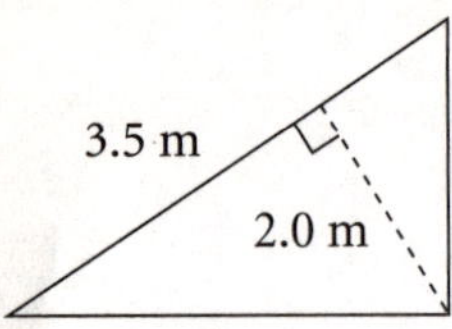

b)

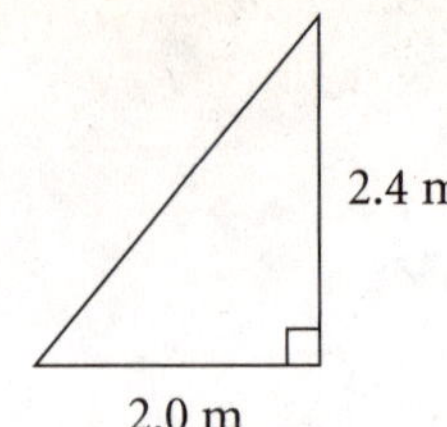

_______________________________   _______________________________

3. Measure and label the base and height of each triangle in centimetres. Then calculate the area.

a)

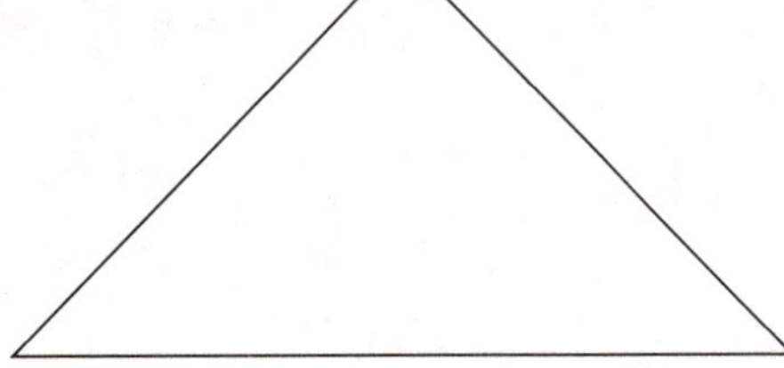

b)

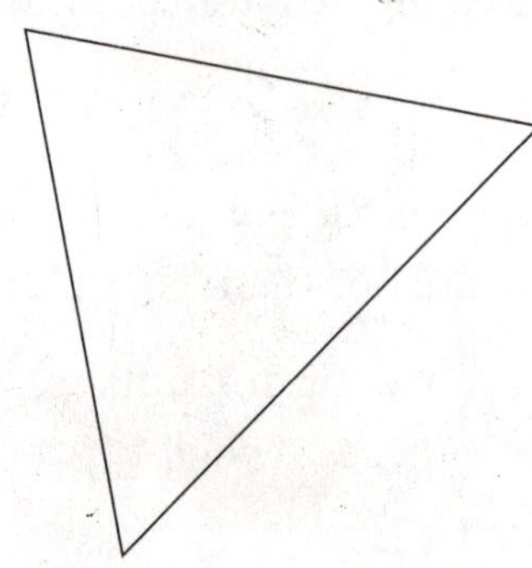

Area = _____________________   Area = _____________________

c)

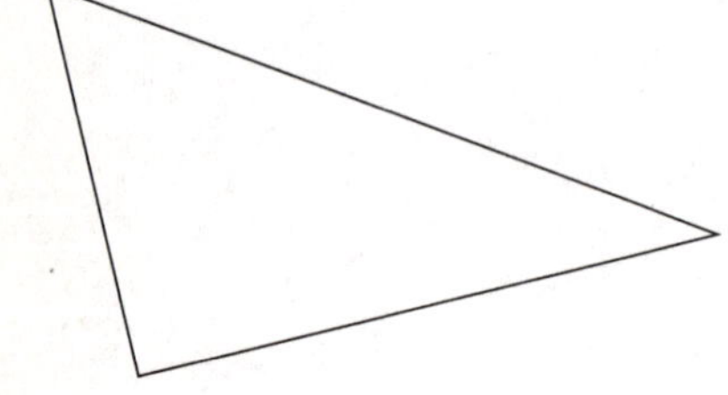

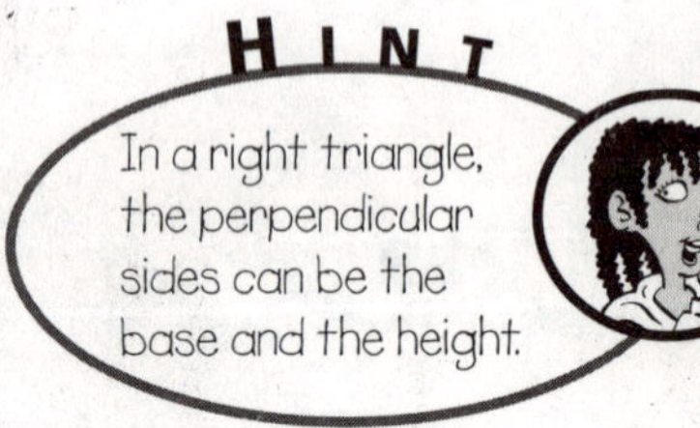

Area = _____________________

4. Draw 3 different triangles each with base 5 units and height 4 units.

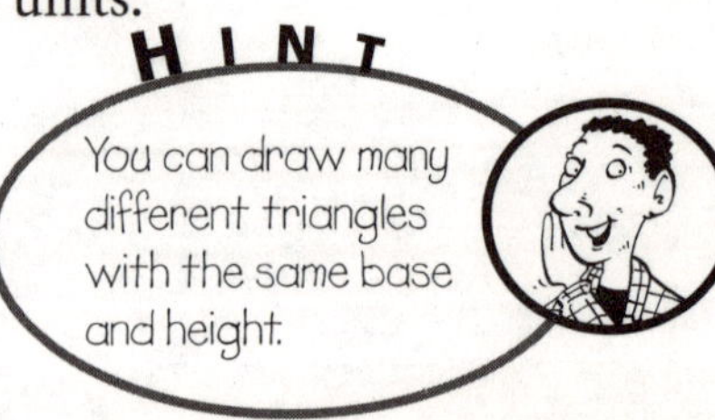

5. Draw 3 different triangles each with area 12 square units.

6. The area, *A*, of each triangle is given.
Find the height, *h*, of each triangle.

a)

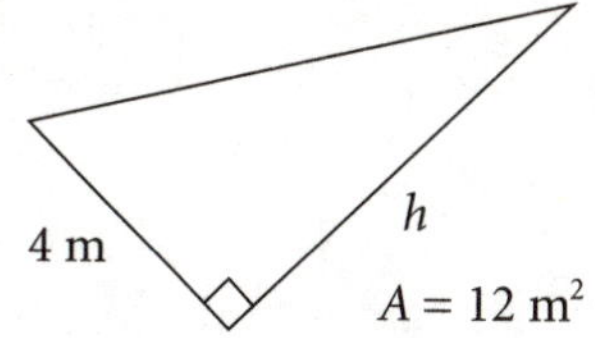

$$\text{Area} = \frac{bh}{2}$$

$$12 = \frac{4 \times h}{2}$$

Height = _______________

b)

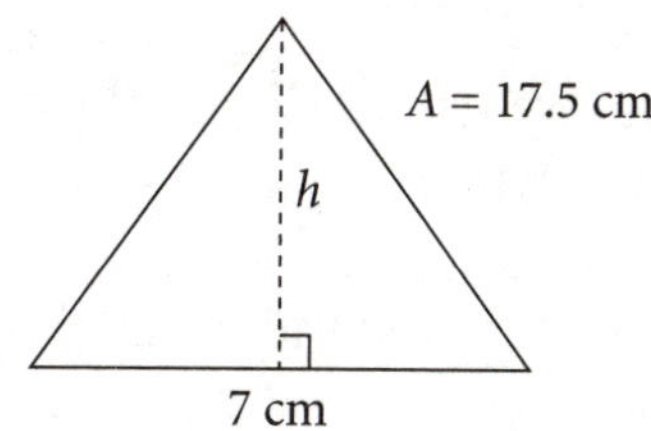

Height = _______________

c)

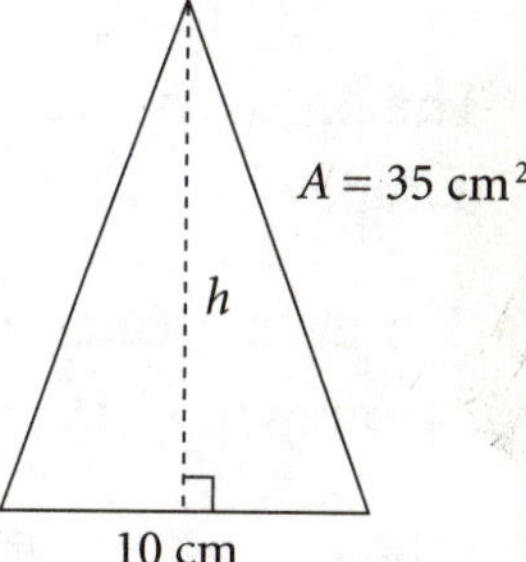

Height = _______________

7. Bernice makes this design on a square sheet of paper.
The paper has a side length of 20 cm.
Each triangle has a base of 12 cm and a height of 10 cm.
Find the area of the white part of the design.
Show your work.

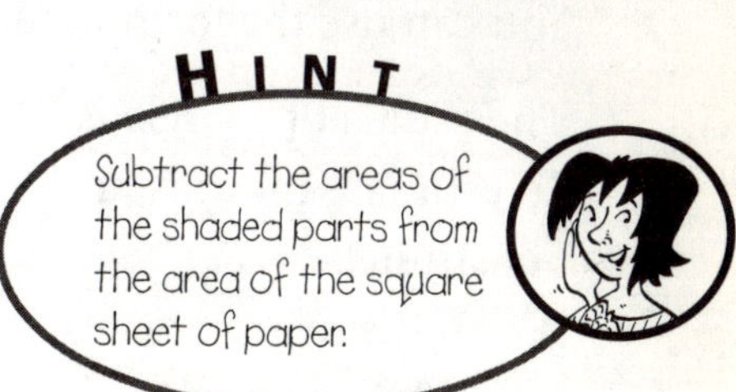

Quick Review

➤ When a circle is divided into many congruent sectors,
the sectors can be arranged to approximate a parallelogram.

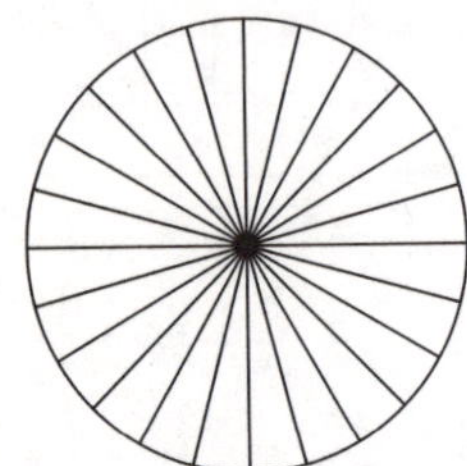
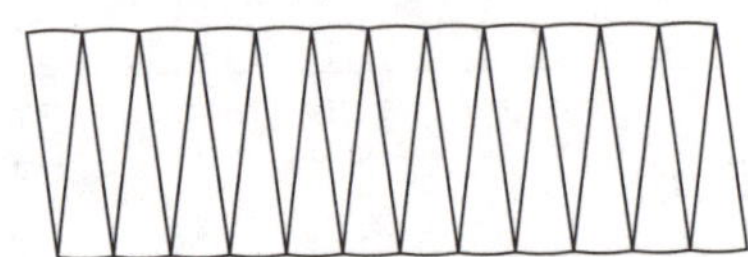

The more congruent sectors we use to divide the circle, the closer the area of the
parallelogram is to the area of the circle.

For even greater numbers of sectors, the parallelogram approaches a rectangle.
So, area of circle = area of rectangle

The sum of the 2 longer sides of the rectangle is equal to the circumference, C.
Length of rectangle: $l = \frac{C}{2} = \frac{2\pi r}{2} = \pi r$
Each of the shorter sides is equal to the radius r.
Width of rectangle: $w = r$

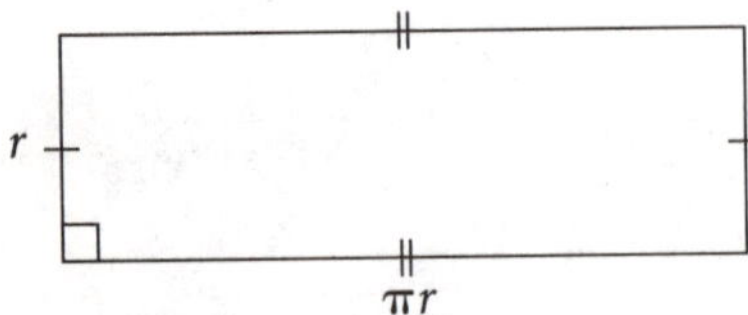

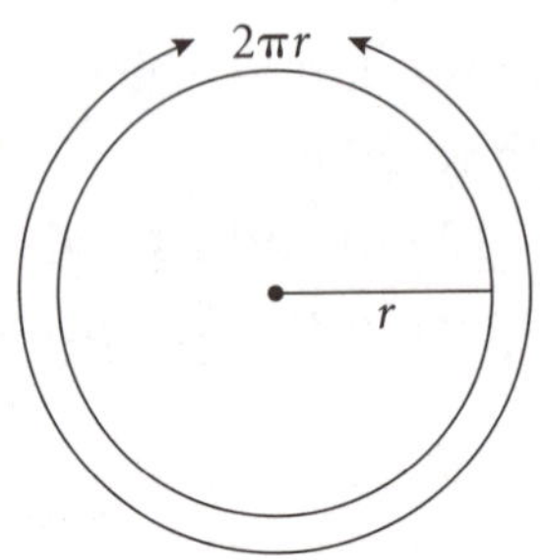

So, the area of a circle with
radius r is:
$A = l \times w$
$\quad = \pi r \times r$
$\quad = \pi r^2$

➤ You can use the formula $A = \pi r^2$ to find the area of any circle given the radius r.

The radius of a circle is 12 cm.

To estimate the area, use: $A = 3r^2$ To calculate the area, use: $A = \pi r^2$
Substitute: $r = 12$ Substitute: $r = 12$
$A = 3(12)^2$ $A = \pi \times 12^2$ Use a calculator.
$\quad = 432$ $\quad \doteq 452.389$
The area is about 432 cm².   The area is 452.39 cm² to 2 decimal places.

1. Estimate the area of each circle.

a)

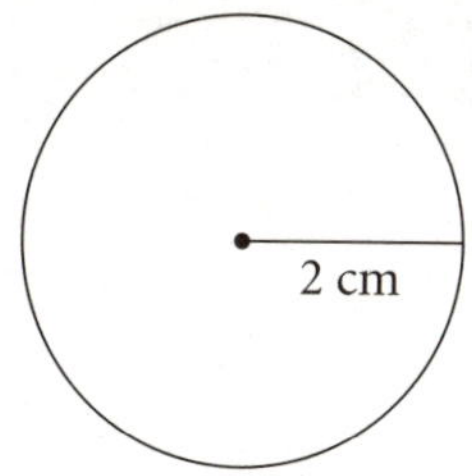

Area: _________________

b)

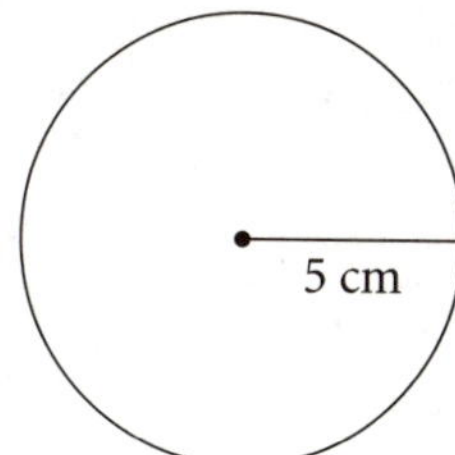

Area: _________________

c)

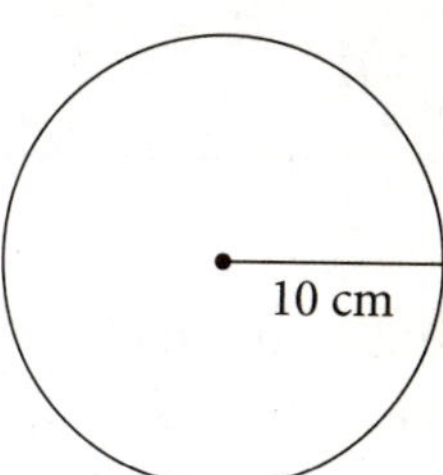

Area: _________________

2. Calculate the area of each circle in question 1.
Give the answers to two decimal places.

a) $r =$ _____________

$A = \pi \times ($_______$)^2$

$\doteq$ ____________

Area: _________________

b) $r =$ ___________

Area: _________________

c) $r =$ ___________

Area: _________________

3. Calculate the area of each circle.
Give the answers to two decimal places.

a)

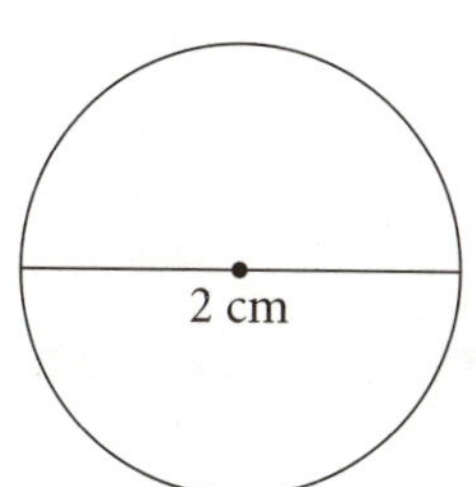

$r =$ ____________

Area: _________________

b)

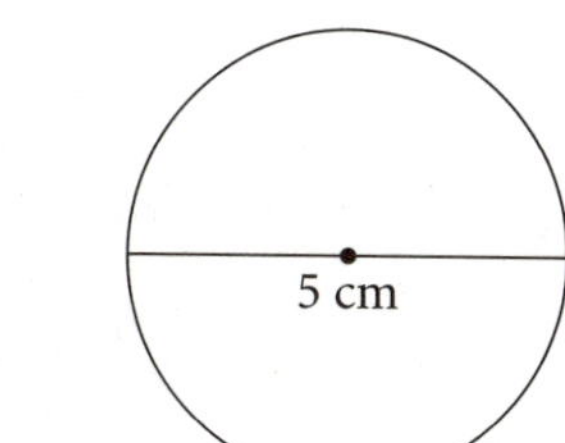

$r =$ ____________

Area: _________________

c)

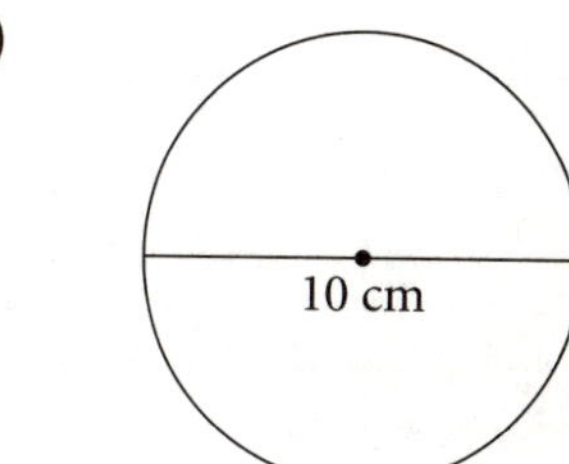

$r =$ ____________

Area: _________________

4. Use the results of questions 2 and 3.
What happens to the area of a circle when
its radius is doubled?

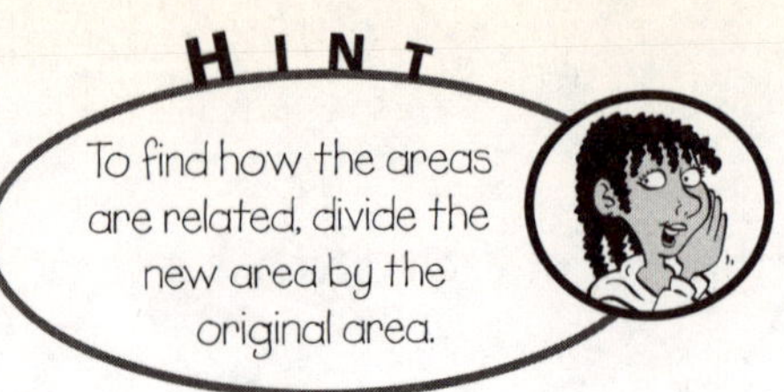

____

What happens to the area of a circle when its radius is halved?

____

5. A machine is cutting circular coasters out of foam.

  a) Each coaster has a diameter of 12 cm. What is its radius? _______________________

  b) What is the area of each coaster? ___________________________________

  c) Each piece of foam is a rectangle measuring 144 cm by 984 cm.

  What is the area of the foam? ___________________________________

  d) The coasters are cut with minimum waste.
How many coasters can be cut from each piece of foam?

____

  e) What area of foam is wasted?

____

6. The circumference of a circle is 92 cm. Calculate the area of the circle.
Give the answer to one decimal place. Show your work.

  The area of the circle is ___________________________.

Quick Review

A **circle graph** shows parts of one whole.
This table and circle graph show how Bobbie spends a typical day.

Activity	Part of the day spent on each activity
Eating	7%
Free time	24%
Homework	9%
Sleeping	33%
At school	27%

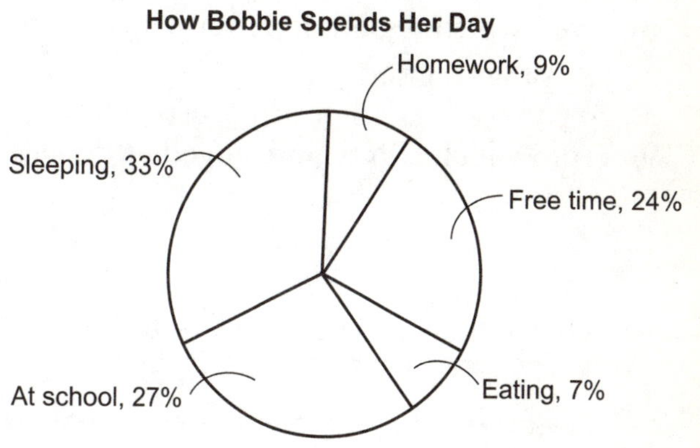

The circle represents 100% of Bobbie's activities.
The sum of the measures of the central angles is 360°.

Each sector of the circle represents a percent
of the whole circle and a percent of Bobbie's day.

The circle graph has a title that describes what it represents.

When a computer is used to draw a circle graph,
a legend shows what each sector represents.

You can interpret the graph to find out about Bobbie's day:

- From the sizes of the sectors, you can see that Bobbie spent about 3 times as long at school as she did doing her homework.

- Also, the most time Bobbie spent doing any activity was sleeping.
  This was about one-third of the day.

- You can find how long Bobbie spent on any activity.
  There are 24 h in a day.
  Bobbie spent 9% of 24 h doing homework.
  This is: $0.09 \times 24 \text{ h} = 2.16 \text{ h}$
  So, Bobbie spent a little more than 2 h doing homework.

1. On the 2006-07 Kootenay Junior Ice Hockey Team, there were 22 players. The circle graph shows where they came from.

Kootenay Ice Roster, 2006/2007

a) From which region do more players come than any other region? _______ *AB*

b) From which region do fewer players come than any other region? _______ *other*

c) From which two regions together do about one-half of the players come?
_______ *B.C / Sask (just under 50%)   or   AB/other (just over 50%)*

d) Why is there a sector labelled "Other"?
_______ *probably just a scattering of regions too small to categorize.*

2. Ms. Reid runs the local convenience store. She keeps track of the types of drinks she sells so she always has stock in the store. The circle graph shows the drinks Ms. Reid sold in one week.

Drinks Sold in the Store

a) Which drink was the most popular? _______ *coffee*

b) Which drink was the least popular? _______ *Energy drinks*

c) Which two drinks together made up about *exactly* one-half the sales? _______ *coffee / juice*

d) Can you find out how much water Ms. Reid sold that week? Explain.
_______ *No. We don't know total drinks she sold + there is no way to figure that out. We only know proportion – relation to other drinks*

3. This graph shows how the budget for the City of Winnipeg was spent in 2004. The budget for 2004 was $692.9 million.

City of Winnipeg 2004 Budget

a) i) Which sector is the smallest?
_______ *Transit / prop. dev.*

ii) What does that tell you about how much money was spent for that sector?
_______ *76.2 million*

b) How much money was spent on Police and fire services?

$242.5 million

c) i) Which 3 sectors together are a little larger that the Police and fire services sector?

Libraries, rec. facilities / transit + prop. dev. / corp. offices.
~ 57%

ii) What does that tell you about how much money was spent on these 3 sectors?

$256.4 million. – they are not most imp. spending priorities / they use less money.

iii) How could you check your answer to part ii?

– use fraction / equation + use decimals
– Use internet to research.

4. Kirabel's father is preparing meals according to the guidelines of the Canada Food Guide. He is planning a total of 25 servings per day, as shown in the graph. The labelling is incomplete.

a) What percent of the servings should be dairy products? *20%*

How do you know? *total of rest is 80%*

b) About how many of the servings should be grains? *9*

Canada Food Guide

Dairy products
Meat/ alternatives, 12%
Vegetables/ fruits, 32%
Grains, 36%

c) About how many servings should be meat or meat alternatives? *3*

not 25 - grains
used 2+

d) About how many servings should be grains, or vegetables and fruits? *17 . 1/29*

5. A survey was taken at school to determine the favourite genre of television shows of the grade 7 students. One hundred twenty students were surveyed. The results are shown in the graph.

120 x .5

Grade 7 Students' Favourite TV Genre

Sit.Com., 35%
Reality/game, 25%
Drama/soap, 20%
Talk/news, 5%
Sports, 15%

a) Which genre had about one-third of the votes? *Sit com*

b) Which two genres together did one-quarter of the students vote for? *Drama/soap + talk/news*

c) Which category received the fewest votes? *talk / news*

Why do you think that happened? *– varied*

d) How many students picked sports as their favourite? *15% – 18*

Quick Review

➤ A circle graph shows how parts of a set of
data compare with the whole set.

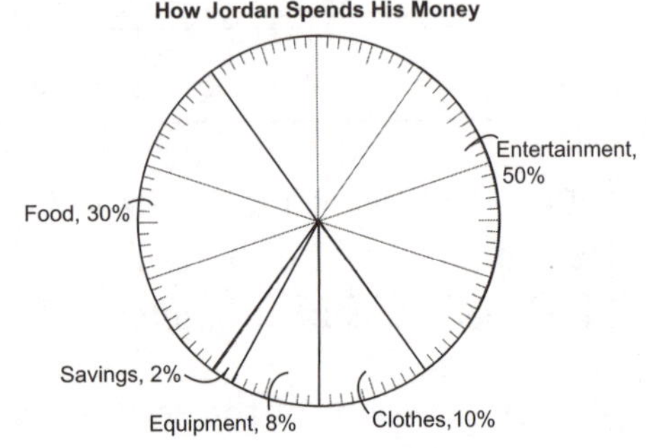

To draw a circle graph, follow these steps:

* Write each number in the data set as a fraction
  of the sum of the numbers in the data set.

  For example, suppose one number in the set is 8 and the total is 80.

  Then the fraction is $\frac{8}{80}$.

* Write each fraction as a percent.

  For example, the fraction $\frac{8}{80} = \frac{1}{10} = 0.10 = 10\%$

* If you use a percent circle to draw a circle
  graph, mark a sector for each percent. Then
  label each sector and give the graph a title.

* If you do not have a percent circle, write each
  percent as a decimal, then multiply by 360°
  to determine the size of each sector angle.
  For example, the sector angle for 10% is:
  $0.10 \times 360° = 36°$

H I N T

Remember the percents
should add to 100%.

* Use a compass to draw a circle.
  Use a protractor and the angles
  you calculated to divide the
  circle into sectors.
  Label each sector, and
  give the graph a title.

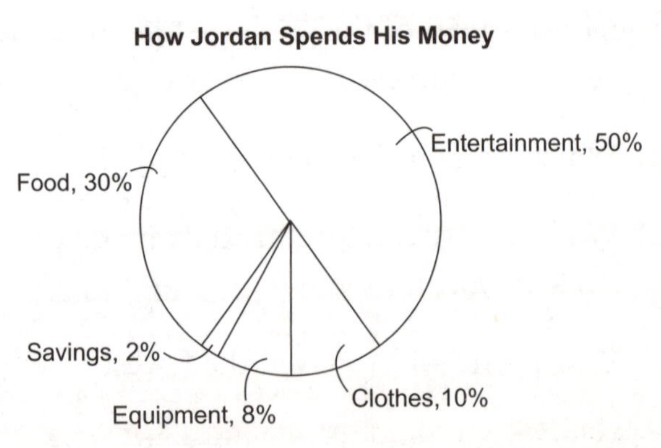

1. Emily and Tasha checked the cars in the teachers' parking lot.
The students grouped the cars according to where the headquarters of
the manufacturer are located. Here are their data.

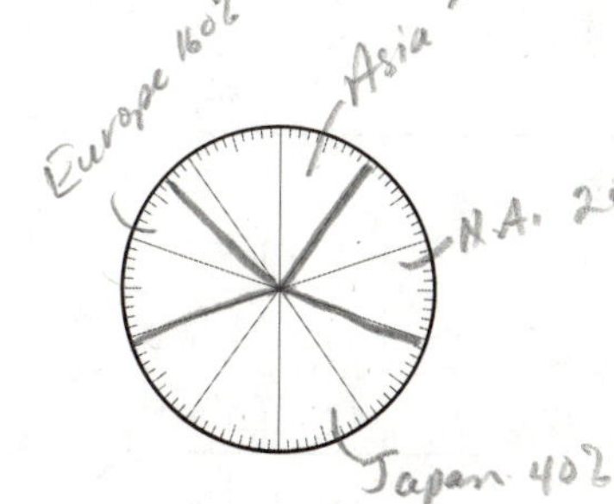

Origin of car	Number of cars
Asia (except Japan)	12
Europe	8
Japan	20
North America	10

a) How many cars are in the lot? __50__

b) Write each type of car as a fraction of the total number of cars in the lot.

$\frac{12}{50}$, $\frac{8}{50}$, $\frac{20}{50}$, $\frac{10}{50}$

c) Write each fraction in part b as a percent.

24%, 16%, 40%, 20%

d) Draw a circle graph in the percent circle.

2. A group of grade 7 students was asked how many of Canada's other provinces and
territories they have visited for at least one day. The data are shown below.

Number of provinces and territories visited	Number of students	Each number of students as a fraction of the total	Each fraction as a percent	Each percent as an angle
0	2	$\frac{2}{25}$	8%	28.8 → 29°
1	4	$\frac{4}{25}$	16%	57.6 → 58°
2 or 3	10	$\frac{10}{25}$	40%	144 → 144°
4 to 6	5	$\frac{5}{25}$	20%	72 → 72°
7 to 10	3	$\frac{3}{25}$	12%	43.2 → 43°
11 or 12	1	$\frac{1}{25}$	4%	14.4 → 14°

a) Find the total number of students surveyed. __25__   360

b) Complete the table. For the last column, write each
percent as a decimal, then multiply by 360°. Write each
angle to the nearest degree where necessary.

c) Draw and label a circle graph.

3. Here are data for the students who wrote Diploma Exams in Alberta, in 2004/2005:

Alberta Diploma Exams Written, 2004/2005

Number of exams written	Percent of students	Each percent as an angle
0	18%	64.8 → 65°
1	4%	14.4 → 14°
2	13%	46.8 → 47°
3	12%	43.2 → 43°
4	19%	68.4 → 68°
5	21%	75.6 → 76°
6 or more	13%	46.8 → 47°

a) Draw and label a circle graph to display the data in the table.

b) Approximately what fraction of the students wrote 4 or 5 exams? $40\% = \frac{40}{100} = \frac{2}{5}$

How do you know? graph tells us

____

4. The table below shows some First Nations' Treaties in Saskatchewan and the approximate percent of land area controlled within each treaty.
The table is not complete.

Saskatchewan's First Nations' Land by Treaty

Treaty number	Land area as a percent	Sector angle in degrees
2	5%	18°
4	21%	75.6 → 76°
5	3%	10.8 → 11°
6	25%	90°
8	14%	50.4 → 50°
10	32%	115.2 → 115°

a) Find the percent of land controlled within treaty number 4.
Complete the table.

b) Display the data in a circle graph.

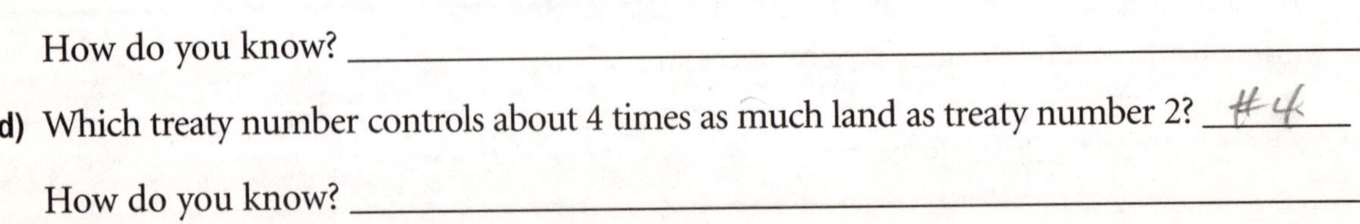

c) Which treaty number controls one-quarter of the land? #6

How do you know? ____

d) Which treaty number controls about 4 times as much land as treaty number 2? #4

How do you know? ____

5. A group of adults was asked this question: "How do you regularly listen to music?"
Here is what the adults said.

Adults' Listening Preferences

Category	Number of adults	Fraction of adults	Percent of adults	Each percent as an angle
CD	4	$\frac{4}{40}=\frac{1}{10}$	10%	36°
MP3 player	12	$\frac{12}{40}=\frac{3}{10}$	30%	108°
Radio	18	$\frac{18}{40}=\frac{9}{20}$	45%	162°
Tape/walkman	4	$\frac{4}{40}$	10%	36°
Vinyl	2	$\frac{2}{40}$	5%	18°

a) Complete the table.

b) Draw a circle graph.

c) Write, then answer a question about your graph.

____

____

6. Matt loves to race his BMX bicycle.
Last summer, he attended a race in Kelowna, B.C.
The registration in each class is given in the table below.

Class	Number of riders
20" elite women	19
20" elite men	65
20" elite junior women	31
20" elite junior men	96
Elite cruiser	29

$\frac{19}{240} = 8\% = 29°$

$\frac{65}{240} = 27\% = 97°$

$\frac{31}{240} = 13\% = 47°$

$\frac{96}{240} = 40\% = 144°$

$\frac{29}{240} = 12\% = 43°$

100 360

a) Display the data on a circle graph.
Write the percents and angles to the nearest whole number where necessary.

b) Colour the graph and include a legend.

c) Which class did about one-quarter of the riders enter? _________________________
How do you know?

____

d) Write a question you could answer using your circle graph. _________________________

____

Answer your question. ____

In Your Words

Here are some of the important words of this unit.
Build your own glossary by recording definitions and examples here. The first one is done for you.

radius _distance between_ _a point on a circle and the centre of_ _the circle_ _For example,_ _the radius of this_ _circle is 1 cm._

1 cm

diameter

circumference

area of a circle

area of a triangle

circle graph

List other mathematical words you need to know.

4.1   **1.** This circle has its centre at point O.

     a) Draw a radius of the circle.
        What is the length of the radius? __________

     b) Draw a diameter of the circle.
        What is the length of the diameter? ________

     c) Write a relationship between the radius, r, and the diameter, d, of a circle.

____

4.2   **2.** Billy plans to put some plastic edging around his circular fish pond.
The diameter of the pond is 5 m.
Find the amount of plastic edging that Billy will need.

____

4.3
4.4   **3.** Find the area of each shape.

a)

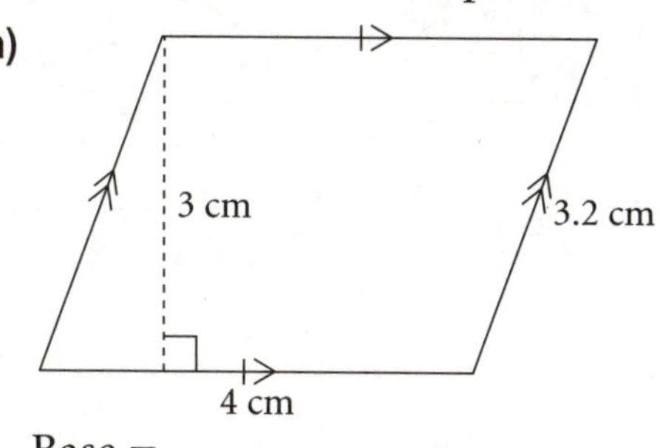

Base = ________
Height = ______
Area = base × height
Area = _______ × _______ = _______
The area is ___________.

b)

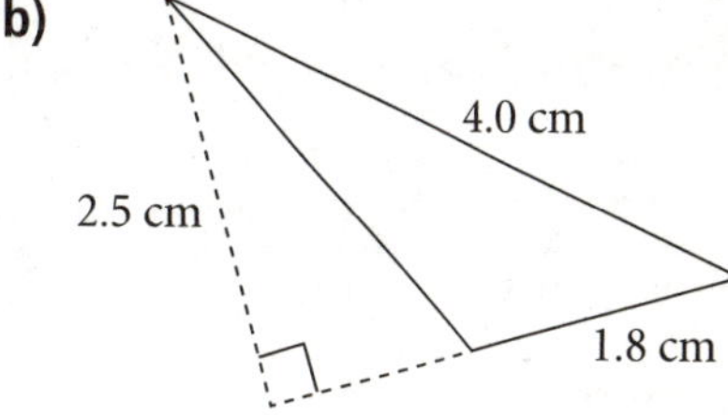

The area is ___________.

4.5   **4.** Estimate the area of each circle, then calculate the area to the nearest square unit.

     a) radius of 4 mm   **b)** diameter of 10.1 m

        Estimate: ________________   Estimate: ________________

        Area: ___________________   Area: ___________________

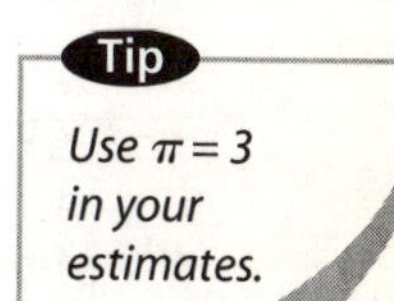

5. Kelly and her friends plan to start a rock band.
They will play in their town and in the surrounding area.
The band has made this table to show its expenses
as percents of what it will earn.

Expenses of Kelly and the Rockers

Type of Expense	Percent of budget	Each percent as an angle
Advertising	10%	
Clothes	20%	
Equipment	25%	
Food	15%	
Travel	30%	

a) Complete the table.

b) Draw and label a circle graph.

c) The band estimates it will earn $10 000 from its gigs.

How much money will the band spend on food? _________

d) Which type of expense is one-half the amount spent on clothes? _______________
How can you tell this:

i) from the table? ____

ii) from the graph? ____

____

e) The band wants to spend $5000 on equipment upgrades.
How much will the band have to earn to be able to do this? _____________

f) Write a question you can answer from the graph.

____

____

g) Answer your question.

____

Operations with Fractions

Just for Fun

Toothpick Puzzle

Make this shape with 12 toothpicks:

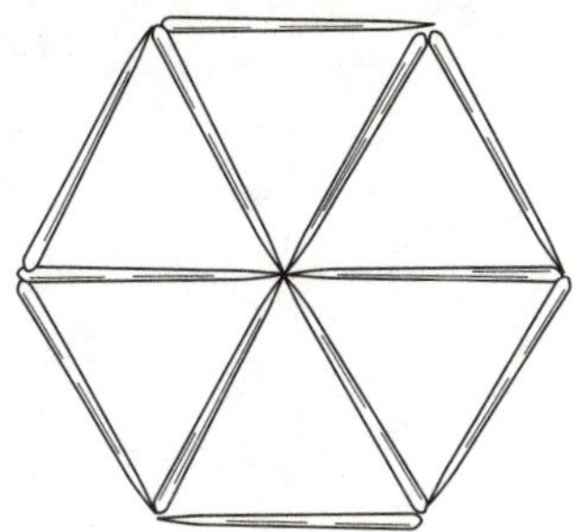

Remove 4 toothpicks to leave 3 triangles.

Penny Puzzle

Arrange 10 pennies in this pattern:

Move 3 pennies to make this pattern:

Compose It!

A Game for 2 or more

Make as many words as you can from the letters of the word EQUIVALENT.
The person who makes the most words in 1 minute wins!

Equivalent Fractions

$\frac{1}{2}$, $\frac{2}{4}$, $\frac{3}{6}$, and $\frac{6}{12}$ are **equivalent fractions.**

They name the same fractional parts.

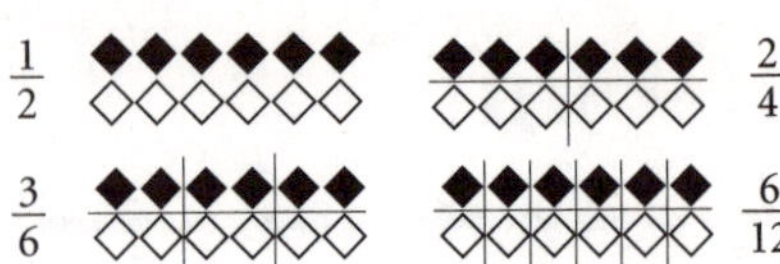

➤ To find equivalent fractions, multiply or divide the numerator and denominator by the same number.

$\frac{6}{8}$ is equivalent to $\frac{3}{4}$. $\frac{3}{4}$ is equivalent to $\frac{9}{12}$.

So, $\frac{3}{4}$, $\frac{6}{8}$, and $\frac{9}{12}$ are all equivalent fractions.

➤ You can use number lines to find equivalent fractions.

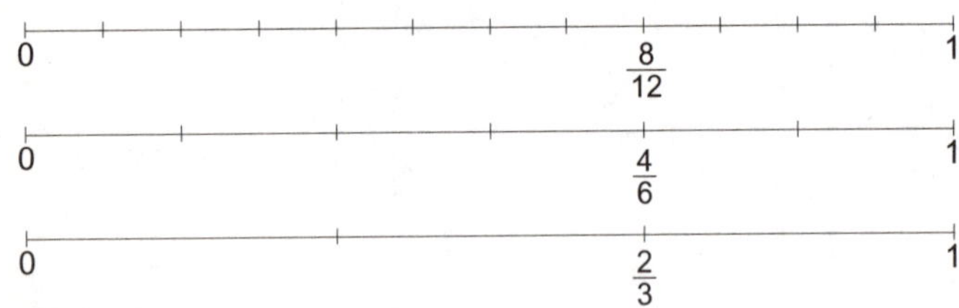

$\frac{2}{3}$, $\frac{4}{6}$, and $\frac{8}{12}$ align vertically; they are equivalent fractions.

✓ Check

1. Write 3 equivalent fractions to represent each shaded part.

a) ____________   b) ____________   c) ____________

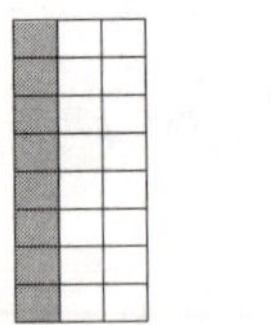   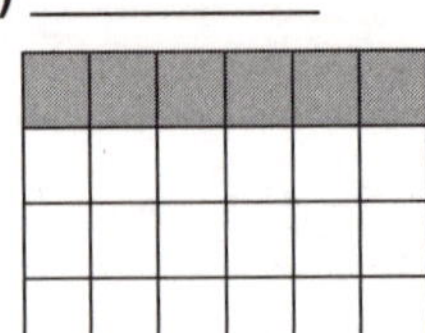   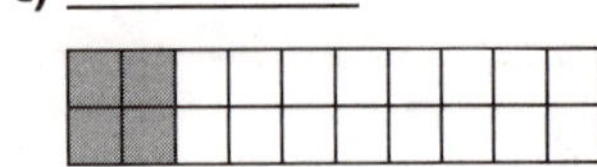

2. Write 3 equivalent fractions for each fraction.

a) $\frac{10}{8}$ ____________   b) $\frac{2}{5}$ ____________   c) $\frac{10}{60}$ ____________

Relating Mixed Numbers and Improper Fractions

➤ This diagram models the **mixed number** $2\frac{3}{5}$:

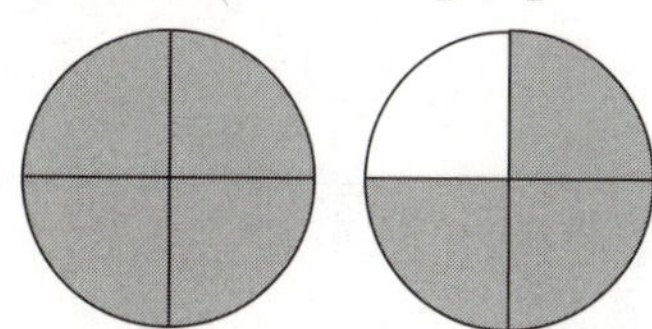

The diagram shows 2 wholes and 3 fifths.
Two wholes are the same as 10 fifths.
Ten-fifths and 3 fifths are 13 fifths.

$$2\frac{3}{5} = \frac{10}{5} + \frac{3}{5} = \frac{13}{5}$$

$\frac{13}{5}$ is an **improper fraction.**
It represents the same amount as $2\frac{3}{5}$.

➤ To write the improper fraction $\frac{7}{4}$ as a mixed number, picture 7 fourths.

There are 4 fourths in 1 whole.

So, $\frac{7}{4}$ is 1 whole and 3 fourths.

So, $\frac{7}{4}$ is the same as $1\frac{3}{4}$.

✓ Check

3. Write an improper fraction and a mixed number to represent each diagram.

a) ______

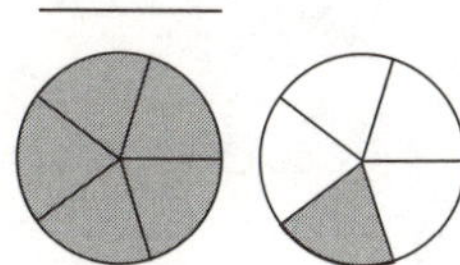

b) ______

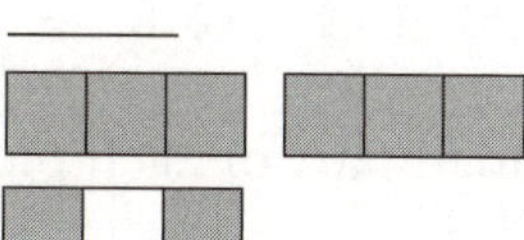

c) ______

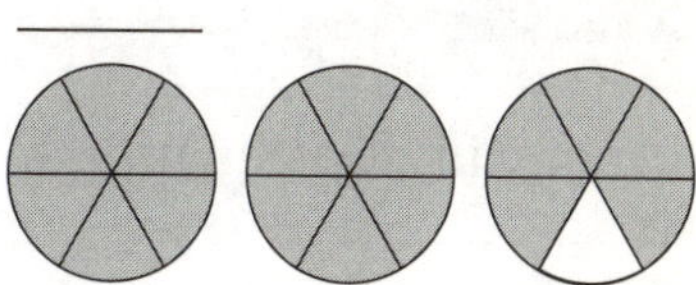

4. Write each mixed number as an improper fraction.

a) $2\frac{3}{8}$ ___

b) $4\frac{1}{3}$ ___

c) $3\frac{4}{5}$ ___

5. Write each improper fraction as a mixed number.

a) $\frac{20}{9}$ ____

b) $\frac{18}{12}$ _________

c) $\frac{20}{8}$ _________

Quick Review

Here is one way to add $\frac{1}{2}$ and $\frac{5}{6}$.

Use Pattern Blocks.
The yellow hexagon represents one whole.

➤ Model $\frac{1}{2}$ and $\frac{5}{6}$.

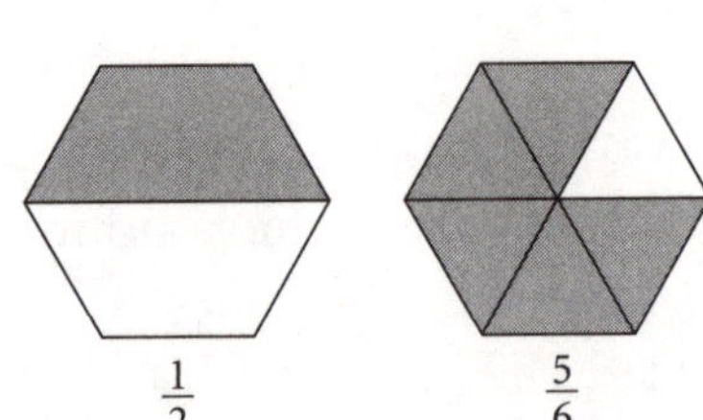

➤ Take 3 sixths from $\frac{5}{6}$.

Put $\frac{3}{6}$ with the $\frac{1}{2}$ to make 1 whole.

That leaves 2 sixths.

1 whole and 2 sixths equals 1 and 2 sixths,

or 1 and 1 third.

So, $\frac{1}{2} + \frac{5}{6} = 1\frac{2}{6}$

$\qquad\qquad = 1\frac{1}{3}$

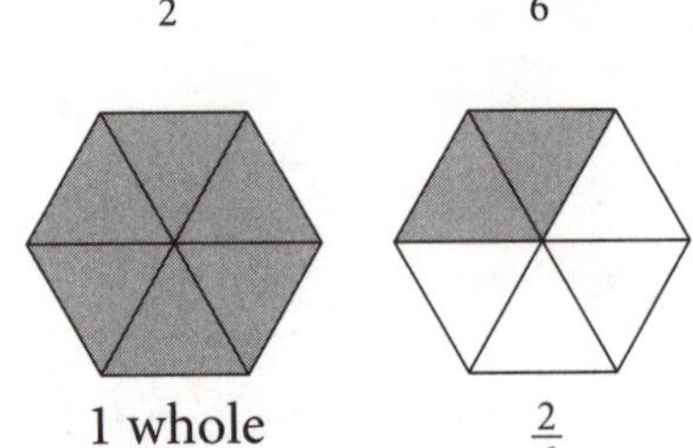

Practice

1. Write an addition equation for the shaded part of each picture.

a)

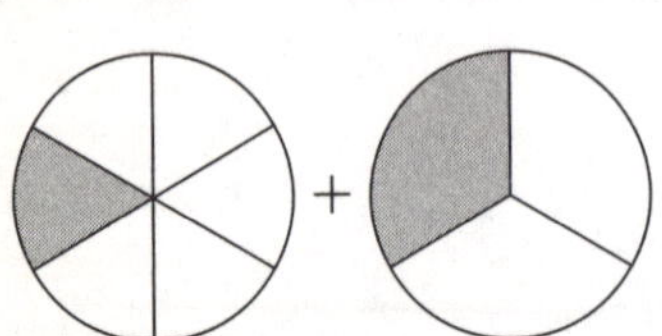

b)

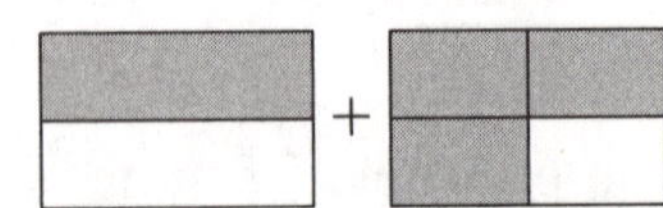

c)

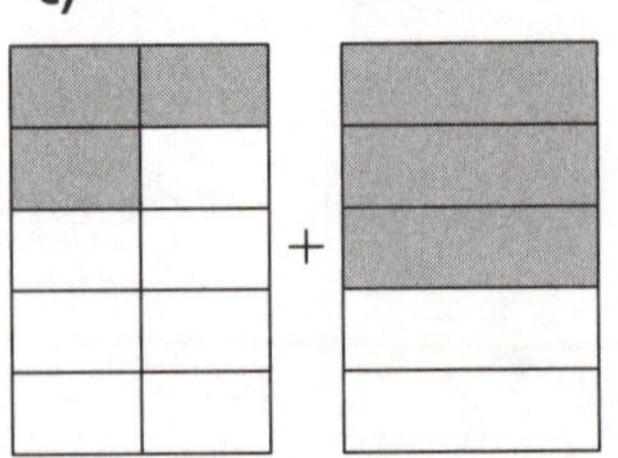

2. Colour the Pattern Blocks to find each sum.

a)

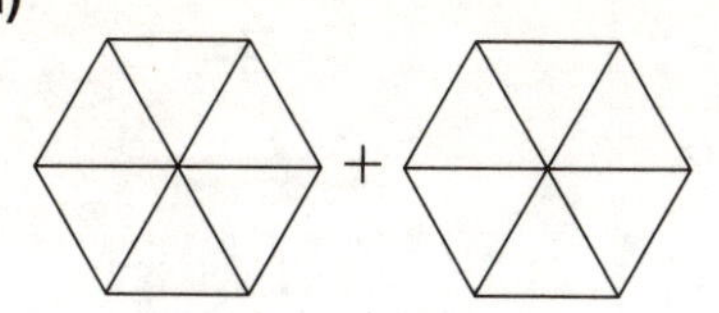

$$\frac{2}{3} + \frac{1}{6} = \underline{\hspace{2cm}}$$

b)

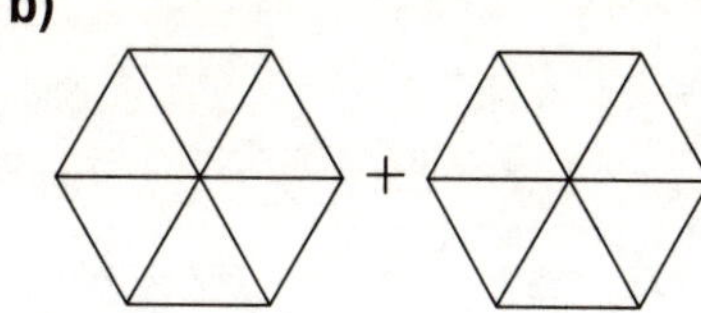

$$\frac{1}{2} + \frac{1}{3} = \underline{\hspace{2cm}}$$

c)

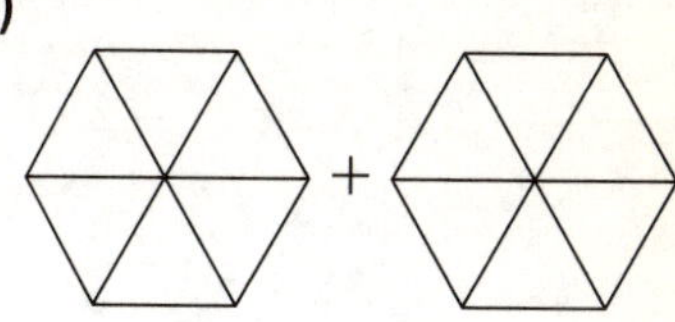

$$\frac{5}{6} + \frac{1}{3} = \underline{\hspace{2cm}}$$

3. Add.

a) $\frac{4}{5} + \frac{1}{5} = \underline{\hspace{2cm}}$

b) $\frac{1}{4} + \frac{2}{4} = \underline{\hspace{2cm}}$

c) $\frac{1}{6} + \frac{4}{6} = \underline{\hspace{2cm}}$

d) $\frac{3}{4} + \frac{3}{4} = \underline{\hspace{2cm}}$

e) $\frac{3}{5} + \frac{4}{5} = \underline{\hspace{2cm}}$

f) $\frac{3}{10} + \frac{6}{10} = \underline{\hspace{2cm}}$

4. Divide and colour the shapes to find each sum.

a)

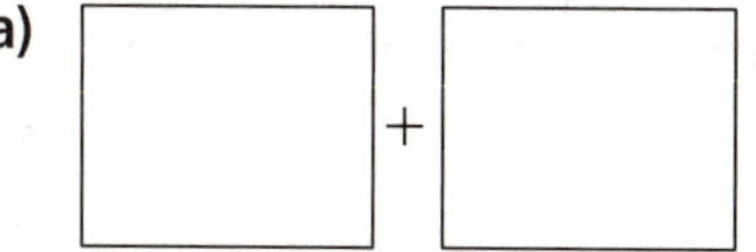

$$\frac{1}{2} + \frac{1}{4} = \underline{\hspace{2cm}}$$

b)

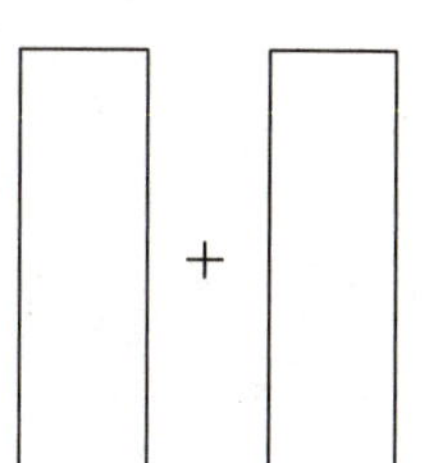

$$\frac{1}{3} + \frac{3}{6} = \underline{\hspace{2cm}}$$

c)

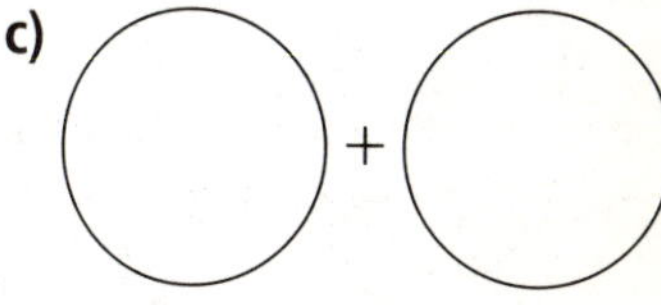

$$\frac{3}{4} + \frac{1}{2} = \underline{\hspace{2cm}}$$

5. Draw a diagram to find each sum.

a) $\frac{1}{4} + \frac{5}{8} = \underline{\hspace{2cm}}$

b) $\frac{1}{2} + \frac{1}{4} = \underline{\hspace{2cm}}$

c) $\frac{1}{3} + \frac{5}{6} = \underline{\hspace{2cm}}$

6. Divide and colour the circles to find each sum.

a) $\frac{1}{2} + \frac{2}{4} = $ ___

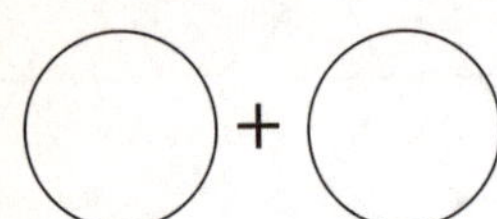 +

b) $\frac{1}{2} + \frac{1}{8} = $ ___

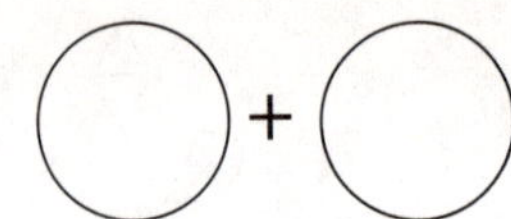 +

c) $\frac{1}{4} + \frac{1}{8} = $ ___

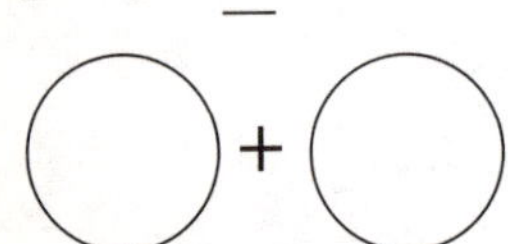 +

d) $\frac{3}{4} + \frac{1}{8} = $ ___

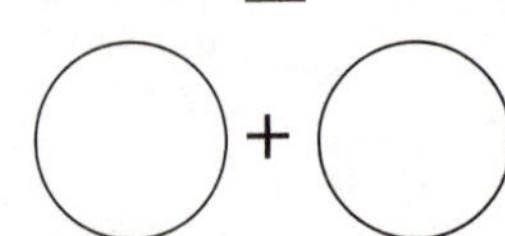 +

7. Draw pictures to show if each sum is greater than or less than 1.

a) $\frac{3}{4} + \frac{2}{4} = $ ______

b) $\frac{1}{2} + \frac{1}{2} = $ ______

c) $\frac{3}{8} + \frac{7}{8} = $ ______

d) $\frac{2}{5} + \frac{2}{5} = $ ______

8. During his first training session, Milo walked for 30 min and ran for 20 min.

a) How many minutes did Milo train the first day? ________

b) Use fractions of an hour.

Write an addition equation that represents Milo's training session. ___________

9. Find as many pairs of fractions as you can that have a sum of 1.

____

Quick Review

There are many models that help you add fractions.
Circle models are useful when the sum of the fractions is less than 1.
Use fraction strips and a number line when the sum of the fractions is greater than 1.

To add $\frac{2}{3} + \frac{1}{2}$, model each fraction with a fraction strip.
Place the fraction strips end-to-end on a number line that shows halves.

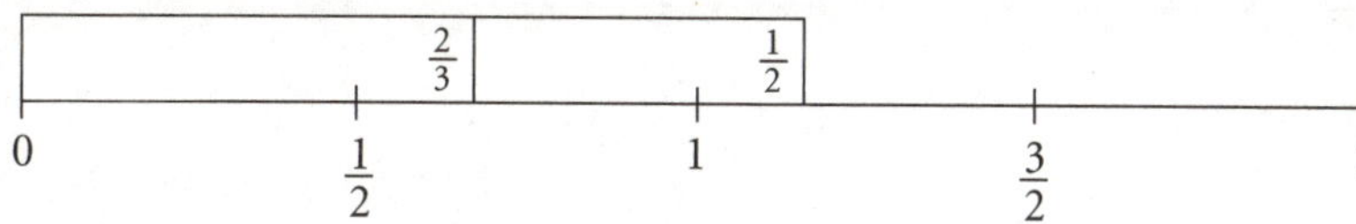

The right end of the strips does not line up with a fraction.
Try using a number line that shows thirds.

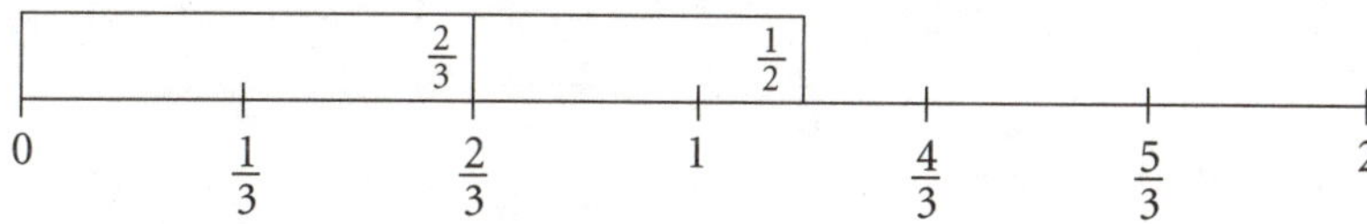

The right end of the strips still does not line up with a fraction.
Find a number line that shows sixths.

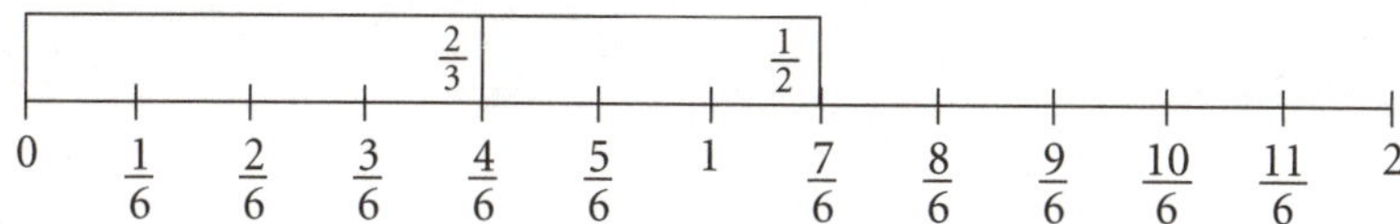

The right end of the strips lines up with $\frac{7}{6}$.

So, $\frac{2}{3} + \frac{1}{2} = \frac{7}{6}$

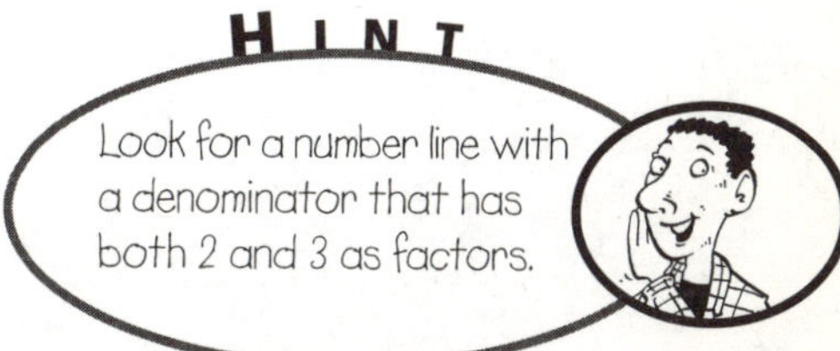

Practice

1. Use fraction strips to add: $\frac{3}{8} + \frac{1}{4}$

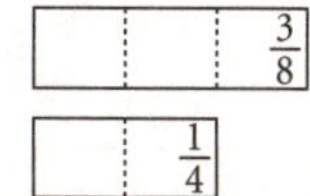

$\frac{3}{8} + \frac{1}{4} = \underline{}$

Key to Success

Form a contact circle with
2 classmates in case you
miss a class.

2. Use fraction strips to add: $\frac{1}{2} + \frac{1}{5}$

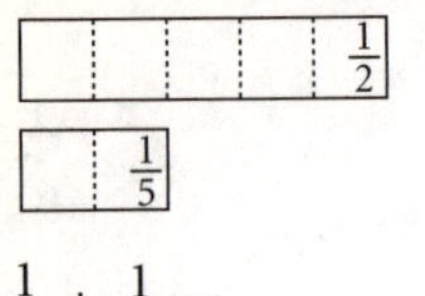

$$\frac{1}{2} + \frac{1}{5} = \underline{\qquad}$$

3. Use the number lines below.
List fractions equivalent to each fraction.

a) $\frac{1}{2}$ _____________ **b)** $\frac{1}{4}$ _________ **c)** $\frac{1}{3}$ _________

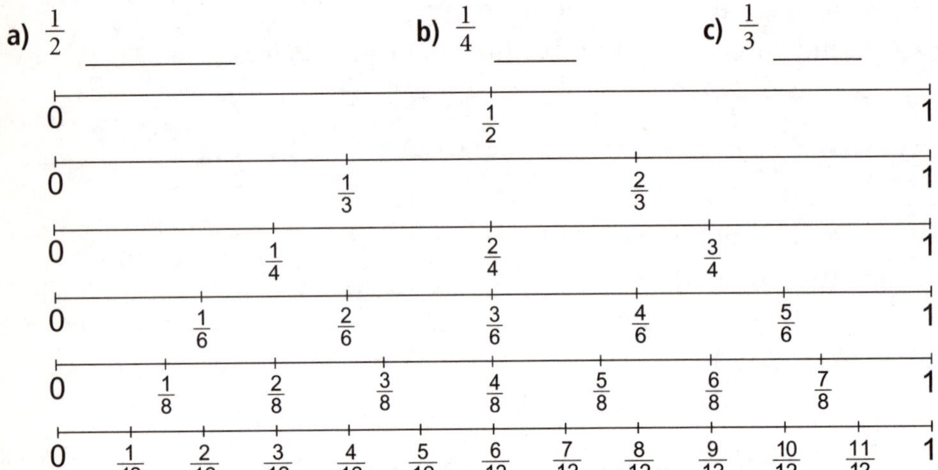

4. Write an addition equation for each picture.

a) _________________________

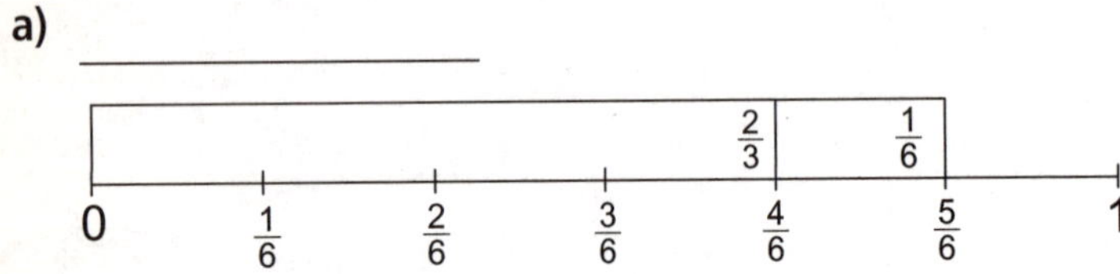

b) _________________________

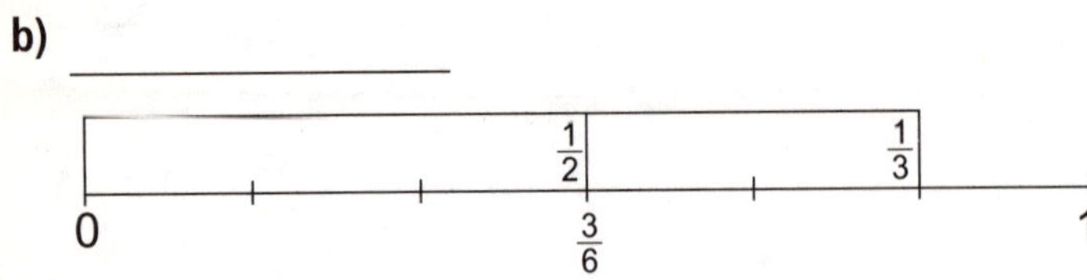

c) _________________________________

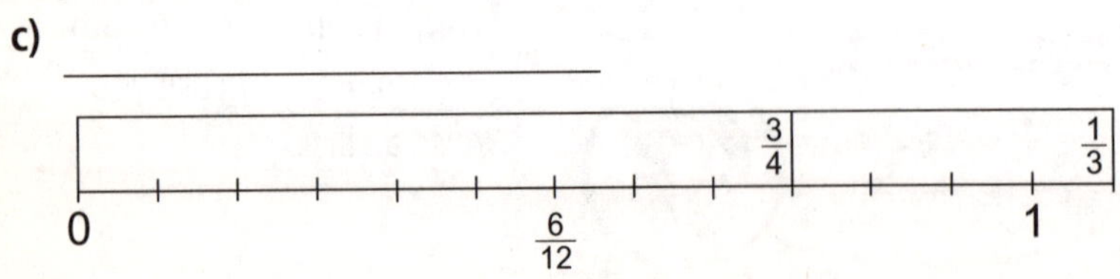

5. Add. Use your fraction strips and a number line like this to help.

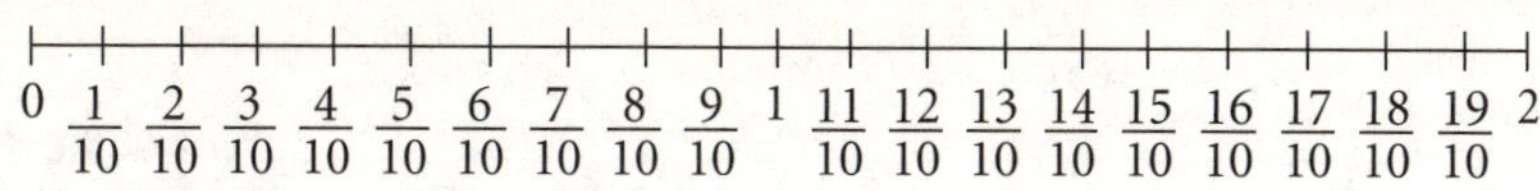

$$\frac{3}{5} + \frac{3}{10} = \underline{\quad}$$

6. Use fraction strips and number lines like these to help you add fractions.

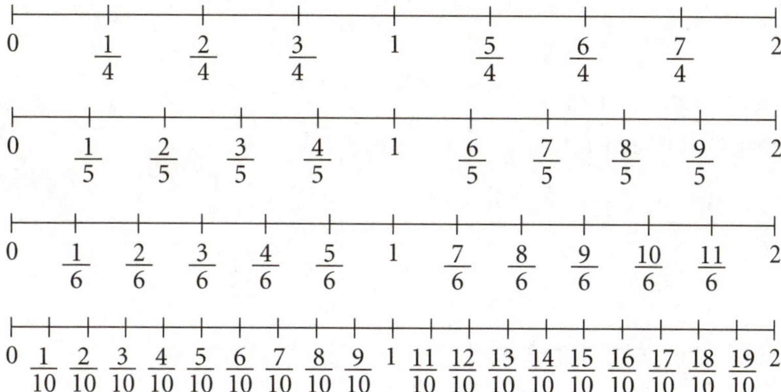

a) $\frac{3}{2} + \frac{2}{4} = \underline{\quad}$

b) $\frac{6}{6} + \frac{3}{4} = \underline{\quad}$

c) $\frac{9}{10} + \frac{3}{5} = \underline{\quad}$

7. Add.

a) $\frac{1}{10} + \frac{1}{5} = \underline{\quad}$

b) $\frac{1}{6} + \frac{1}{2} = \underline{\quad}$

c) $\frac{2}{3} + \frac{2}{6} = \underline{\quad}$

d) $\frac{2}{5} + \frac{3}{10} = \underline{\quad}$

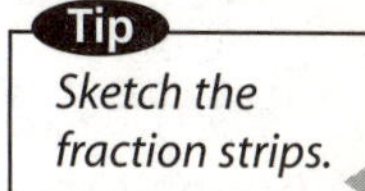

8. Robert and his brother ordered a pizza. Robert ate $\frac{1}{4}$ of the pizza.

His brother ate $\frac{3}{8}$ of the pizza.

How much pizza was eaten? $\underline{\quad}$

9. Three friends shared a chocolate bar.

Anika ate $\frac{1}{3}$ of the chocolate bar, Ali ate $\frac{1}{6}$, and Augusto ate $\frac{1}{3}$.

a) What fraction of the chocolate bar did Anika and Ali eat? $\underline{\quad}$

b) What fraction of the chocolate bar did the 3 friends eat? $\underline{\quad}$

Quick Review

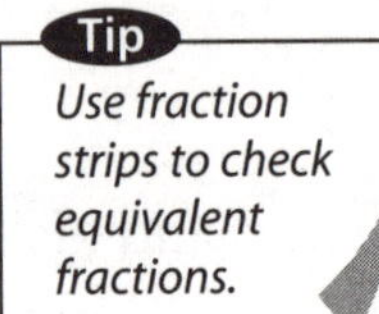

➤ To add fractions with the same denominator, add the numerators.
Then write the sum of the numerators over the common denominator.

For example, $\frac{1}{12} + \frac{4}{12} = \frac{5}{12}$

➤ To add fractions with different denominators,
first write them with the same denominator.

For example, to add $\frac{1}{2} + \frac{3}{5}$, estimate first.

Think: $\frac{3}{5} > \frac{1}{2}$; so, $\frac{1}{2} + \frac{3}{5} > 1$

To add $\frac{1}{2} + \frac{3}{5}$, find equivalent fractions for $\frac{1}{2}$ and $\frac{3}{5}$
with a common denominator.

The common denominator is a multiple of 2 and 5.
Multiples of 2 are: 2, 4, 6, 8, **10**, 12, 14, . . .
Multiples of 5 are: 5, **10**, 15, . . .
10 is a common multiple of 2 and 5.
So, you can use 10 as the common denominator.

Then, write the equivalent fractions for $\frac{1}{2}$ and $\frac{3}{5}$ with 10 as the denominator.

To get equivalent fractions, multiply the numerator and denominator

by the same number.

$$\overset{\times 5}{\frac{1}{2}} = \frac{5}{10} \underset{\times 5}{\qquad} \qquad \overset{\times 2}{\frac{3}{5}} = \frac{6}{10} \underset{\times 2}{\qquad}$$

> **Tip**
> Use fraction
> strips to check
> equivalent
> fractions.

$$\frac{1}{2} + \frac{3}{5} = \frac{5}{10} + \frac{6}{10}$$

$$= \frac{11}{10}$$

You can write a fraction greater than 1 as a mixed number.

$$\frac{11}{10} = 1\frac{1}{10}$$

1. Write 2 equivalent fractions for each fraction.

a) $\frac{4}{5}$ 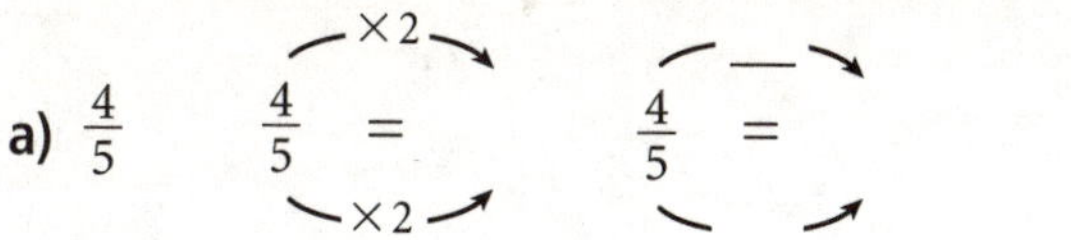

b) $\frac{4}{6}$ 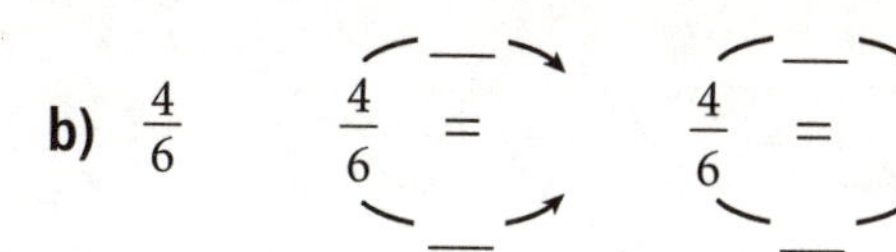

2. Complete each equation to make it true.

a) $\frac{3}{4} = \frac{}{12}$

b) $\frac{1}{2} = \frac{}{10}$

c) $\frac{4}{6} = \frac{}{3}$

d) $\frac{10}{12} = \frac{}{6}$

3. Find a common denominator for each pair of fractions.

a) $\frac{1}{2}$ and $\frac{3}{4}$

The multiples of 2 are: ____

The multiples of 4 are: ____

The lowest common multiple and a common denominator is: ___

b) $\frac{2}{3}$ and $\frac{3}{5}$

The multiples of 3 are: ____

The multiples of 5 are: ____

The lowest common multiple and a common denominator is: ____

4. Add.

a) $\frac{2}{9} + \frac{1}{3}$

The multiples of 9 are: ____

The multiples of 3 are: ____

The lowest common multiple of 9 and 3 is: __

Use this as a common denominator.

$\frac{1}{3} = $ $\times 3$

$\frac{2}{9} + \frac{1}{3} = $ ______

$= \frac{}{}$

b) $\dfrac{7}{10} + \dfrac{1}{6}$

The lowest common multiple of 10 and 6 is: __________.

$$\dfrac{7}{10} + \dfrac{1}{6} = \underline{\hspace{3em}}$$

$$= \underline{\hspace{2em}}$$

$$= \underline{\hspace{2em}}$$

5. Add. Write each sum in simplest form.

a) $\dfrac{5}{6} + \dfrac{1}{3} = \underline{\hspace{2em}}$ **b)** $\dfrac{2}{3} + \dfrac{3}{4} = \underline{\hspace{2em}}$ **c)** $\dfrac{3}{10} + \dfrac{1}{2} = \underline{\hspace{3em}}$

6. Colin is wrapping presents.

He needs $\dfrac{3}{4}$ of a metre of green ribbon and $\dfrac{7}{8}$ of a metre of red ribbon.

How much ribbon does Colin need altogether?

$$\underline{\hspace{8em}}$$

7. Complete this magic square so that the sum of every row, column, and diagonal is 1.

Write all fractions in simplest form.

$\dfrac{8}{15}$	$\dfrac{1}{15}$	
	$\dfrac{1}{3}$	

Quick Review

When you subtract $7 - 3$, you could think:
What do I add to 3 to make 7?
You can use the same strategy to subtract fractions.

To subtract $\frac{7}{12} - \frac{1}{2}$, use fraction strips and a number line.

Think: What do I add to $\frac{1}{2}$ to get $\frac{7}{12}$?

The lowest common multiple of 12 and 2 is 12.
Use a number line that shows twelfths.

Place the $\frac{1}{2}$ strip on the number line with its right end at $\frac{7}{12}$.

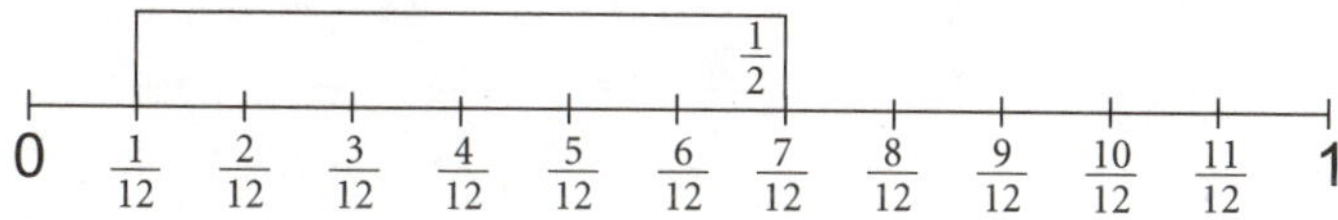

The left end of the strip is at $\frac{1}{12}$.

So, $\frac{7}{12} - \frac{1}{2} = \frac{1}{12}$

Practice

1. Use Pattern Blocks. Subtract.

    a) $\frac{1}{2} - \frac{1}{3} =$ _______   **b)** $\frac{5}{6} - \frac{4}{6} =$ _______   **c)** $\frac{2}{3} - \frac{1}{2} =$ _______

    d) $\frac{2}{3} - \frac{2}{6} =$ _______   **e)** $\frac{1}{2} - \frac{1}{6} =$ _______   **f)** $\frac{1}{2} - \frac{3}{6} =$ _______

2. Use Pattern Blocks. Is each difference greater than $\frac{1}{2}$ or less than $\frac{1}{2}$?
Show how you know.

    a) $\frac{5}{6} - \frac{1}{6}$

    b) $1 - \frac{1}{3}$

    c) $\frac{5}{6} - \frac{1}{2}$

3. Use each diagram to subtract.

a)

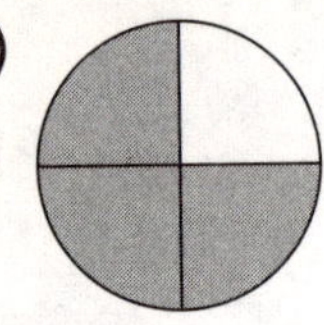

$$\frac{3}{4} - \frac{1}{2} = \underline{\qquad}$$

b)

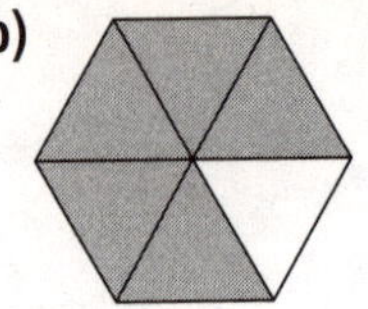

$$\frac{5}{6} - \frac{2}{3} = \underline{\qquad}$$

c)

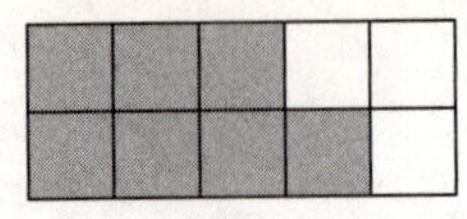

$$\frac{7}{10} - \frac{3}{5} = \underline{\qquad}$$

4. Use fraction circles to subtract.

a) $\frac{9}{10} - \frac{2}{5} = \underline{\qquad}$

b) $\frac{5}{8} - \frac{1}{4} = \underline{\qquad}$

c) $1 - \frac{2}{3} = \underline{\qquad}$

d) $2 - \frac{3}{4} = \underline{\qquad}$

e) $\frac{4}{5} - \frac{1}{2} = \underline{\qquad}$

f) $\frac{1}{2} - \frac{1}{4} = \underline{\qquad}$

5. Write a subtraction equation for each picture.

a) ________________

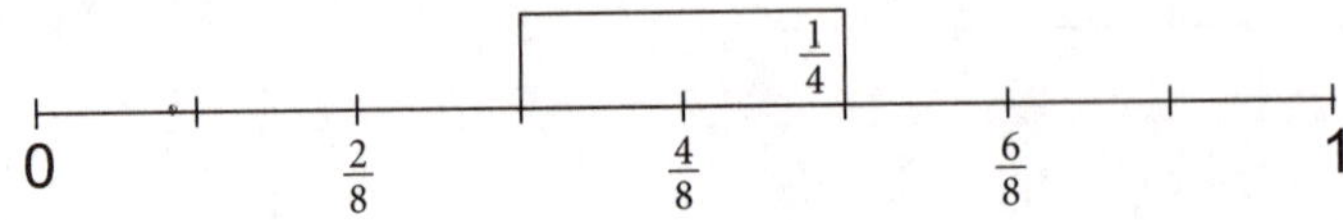

b) ________________

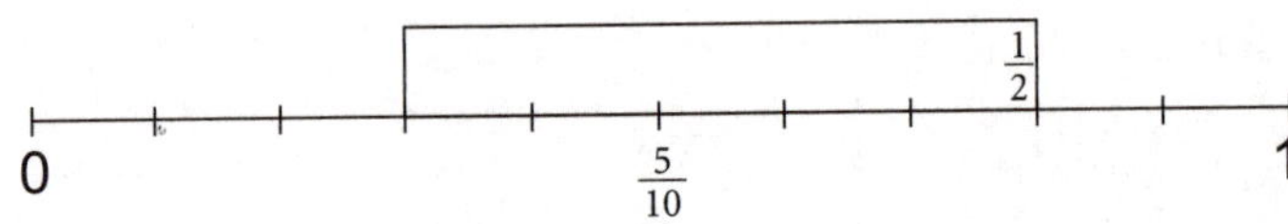

c) ________________

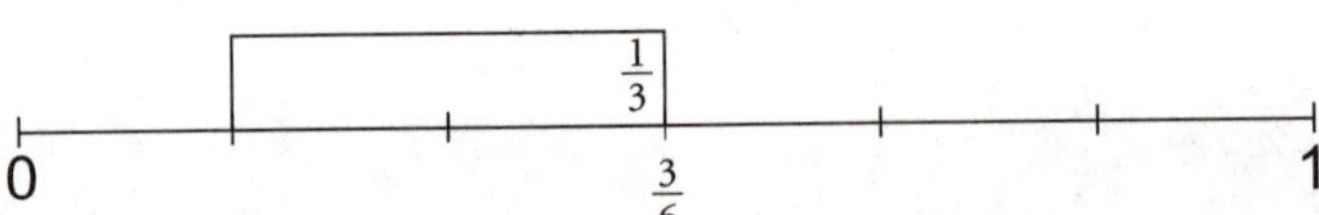

6. Subtract.

$$\frac{6}{10} - \frac{2}{5}$$

The lowest common multiple of 10 and 5 is: _______

Use a number line that shows _______.

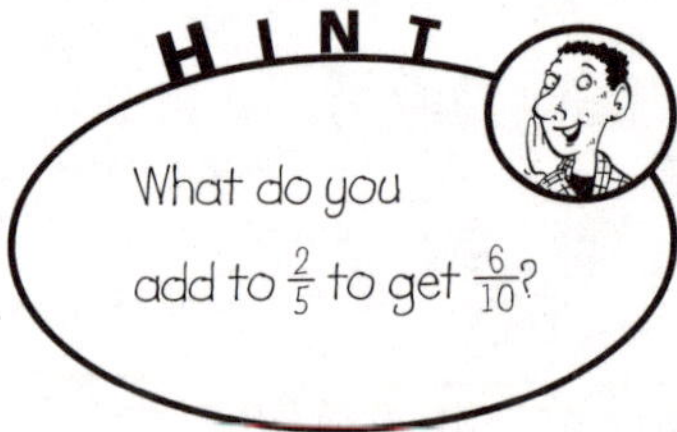

Place the $\frac{2}{5}$ fraction strip on the number line with the right end at $\frac{6}{10}$.

The left end of the $\frac{2}{5}$ strip is at: ___

So, $\frac{6}{10} - \frac{2}{5} = \underline{\qquad}$

7. Subtract.

a) $\frac{5}{6} - \frac{1}{6}$

Use a number line that shows:

____

The left end of the $\frac{1}{6}$ strip is at: __

So, $\frac{5}{6} - \frac{1}{6} =$ ______

b) $\frac{7}{8} - \frac{3}{4}$

Use a number line that shows:

____

The left end of the $\frac{3}{4}$ strip is at: __

So, $\frac{7}{8} - \frac{3}{4} =$ __

8. Subtract.

a) $\frac{9}{10} - \frac{1}{2} =$ ________

b) $\frac{5}{6} - \frac{1}{2} =$ ______

c) $\frac{11}{6} - \frac{1}{3} =$ __________

d) $1 - \frac{5}{8} =$ __

9. Sergio has $\frac{7}{8}$ of a cup of trail mix. He gives Lien $\frac{3}{4}$ of a cup.
How much does Sergio have left? Use pictures, numbers, and words.

____

____

10. Kate drank $\frac{7}{10}$ of a glass of buttermilk.

Vicky drank $\frac{4}{5}$ of a glass.

a) Who drank more buttermilk? ______

b) How much more did she drink? Explain how you know.

____

11. Write 5 subtraction statements with a difference of $\frac{1}{2}$.

_________ _________ _________ _________ _________

Quick Review

The strategies for subtracting fractions are similar to those for adding fractions.

➤ If the denominators are the same, subtract the numerators.
Then write the difference over the common denominator.

4 fifths – 1 fifth = 3 fifths

$$\frac{4}{5} - \frac{1}{5} = \frac{3}{5}$$

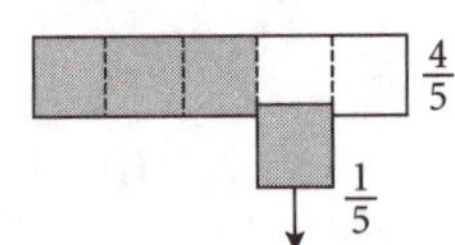

➤ If the denominators are different, subtract equivalent fractions
with the same denominator.

To subtract $\frac{1}{2} - \frac{1}{8}$, find the lowest common multiple of 2 and 8.

Multiples of 2 are: 2, 4, 6, **8**, 10, 12, …

Multiples of 8 are: **8**, 16, 24, …

The lowest common multiple of 2 and 8 is 8.

Write equivalent fractions using 8 as the denominator.

$$\frac{1}{2} \overset{\times 4}{\underset{\times 4}{=}} \frac{4}{8}$$

So, $\frac{1}{2} - \frac{1}{8} = \frac{4}{8} - \frac{1}{8}$

$$= \frac{3}{8}$$

Tip

Since 8 is a multiple of 2, 8 is the lowest common multiple of 2 and 8.

Practice

1. Subtract.

a) $\frac{7}{8} - \frac{3}{8} = $ _______

b) $\frac{3}{5} - \frac{1}{5} = $ __

c) $\frac{9}{10} - \frac{2}{10} = $ __

d) $\frac{8}{9} - \frac{2}{9} = $ ______

e) $\frac{6}{7} - \frac{1}{7} = $ __

f) $\frac{11}{12} - \frac{3}{12} = $ _______

2. Subtract.

a) $\frac{3}{4} - \frac{1}{12}$

The multiples of 4 are: _______________________________

The multiples of 12 are: _______________________________

A multiple of 4 and 12 is: __

Use this as a common denominator.

$\frac{3}{4} - \frac{1}{12} =$ _______

$=$ _______

b) $\frac{2}{3} - \frac{2}{10}$

The multiples of 3 are: _______________________________

The multiples of 10 are: _______________________________

A multiple of 3 and 10, and a common denominator is: ___

$\frac{2}{3} - \frac{2}{10} =$ _______

$=$ _______

c) $\frac{3}{4} - \frac{3}{10}$

Multiples of 4 are: _______________________________

Multiples of 10 are: _______________________________

A multiple of 4 and 10, and a common denominator is: ___

$\frac{3}{4} - \frac{3}{10} =$ _______

$=$ ___

d) $\frac{3}{2} - \frac{7}{10}$

The multiples of 2 are: _______________________________

The multiples of 10 are: _______________________________

A multiple of 2 and 10, and a common denominator is: ___

$\frac{3}{2} - \frac{7}{10} =$ _______

$=$ _______

3. Subtract: $\dfrac{4}{9} - \dfrac{1}{3}$

The lowest common multiple of 9 and 3 is: _________

$$\dfrac{4}{9} - \dfrac{1}{3} = \underline{\hspace{2cm}}$$

$$= \underline{\hspace{1cm}}$$

4. Subtract. Write the answer in simplest form.

a) $\dfrac{5}{8} - \dfrac{1}{6} =$ _____________

b) $\dfrac{2}{3} - \dfrac{5}{12} =$ _____________

c) $\dfrac{5}{7} - \dfrac{2}{5} =$ _____________

d) $\dfrac{2}{5} - \dfrac{1}{6} =$ _____________

5. Complete this magic square so that the sum of every row, column, and diagonal is 1.

Write all fractions in simplest form.

$\dfrac{3}{8}$	$\dfrac{1}{6}$	
	$\dfrac{1}{3}$	

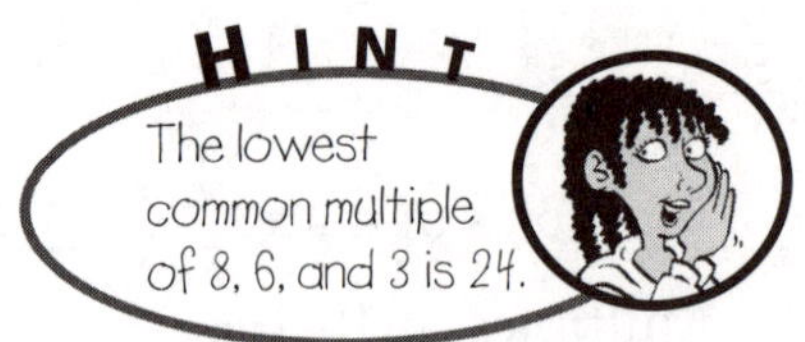

6. Jie weeds $\dfrac{2}{5}$ of her garden on Friday, and $\dfrac{1}{3}$ on Saturday.

How much of the garden still needs to be weeded?

____

Quick Review

To add mixed numbers, follow these steps:

- Change the fractions to equivalent fractions with common denominators.
- Add the fractions.
- Then add the whole numbers.

For example, to add $3\frac{7}{8} + 2\frac{1}{3}$:

$$3\frac{7}{8} + 2\frac{1}{3} = 3\frac{21}{24} + 2\frac{8}{24}$$

$$= 5\frac{29}{24}$$

$$= 5 + \frac{24}{24} + \frac{5}{24}$$

$$= 5 + 1 + \frac{5}{24}$$

$$= 6\frac{5}{24}$$

Practice

1. Write each mixed number as an improper fraction.

a) $4\frac{3}{4} = \frac{16}{4} + \frac{3}{4}$

$= \dfrac{}{4}$

b) $4\frac{7}{10} = \frac{}{10} + \frac{}{10}$

$= \dfrac{}{10}$

c) $2\frac{3}{8} = $ ______

$= $ ____

2. Write each improper fraction as a mixed number.

a) $\frac{8}{5} = \frac{5}{5} + \frac{3}{5}$

$= 1\frac{}{5}$

b) $\frac{16}{3} = \frac{}{3} + \frac{}{3}$

$= $ ____

c) $\frac{17}{5} = $ ______

$= $ ____

d) $\frac{29}{8} = $ ______

$= $ ____

e) $\frac{33}{9} = $ ______

$= $ ______

f) $\frac{41}{7} = $ ______

$= $ ____

3. Write the addition equation represented by each diagram.

a) ______________

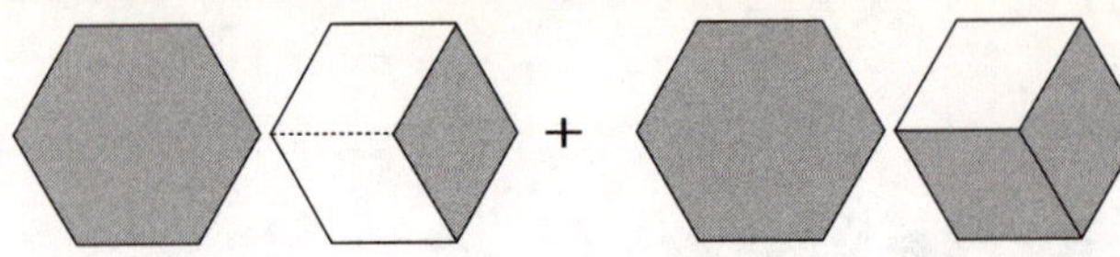

b) ______________

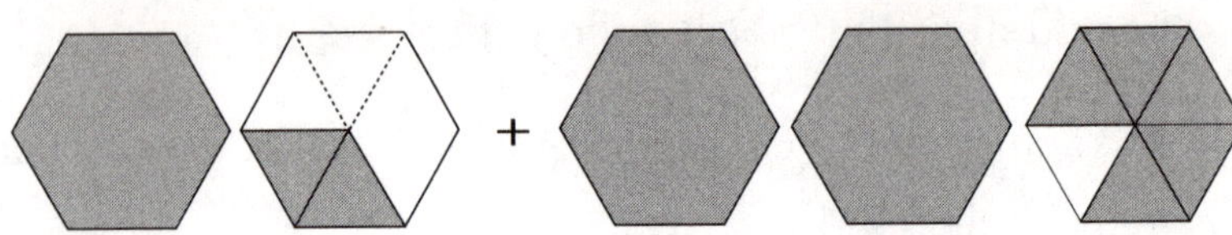

c) ______________

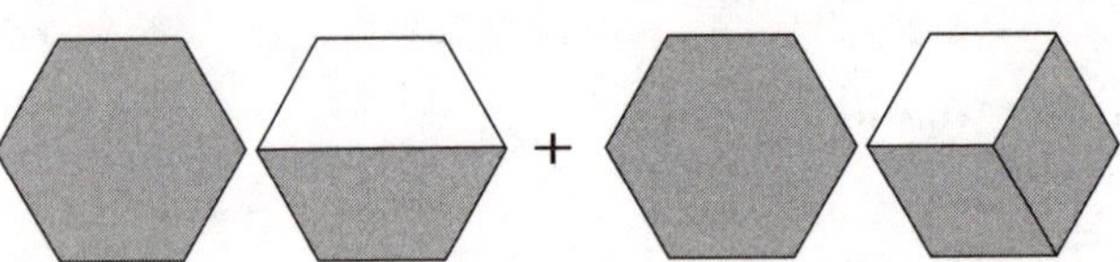

d) ______________

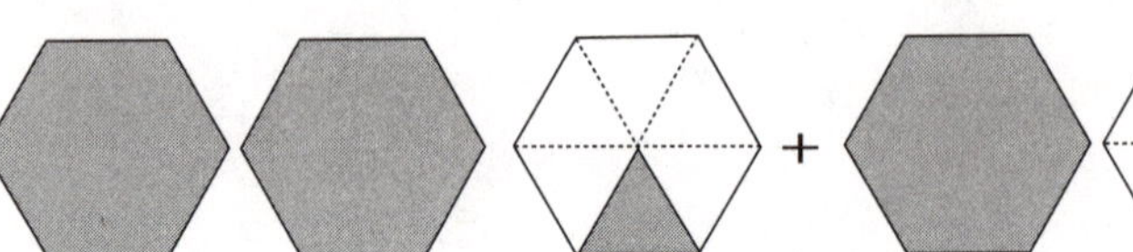

4. Add.

a) $2\frac{1}{2} + 3\frac{2}{5} =$ ______

b) $7\frac{1}{9} + 3\frac{1}{6} =$ ______

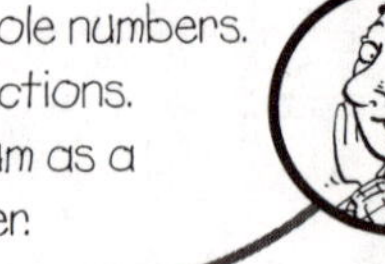

5. Linda is making new curtains for her kitchen and living room windows.

She needs $1\frac{1}{3}$ m of fabric for the kitchen and $2\frac{3}{5}$ m for the living room.

How many metres of fabric does Linda need altogether?

____

6. Last week, Jenna worked $5\frac{2}{3}$ h baby-sitting and $3\frac{1}{2}$ h giving swimming lessons. How many hours did she work in all?

____

Quick Review

To subtract mixed numbers, follow these steps:

- Change the fractions to equivalent fractions with common denominators.
- Subtract the fractions.
- Then subtract the whole numbers.

Sometimes, you need to write improper fractions to subtract mixed numbers.

For example, to subtract: $3\frac{1}{8} - 2\frac{1}{2}$

$3\frac{1}{8} - 2\frac{1}{2} = 3\frac{1}{8} - 2\frac{4}{8}$

Since $\frac{1}{8} < \frac{4}{8}$, write $3\frac{1}{8}$ as $3 + \frac{1}{8}$, then take 1 from 3 and write it as $\frac{8}{8}$.

$3\frac{1}{8} = 2\frac{8}{8} + \frac{1}{8}$

$\quad = 2\frac{9}{8}$

So, $3\frac{1}{8} - 2\frac{1}{2} = 2\frac{9}{8} - 2\frac{4}{8}$

$\qquad\qquad = \frac{5}{8}$

Practice

1. Write a subtraction equation for each picture.

a) _______________

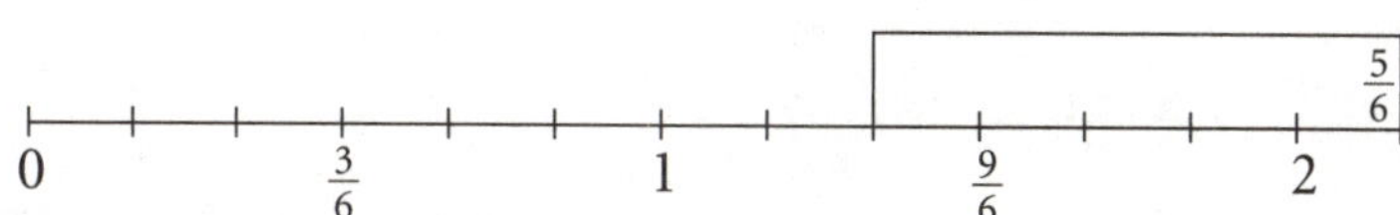

b) _______________

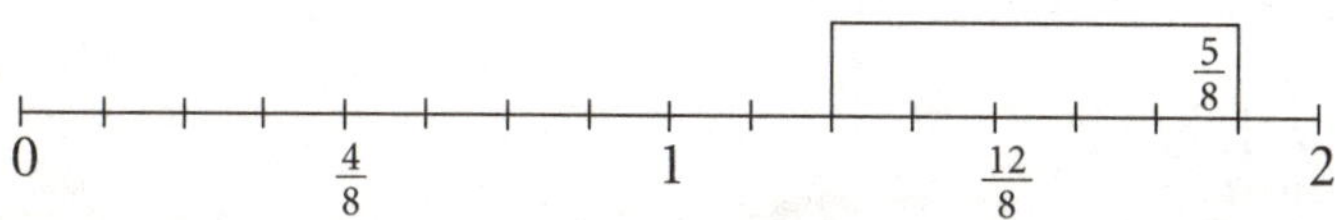

2. Subtract.

a) $3\frac{7}{8} - 1\frac{5}{8} =$ _______

b) $8\frac{3}{4} - 2\frac{1}{4} =$ _______

c) $5\frac{7}{12} - 3\frac{1}{12} =$ _______

3. Write a subtraction equation for each picture.

a) ______________________

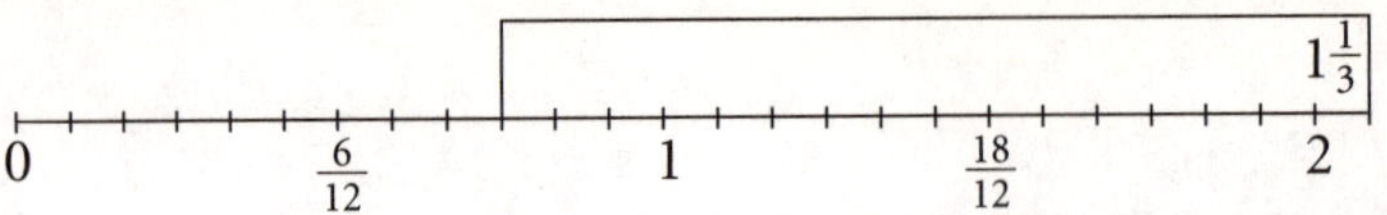

b) ______________________

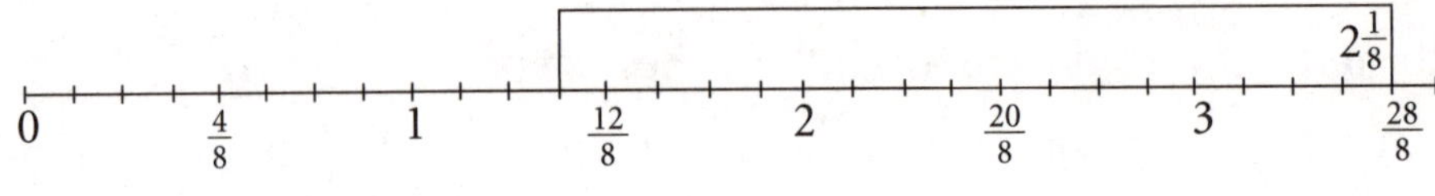

4. We know that $\frac{1}{2} - \frac{1}{3} = \frac{1}{6}$.

Use this result to find each sum.

a) $5\frac{1}{2} - 1\frac{1}{3} =$ ____

b) $2\frac{1}{2} - 1\frac{1}{3} =$ ____

c) $4\frac{1}{2} - \frac{1}{3} =$ ____

5. Regroup to subtract.

a) $2 - \frac{1}{3} = 1\frac{3}{3} -$ ____

$=$ ____

b) $3 - 1\frac{5}{8} =$ ______

$=$ ____

c) $4 - \frac{2}{5} =$ ______

$=$ ____

6. Subtract. Regroup if necessary.

a) $4\frac{1}{9} - 2\frac{2}{3} =$ __________

b) $4 - 1\frac{1}{2} =$ __________

c) $3\frac{4}{7} - 1\frac{1}{2} =$ __________

d) $7\frac{1}{4} - 3\frac{5}{6} =$ __________

7. George swam $8\frac{3}{4}$ laps on Monday and $6\frac{1}{5}$ laps on Tuesday.

How many more laps did he swim on Monday than on Tuesday?

____

8. Armin has 3 flower gardens. He bought 5 bags of mulch.

Armin used $1\frac{1}{2}$ bags of mulch on each garden.

How much mulch is left? ______

In Your Words

Here are some of the important mathematical words of this unit.
Build your own glossary by recording definitions and examples here. The first one is done for you.

improper fraction

a fraction where the numerator is greater than the denominator; for example, $\frac{3}{2}$ is an improper fraction

common denominator

mixed number

unit fraction

related denominators

unrelated denominators

List other mathematical words you need to know.

5.1

1. Colour each pair of Pattern Block shapes to help you to add the fractions.

a) $\frac{1}{2} + \frac{1}{6} =$ _______

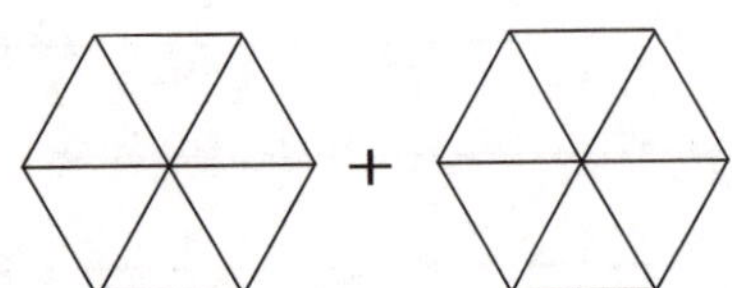

b) $\frac{1}{2} + \frac{1}{3} =$ _______

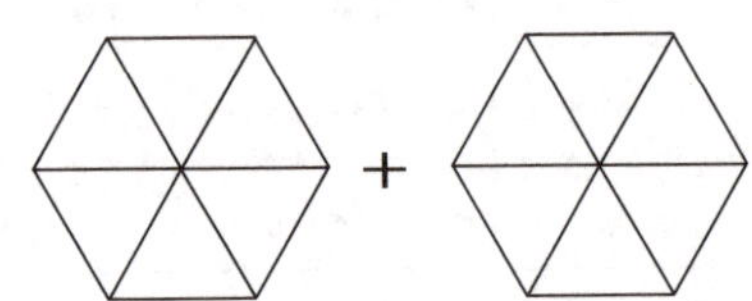

c) $\frac{1}{3} + \frac{1}{6} =$ _______

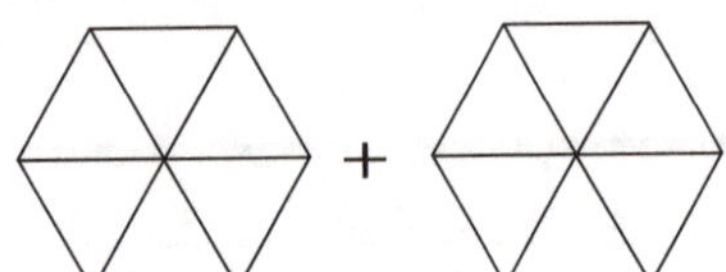

d) $\frac{2}{3} + \frac{1}{2} =$ _______

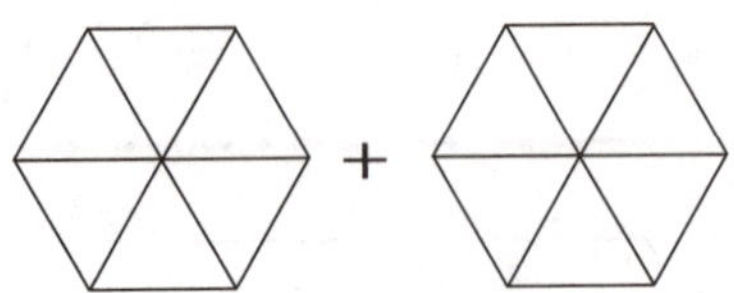

2. Use fraction circles to find each sum.

a) $\frac{3}{5} + \frac{3}{10} =$ ___

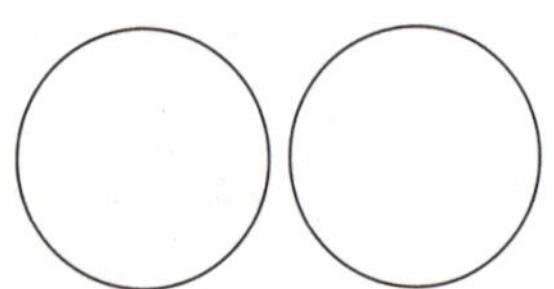

b) $\frac{5}{8} + \frac{1}{4} =$ __

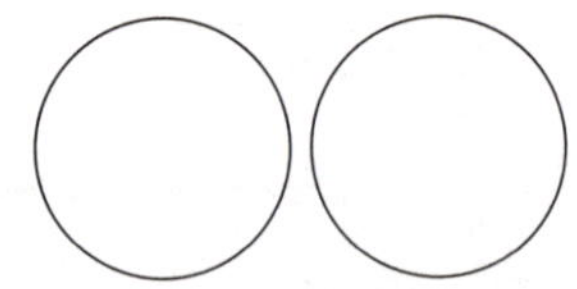

c) $\frac{5}{12} + \frac{3}{4} =$ _______________

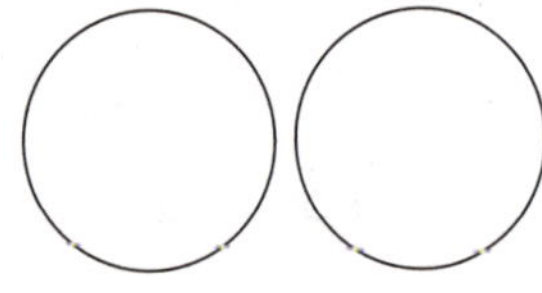

d) $\frac{5}{6} + \frac{7}{12} =$ __________

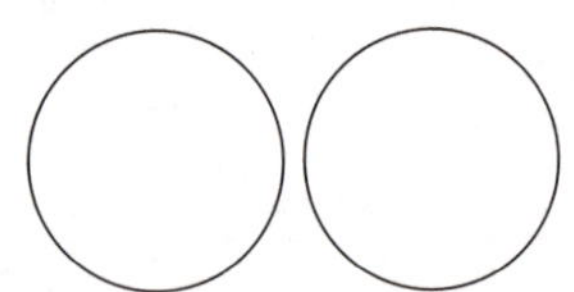

5.2

3. Write the addition equation represented by the diagram.

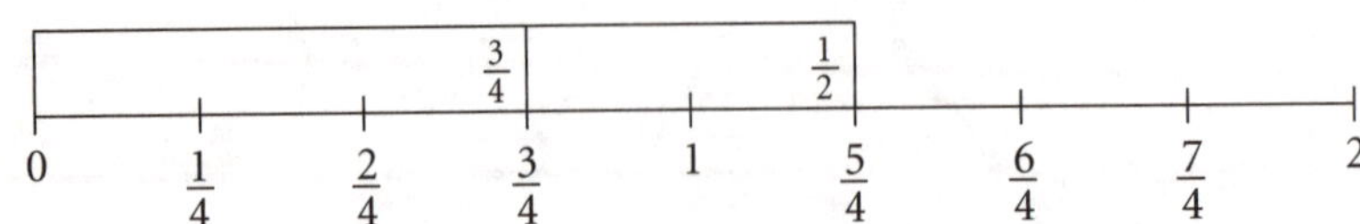

____

5.2   **4.** Use fraction strips and number lines to add.

a) $\frac{2}{3} + \frac{1}{6} =$ _____

b) $\frac{1}{2} + \frac{3}{10} =$ _____

c) $\frac{3}{4} + \frac{11}{12} =$ _____

d) $\frac{3}{2} + \frac{2}{5} =$ _____

e) $\frac{7}{8} + \frac{1}{2} =$ _____

f) $\frac{2}{3} + \frac{3}{4} =$ _____

5.3   **5.** Zach took $\frac{5}{12}$ of an hour to drive to work and $\frac{2}{3}$ of an hour to drive home.

a) Write the total time it took Zach to drive to and from work as a fraction of an hour.

____

b) Write the time in part a in minutes. _________

6. Estimate, then add.

a) $\frac{3}{4} + \frac{2}{5}$ Estimate: ___   Sum: _______

b) $\frac{5}{8} + \frac{1}{3}$ Estimate: ___   Sum: ___

c) $\frac{5}{9} + \frac{1}{6}$ Estimate: ___   Sum: ___

d) $\frac{1}{2} + \frac{3}{7}$ Estimate: ___   Sum: ___

e) $\frac{2}{3} + \frac{3}{5}$ Estimate: ___   Sum: _______

f) $\frac{4}{5} + \frac{5}{6}$ Estimate: ___   Sum: _______

5.4   **7.** Use each diagram to find the difference.

a) $\frac{5}{6} - \frac{1}{3} =$ _______

b) $\frac{9}{10} - \frac{3}{5} =$ ___

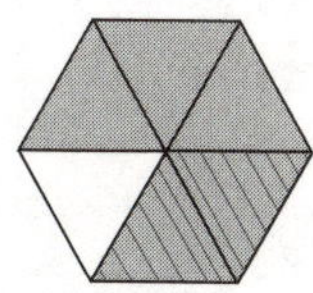
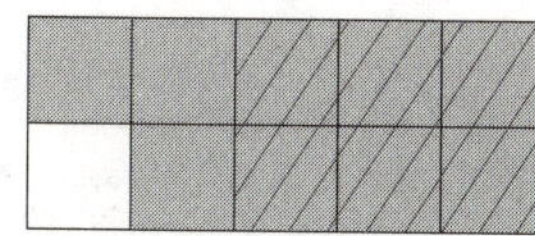

c) $\frac{11}{12} - \frac{2}{3} =$ _______

d) $\frac{4}{5} - \frac{3}{4} =$ ___

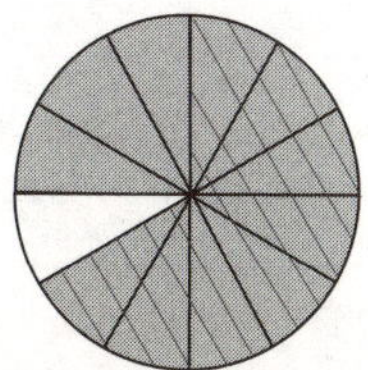
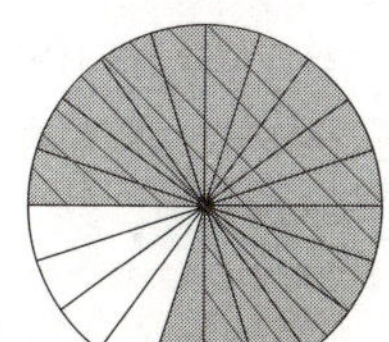

5.4 **8.** Write the subtraction equation represented by each diagram.

a) ____________

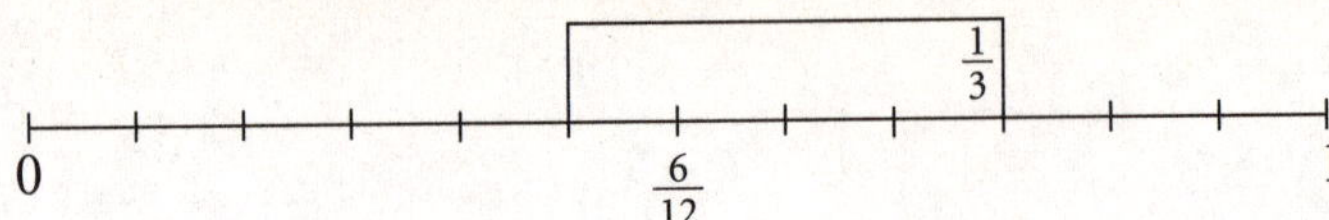

b) ____________

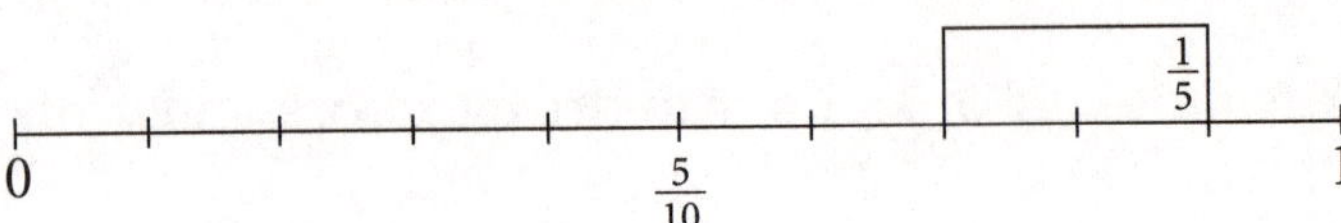

5.5 **9.** Estimate, then subtract.

a) $\frac{7}{8} - \frac{3}{4}$ Estimate: ___   Difference: ___

b) $\frac{3}{2} - \frac{3}{8}$ Estimate: ___   Difference: ________

c) $\frac{5}{4} - \frac{7}{12}$ Estimate: ___   Difference: ________

d) $\frac{2}{3} - \frac{2}{9}$ Estimate: ___   Difference: ___

5.6 **10.** Add.

a) $3\frac{7}{8} + 1\frac{5}{8} =$ ________   b) $2\frac{2}{3} + 4\frac{5}{12} =$ ____

11. On Sunday, Maya studied $1\frac{1}{4}$ h for her math exam.

On Monday she studied $1\frac{2}{3}$ h.

What is the total time Maya studied?

____

5.7 **12.** Subtract.

a) $5\frac{11}{12} - 1\frac{7}{12} =$ __________   b) $2\frac{5}{7} - 1\frac{3}{14} =$ __________

13. Leigh has $4\frac{1}{2}$ m of ribbon.

He uses $1\frac{3}{4}$ m to wrap a present and $\frac{1}{3}$ m to make a bow.

How much ribbon is left?

____

128

Just for Fun

Pharaoh's Staircase

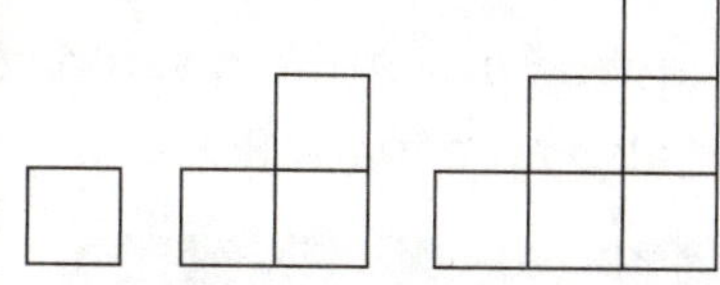

You need 6 blocks to make a *Pharaoh's Staircase* with a height of 3 blocks.

You will need _____ blocks for a staircase with a height of 5 blocks.

You will need _____ blocks for a staircase with a height of 10 blocks.

Pairing Up

Find the missing numbers.

6	3	5	1
4		5	9

5	8	7	11
3	6		9

3	5	8	
6	10		20

Heading Home

A Game for 2

Use the dot grid. Start at the centre, O.

You may move up, down, left, or right, but not diagonally.

Player A draws an arrow 1 grid unit long in any direction from O.

Player B adds an arrow 1 grid unit long to Player A's arrow to make a continuous route. Take turns drawing arrows.

Player A tries to head home to A, while player B tries to head home to B.

You may not go over a dot more than once.

The first player to get home wins.

Activating Prior Knowledge

Writing Expressions and Equations

You can use algebraic expressions to represent word statements.

In an algebraic expression, a letter, such as x or n, is used to represent a number.

This letter is called a **variable**.

Multiplication of a number and a letter is written as the number followed by the letter.

For example, $4n$ means $4 \times n$.

An equation is a statement that two algebraic expressions are equal. One of them can be a number. For example, $4n = 8$ is an equation and $4n + 2 = 10$ is also an equation.

Example 1

a) Write an algebraic expression for this statement:

Five times a number minus 3

b) Write an equation for this sentence:

Three less than five times a number is 2.

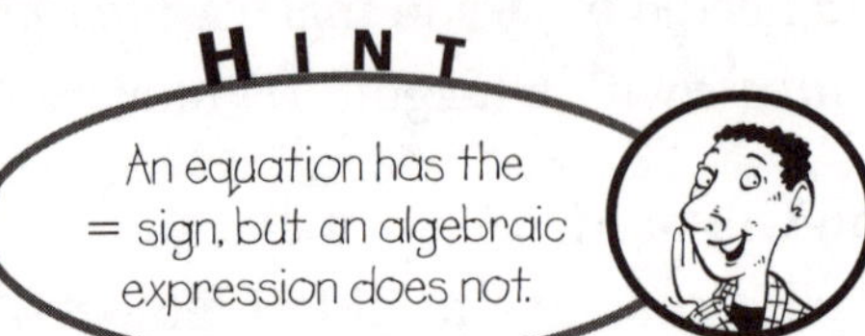

Solution

Let x be the number.

a) Then, five times a number is $5x$.

$5x$ minus 3 is: $5x - 3$

$5x - 3$ is an algebraic expression.

b) Three less than five times the number is 2.

So, $5x - 3 = 2$

$5x - 3 = 2$ is an equation.

✓ Check

1. Write an algebraic expression for each statement.

a) eight more than a number ___________________________

b) two less than seven times a number ___________________________

c) a number divided by 6 ___________________________

2. Write an equation for each sentence.

a) The sum of 10 and a number is 15. ___________________________

b) The product of a number and nine is 63. ___________________________

c) Eleven decreased by 2 times a number is 1. ___________________________

Evaluating Expressions

To find the value of an expression, replace each variable with its given value.
Then use the order of operations to simplify.

Example 2

Evaluate the expression $a + 2$ for $a = -3$.

Solution

Substitute $a = -3$ into the expression.

$$a + 2 = -3 + 2$$
$$= -1$$

✔ Check

3. Evaluate each expression.

a) $x - 9$ for $x = -5$

$$x - 9 = \underline{\quad} - 9$$

$$= \underline{\qquad}$$

b) $4x$ for $x = 3$

$$4x = 4(\underline{\ })$$

$$= \underline{\qquad}$$

c) $-6 + x$ for $x = -2$

$$-6 + x = -6 + (\underline{\ })$$

$$= \underline{\qquad}$$

4. Evaluate each expression for $m = -3$.

a) $m - 2$

$$= \underline{\quad} - 2$$

$$= \underline{\quad}$$

b) $m + 2$

$$= \underline{\quad} + 2$$

$$= \underline{\quad}$$

c) $2 - m$

$$= 2 - \underline{\quad}$$

$$= \underline{\qquad}$$

$$= \underline{\qquad}$$

5. Evaluate each expression.

a) $a - 4$, when $a = -3$: ________

b) $-a + 3$, when $a = -4$: ______

c) $-a - 3$, when $a = -3$: ______

d) $-a - 4$, when $a = -4$: ______

e) $-a + 4$, when $a = -3$: ______

Quick Review

➤ When you **solve an equation** you find the value of the variable that makes the equation true.

You can solve an equation by *systematic trial* or by *inspection*.

➤ Sharon baby-sits for an hourly wage.
She works for 2 h and is given an extra $3 as a tip.
Sharon earns $17. What is her hourly rate?

Let d dollars per hour represent Sharon's hourly rate.

Then $2 \times d$, or $2d$ is how much she earns for 2 h work.
Include the $3 tip, then an equation that
represents this situation is: $2d + 3 = 17$

> **Tip**
>
> *Each trial provides information to guide you in choosing a value for the next trial.*

Solve by Systematic Trial

$2d + 3 = 17$

Choose a value for d and substitute.
Try $d = 10$; then $2 \times 10 + 3 = 23$ 23 is too large. Try a lesser value.
Try $d = 5$; then $2 \times 5 + 3 = 13$ 13 is too small. Try a value between 5 and 10.
Try $d = 6$; then $2 \times 6 + 3 = 15$ 15 is too small. Try a value between 6 and 10.
Try $d = 7$; then $2 \times 7 + 3 = 17$ $d = 7$ makes the equation true.

So, $d = 7$

Solve by Inspection

$2d + 3 = 17$

To solve the equation by inspection, ask yourself:
"Which number added to 3 gives 17?"

$$2d + 3 = 17$$
You know that $14 + 3 = 17$
$$\text{So, } 2d = 14$$

Then ask yourself, "Two times which number gives 14?"
You know that $2 \times 7 = 14$.
So, $d = 7$
Sharon earns $7/h.

1. Look at these algebraic expressions and equations.

$$2p = 16 \qquad x + 12$$

$$\frac{n}{5} = 4 \qquad z - 6 = 20$$

$$\frac{k + 3}{2}$$

a) Which are expressions? _______________________

b) Which are equations? _______________________

2. Solve by inspection.

a) $2n = 12$ **b)** $x + 10 = 30$ **c)** $25 - p = 20$

_______________   _______________   _______________

d) $x - 8 = 2$ **e)** $5n = 15$ **f)** $\frac{x}{2} = 5$

_______________   _______________   _______________

3. Solve the equation $2x + 5 = 37$ by systematic trial.

Input	Evaluate $2x + 5$	Too large or too small?
$x = 30$	$2 \times 30 + 5 = 65$	This is too large.
$x = 20$	$2 \times 20 + 5 = 45$	This is too large.
$x = 5$	$2 \times 5 + 5 = 15$	This is too small.
$x = 10$	$2 \times 10 + 5 =$	
$x = 15$	$2 \times 15 + 5 =$	

4. Solve.

a) $3x = 60$ **b)** $x + 12 = 30$ **c)** $\frac{x}{5} = 9$ **d)** $5x - 4 = 26$

_______   _______   _______   _______

5. Which value of n makes the equation $\frac{20}{n} + 5 = 9$ true? Circle your answer.

a) $n = 1$ **b)** $n = 2$ **c)** $n = 4$ **d)** $n = 5$ **e)** $n = 10$ **f)** $n = 20$

6. Jasmine has 135 butterfly stickers.
   She gave 15 to her little sister and the rest to her friends.
   Each friend has 20 stickers. How many friends did she give stickers to?
   Fill in the missing expressions to create an equation you can solve.
   Let f represent the number of friends.

   ____________ + ____________ = ____________

   number of   number of   total number of
   stickers to sister   stickers to friends   stickers

   Jasmine gave stickers to __________ friends.

7. Write an equation you could use to solve each problem.
   Solve each equation.

   a) Joshua purchased tennis balls for $8 each. He spent $128.
      How many tennis balls did Joshua buy?

      The equation is: __________

      Joshua bought _____ tennis balls.

   b) Five more than three times a number is 35.
      What is the number?

      The equation is: ___________

      The number is: _____

   c) A box of apples is divided among 6 people.
      Each person received 3 apples.
      How many apples were in the box?

      The equation is: _______

      There were _____ apples in the box.

   d) Petra works for 5 h. She gets a bonus of $10.
      Petra's total earnings are $70. What is her hourly rate?

      The equation is: __________

      Petra's hourly rate is ______.

Quick Review

Balance scales can be used to model an equation.
When the pans are balanced, the masses on both pans are equal.
This two-pan balance models the equation $2x + 5 = 7 + 4$.

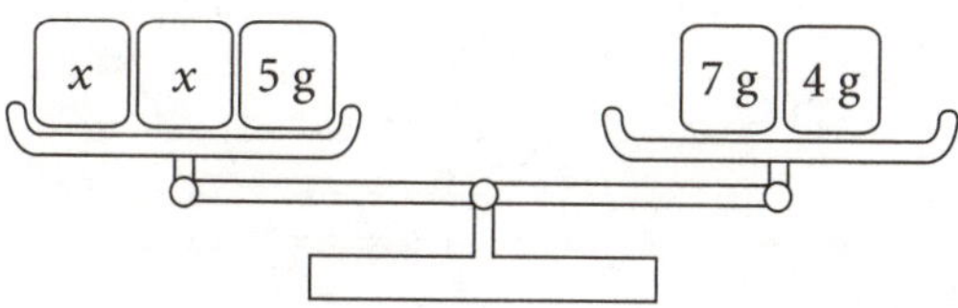

To find each unknown mass, x, replace the 7 g in the right pan with 5 g and 2 g.
Then remove 5 g from each pan.

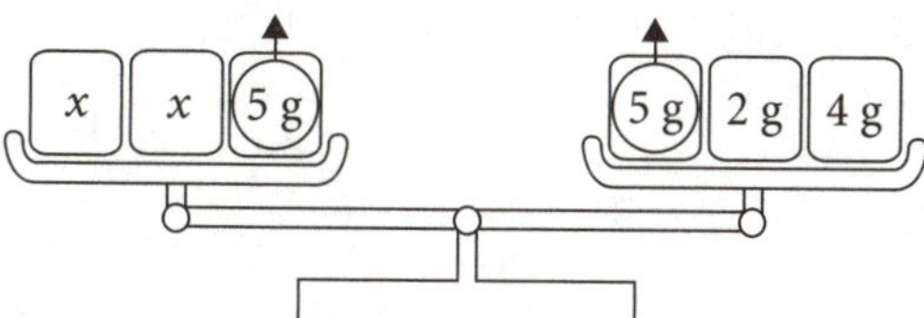

The unknown masses have been isolated in the left pan, and 6 g is left in the right pan.

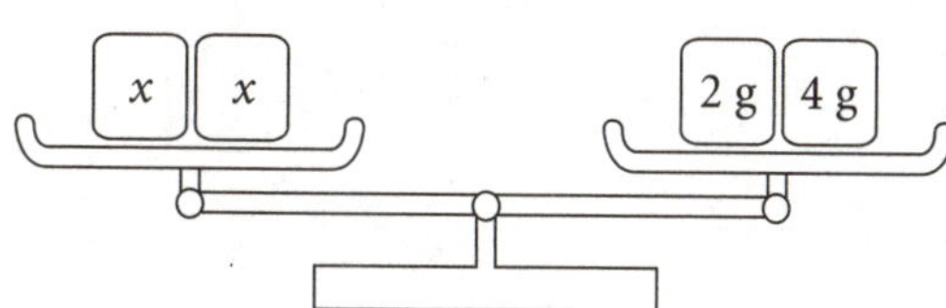

The two unknown masses balance 6 g.
So, each unknown mass is 3 g.

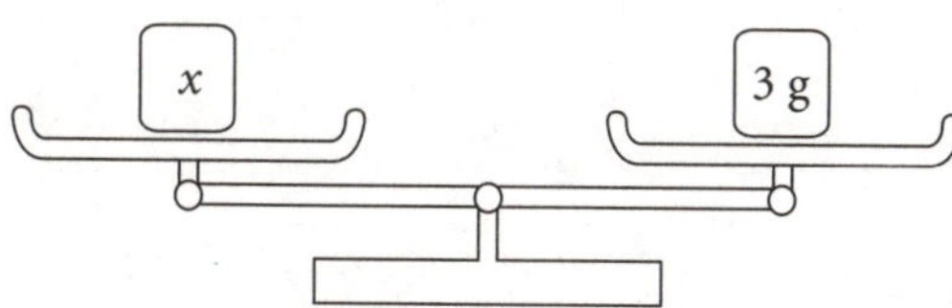

The solution to the equation is $x = 3$.
You can verify the solution by replacing each unknown mass
in the original balance scales with 3 g.
Then, in the left pan: $3\text{ g} + 3\text{ g} + 5\text{ g} = 11\text{ g}$
And, in the right pan: $7\text{ g} + 4\text{ g} = 11\text{ g}$
Since the masses are equal, the solution is correct.

1. Match each balance scales with an equation below.

A.
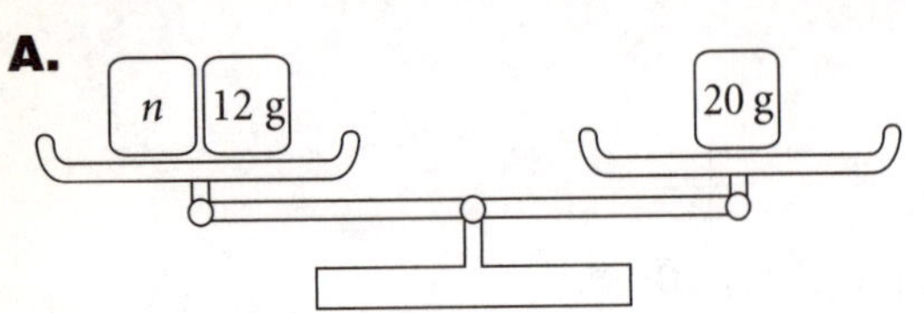

B.
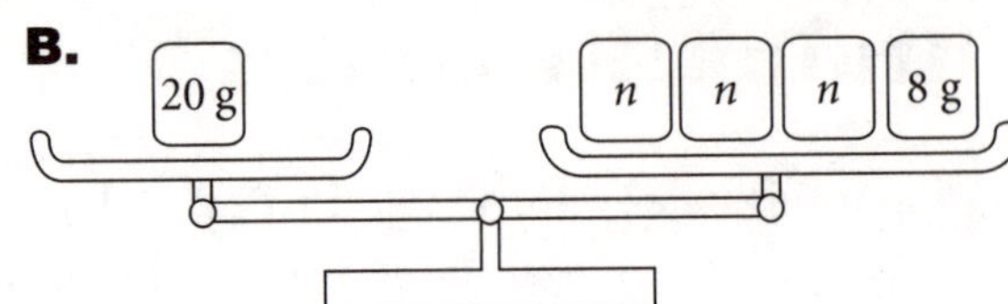

C.
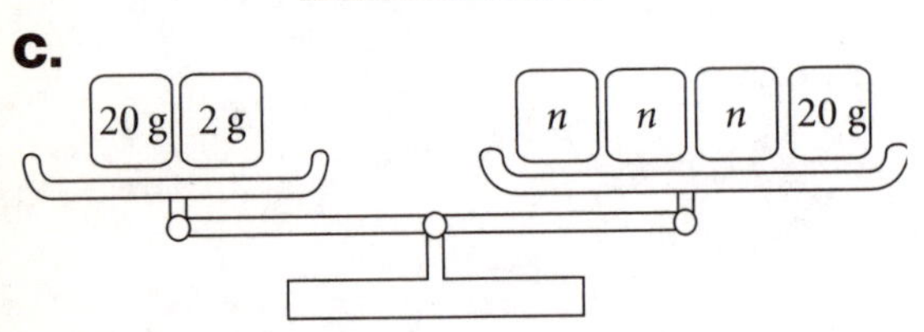

D.
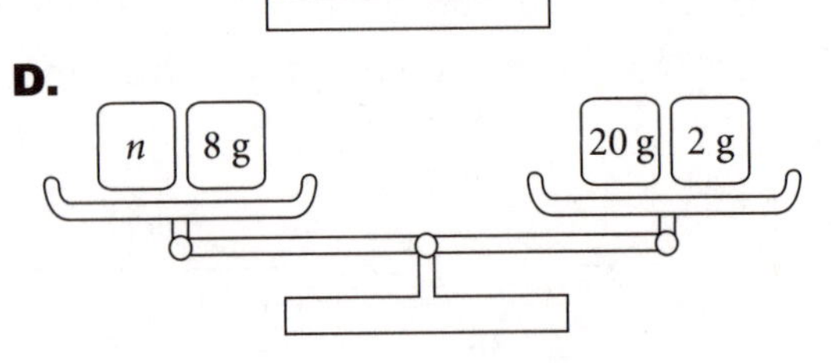

i) $n + 8 = 22$ ___   **ii)** $3n + 8 = 20$ ___   **iii)** $3n + 20 = 22$ ___   **iv)** $n + 12 = 20$ ___

2. Write the equation modelled by each two-pan balance. Then solve the equation.

a)
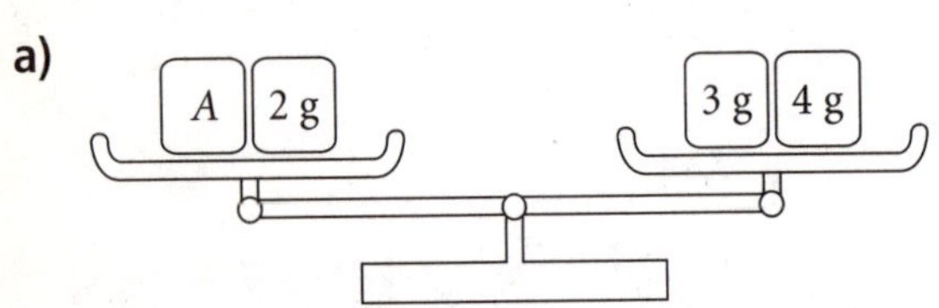

____

b)
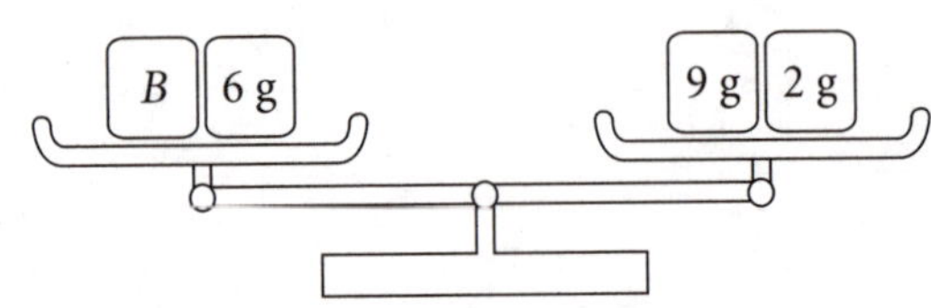

____

c)
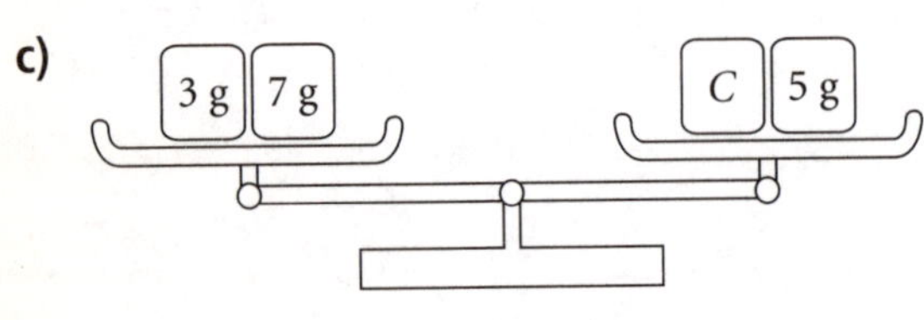

____

d)
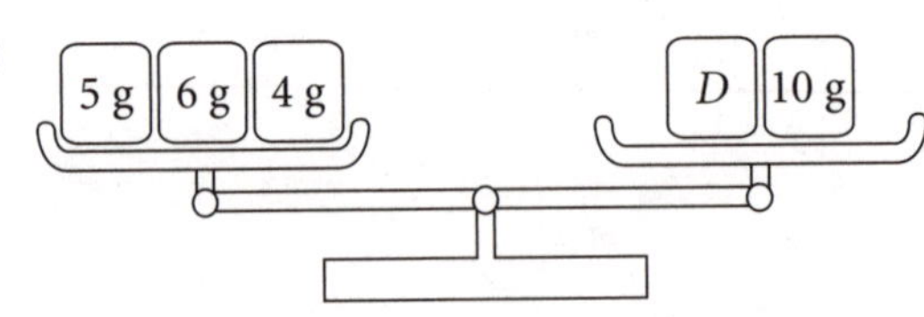

____

3. Find the value of the unknown mass on each balance scales.

a)
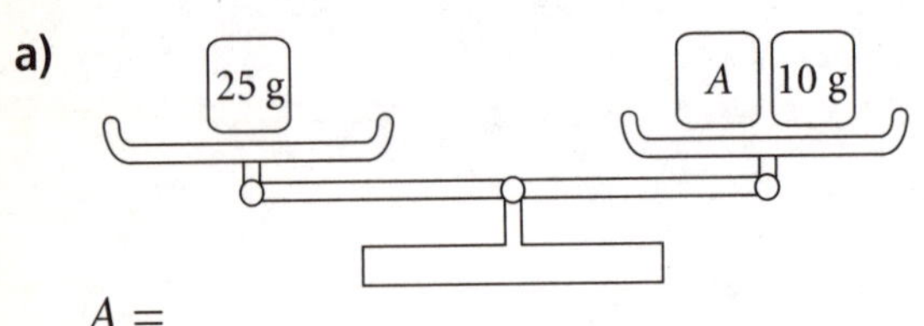

$A =$ ____

b)
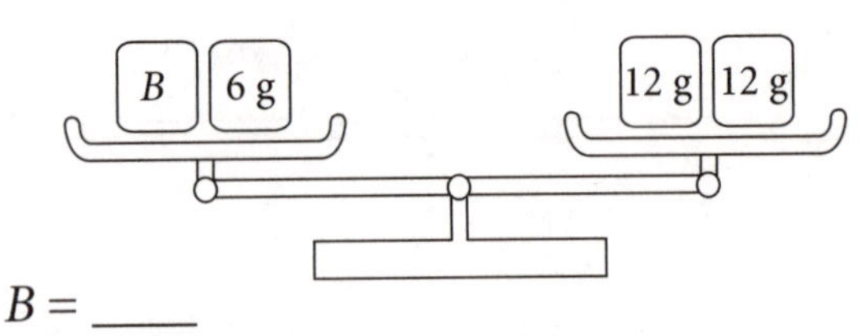

$B =$ ____

c)
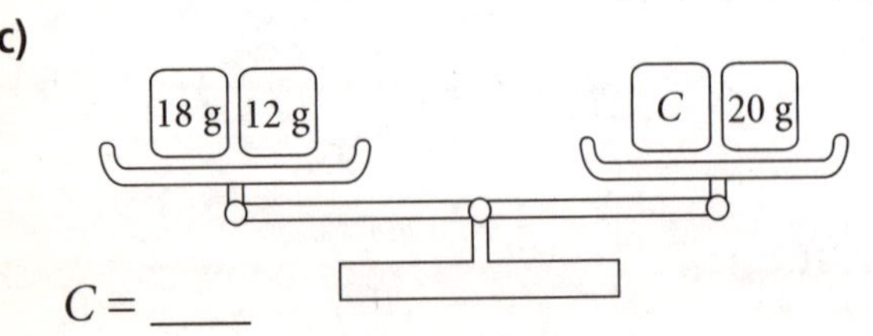

$C =$ ____

d)
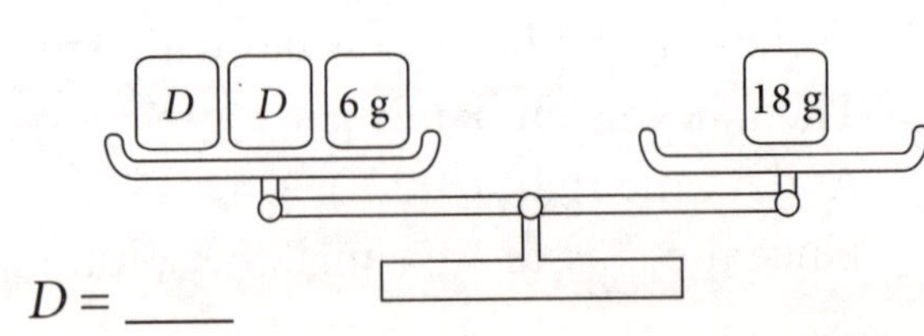

$D =$ ____

4. a) Sketch balance scales to represent each equation.
   b) Solve each equation. Verify the solution.

   i) $x + 7 = 12$

   ii) $n + 18 = 22$

   $x =$ _____

   $n =$ ___

   iii) $2m = 26$

   iv) $27 = 9 + 3k$

   $m =$ _____

   $k =$ _____

5. a) Write an equation for each sentence.
   b) Solve each equation. Verify the solution.

   i) Two more than a number is 12.

   ii) A number increased by nine is 21.

   ____

   ____

   iii) Four times a number is 24.

   iv) Four more than three times a number is 28.

   ____

   ____

6. The perimeter of this rectangle is 44 cm and the base is 8 cm.
   What is the height, h?

   a) Write an equation to represent this problem.

   ____

   b) Model the equation with balance scales.

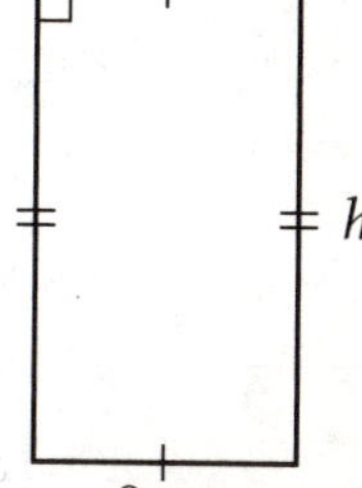

   c) Solve the equation for h to find the height. _________

7. The area of a rectangle is given by the formula $A = bh$,
   where b is the base of the rectangle and h is the height.
   The area of a rectangle is 120 cm², and its base is 15 cm.
   What is the height of the rectangle? _______

Quick Review

As with balance scales, algebra tiles can be used to model and solve equations.

$\square$ +1   ■ −1 $\boxed{}$ x

The +1 tile and −1 tile are called **unit tiles**. The x-tile is a **variable tile**.

One white unit tile and one black unit tile form a **zero pair**. $\square$ +1 ■ −1

To solve the equation $x - 3 = 1$, use tiles to represent the equation.
What you do to one side of the equation, you also do to the other side.

Isolate the x-tile by adding 3 white tiles to each side.
The tiles on the left side make zero pairs. Remove the zero pairs.

This arrangement becomes:

One x-tile equals 4 white tiles. So, $x = 4$

To verify the solution: Replace the variable tile in the original equation with 4 white tiles.

Remove zero pairs. One white tile remains on the left side.
This matches the right side of the equation.
So, the solution is correct.

1. Match each equation with an arrangement of tiles.

A.

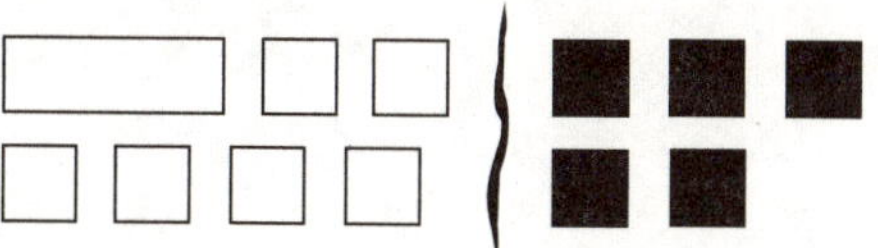

B.

C.

D.

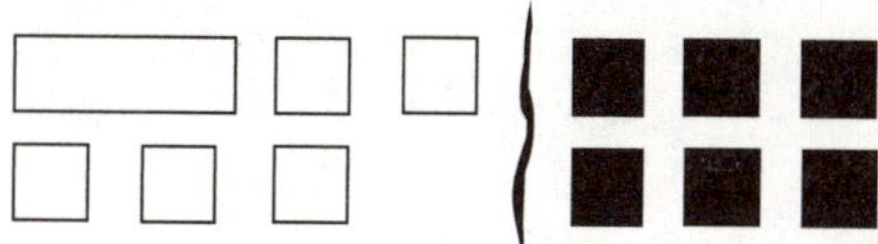

a) $x + 5 = -6$ _____   **b)** $x + 6 = -5$ _____   **c)** $x - 5 = 6$ _____   **d)** $x - 6 = -5$ _____

2. Write the equation modelled by each set of algebra tiles. Then solve the equation.

a)

> **Tip**
> To isolate the x-tile, make zero pairs.

____

b)

____

3. Sketch a set of algebra tiles that represents each equation. Then solve the equation.

a) $x + 3 = 9$ ___________   **b)** $3 = x - 5$ ___________

4. Use tiles to solve each equation. Verify each solution.

a) $3 + x = 9$

   $x =$ ___

b) $x - 3 = 9$

   $x =$ ___

c) $5 + x = 7$

   $x =$ ___

d) $7 = x - 5$

   $x =$ ___

5. Solve each equation.
Use tiles to help you.
Verify each solution.

a) $8 = n - 6$

   $n =$ ___

b) $n + 5 = 3$

   $n =$ ___

c) $7 = n - 8$

   $n =$ ___

d) $n + 9 = -4$

   $n =$ ___

6. a) Eight less than a number is 10.
Let n represent the number.
Then, an equation is: $n - 8 = 10$
Solve the equation.
What is the number? ___________________

b) Sixteen more than a number is 22.
Write an equation, then solve it to find the number.

____

7. Between 5 P.M. and midnight, the temperature dropped by 7°C to −5°C.

a) Write an equation you can solve to find the temperature at 5 P.M. ___________________

b) Use tiles to solve the equation. ___________________________________

8. Jamal thinks of an integer.
He adds 8 to this number and the sum is 3.
What is the integer?
Write an equation, then solve it using algebra tiles.

____

9. Solve each equation. Verify each solution.

a) $x - 25 = 34$

   ____

b) $x - 132 = -97$

   ____

c) $54 = 130 + x$

   ____

d) $176 + x = -24$

   ____

Quick Review

When you use *algebra* to solve an equation, you always perform the same operation on both sides of the equation. That is, whatever you do to one side of an equation, you must do the same to the other side.

Five more than three times a number is 23.
What is the number?

Let x represent the number.
Then 3 times the number is: $3x$
Five more than 3 times the number is: $3x + 5$
The equation is: $3x + 5 = 23$
Here are the steps to solve this equation:

Step 1: Isolate the variable by adding to or subtracting from each side.
In this case, to remove $+5$ from the left side, subtract 5 from each side.

$$3x + 5 - 5 = 23 - 5$$
$$3x = 18$$

Step 2: Divide each side by the numerical coefficient.
In this case, divide each side by 3.

$$\frac{3x}{3} = \frac{18}{3}$$

$$x = 6$$

Step 3: Verify the solution by substitution.
Left side $= 3x + 5$ Right side $= 23$
$= 3(6) + 5$
$= 23$

Since the left side equals the right side, $x = 6$ is correct.
The number is 6.

In some equations, such as $5x = 40$, you can omit Step 1 because the variable term is already isolated. In this case, start with Step 2 and divide each side by 5 to get $x = 8$.

1. Solve each equation.

a) $8x - 7 = 9$

$8x - 7 +$ _______ $= 9 +$ _______

$8x =$ _______

$x =$ _______

b) $9 = 3n - 6$

$n =$ _______

2. Four less than two times a number is 6.
What is the number?

Let x represent the number.
Then 2 times the number is: ___
Four less than 2 times the number is: _______

The equation is: _________

Solve this equation:
To remove _______ from the left side, add _______ to each side.

$2x$ _____________ $= 6 +$ _________
$2x \qquad\qquad = 10$

Divide each side by ______

$x =$ ___

Verify the solution.
Left side $= 2x - 4$ Right side $= 6$

$= 2(\underline{}) - 4$

$=$ ___

Since the left side equals the right side, $x =$ _______ is correct.
The number is ______.

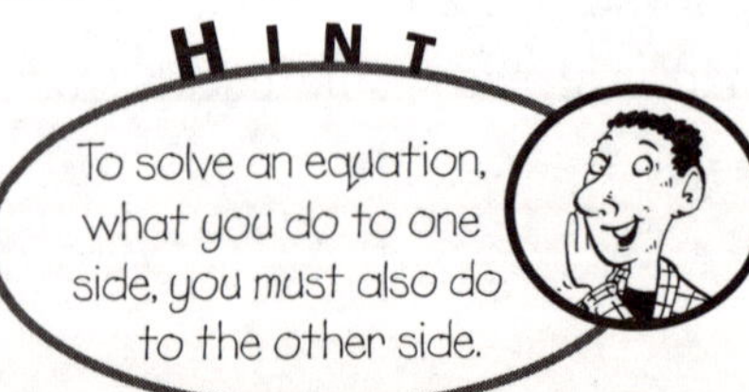

3. Write, then solve, an equation to answer each question. Verify the solution.

a) Twice a number added to 8 is 14. Let n represent the number.

Equation: _______________

To verify the solution, substitute $n =$ _______ into the equation.

Left side: Right side:

b) Fourteen less than four times a number is equal to 6.
Let y represent the number.

Equation: _________________

To verify the solution, substitute $y =$ _______ into the equation.
Left side: Right side:

4. Solve each equation. Show your steps. Verify your solution.

a) $3w = 15$ **b)** $2x = 28$

_______   _______

c) $5y = 40$ **d)** $8z = 56$

_______   _______

5. Solve each equation. Show your steps. Verify your solution.

    a) $3w - 2 = 13$ **b)** $2x - 4 = 12$

    c) $5y - 6 = 14$ **d)** $7z - 16 = 12$

6. Solve each equation. Show your steps. Verify your solution.

    a) $2w + 5 = 11$ **b)** $3x + 2 = 17$

    c) $5y + 6 = 26$ **d)** $4z + 10 = 30$

7. Solve each equation. Verify your solution.

    a) $2w - 5 = 11$ **b)** $5x + 12 = 52$ **c)** $13y = 91$ **d)** $6z - 15 = 57$

8. Write, then solve an equation to find each number. Verify your solution.

    a) Seven less than three times a number is 17.

    b) Eight more than four times a number is 20.

9. For each problem, write an equation you can use to solve the problem. Solve the equation. Verify the solution.

    a) Max has $34 in his bank account.
         He plans to deposit $12 a week until he has $130.

         How many weeks will it take him? _______________________

    b) Kenji is saving nickels in a jar. He has $35 in nickels.

         How many nickels are in the jar? _______________________

Quick Review

➤ Use algebra tiles to solve equations that involve integers.
For example, to solve $x - 2 = -5$:

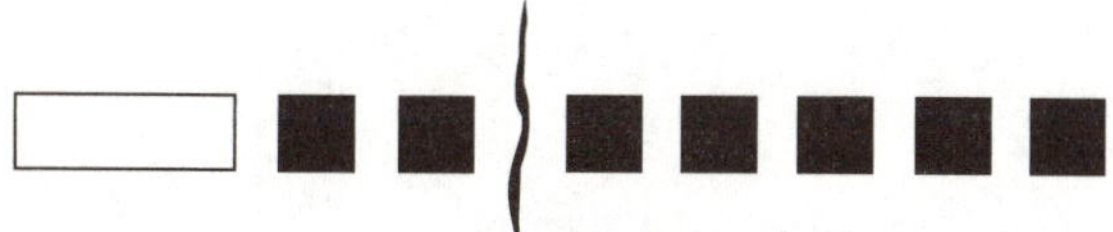

Add 2 white tiles to each side, then remove zero pairs.

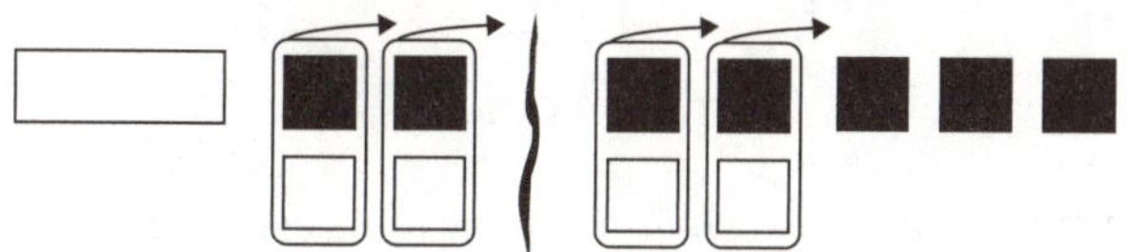

The solution is $x = -3$.

➤ Solve *by inspection* for simple equations that involve whole numbers.
For example, to solve $2x + 1 = 9$:
Think: Which number added to 1 gives 9?
Answer: $8 + 1 = 9$
Now think: Which number multiplied by 2 gives 8?
Answer: $4 \times 2 = 8$
So, the solution is $x = 4$.

➤ Use *algebra* to solve any equation.
For example, to solve $\frac{n}{5} = 10$:

$$\frac{n}{5} = 10 \qquad \text{Multiply each side of the equation by 5 to isolate } n.$$

$$\frac{n}{5} \times 5 = 10 \times 5$$

$$n = 50$$

➤ Use *systematic trial* to solve an equation if you are not sure how to start.

➤ Use the *balance-scales model* to help you visualize the equation.
Whichever method you choose, always *verify* your solution by
substituting the solution into the original equation.

For questions 1 to 4, use algebra, a balance-scales model, inspection, systematic trial, or tiles to solve each equation. Verify your solutions.

1. **a)** $\frac{x}{3} = 12$

The solution is: _________

b) $\frac{x}{2} = 8$

The solution is: _________

c) $3x = 12$

The solution is: _________

d) $2x = 8$

The solution is: _________

2. **a)** $n - 5 = -3$

The solution is: _________

b) $n + 10 = 6$

The solution is: _________

c) $n + 8 = -2$

The solution is: _________

d) $n - 6 = -10$

The solution is: _________

3. **a)** $2x + 5 = 19$

The solution is: _________

b) $7x + 4 = 18$

The solution is: _________

c) $4x - 3 = 13$

The solution is: _________

d) $3x - 10 = 14$

The solution is: _________

4. a) $p + 4 = 11$ **b)** $t - 6 = 14$

The solution is: _______   The solution is: _______

c) $\frac{k}{8} = 5$ **d)** $5x = 45$

The solution is: _______   The solution is: _______

For questions 5 to 9, write then solve an equation to solve the problem.

5. One adult ticket costs \$5. One child ticket costs \$3.
The total cost of 2 adult tickets and n child tickets is \$25.
How many child tickets are there?

____

6. Four years ago, Ellie was 12 years old.
How old is Ellie now?

____

7. A square has perimeter 28 cm.
What is the length of a side of the square?

____

8. Phillipe shared his beads with three friends.
Each person had 6 beads.

How many beads did Phillipe start with?

____

9. Julie sorted 52 sports cards. She divided them into 5 equal groups.
Julie had 12 cards left over. How many cards were in each group?

____

10. Write a problem that can be described by the equation $2x + 3 = 21$.
Solve the equation. Solve the problem.

____

____

____

In Your Words

Here are some of the important mathematical words of this unit.
Build your own glossary by recording definitions and examples here. The first one is done for you.

solve by inspection

I solve an equation by thinking about the numbers in the equation and how they are related. For example, to solve $x + 7 = 10$; I think, "Which number do I add to 7 to get 10?" The answer, 3, is the solution to the equation, so I write $x = 3$.

solve by systematic trial

verify a solution

balance-scales model

preserving equality

solve using algebra

List other mathematical words you need to know.

Unit Review

6.1 **1.** Write an equation you can use to solve each problem.
Solve each equation by inspection or systematic trial.

a) Gabrielle wants to buy a new snowboard that costs $300.
She has $180 in her bank account.
How much more must Gabrielle save so she can buy the snowboard?

____

b) Freddy bought a new music player for $250.
He then had $380 left in his bank account.
How much was in Freddy's account before he bought the player?

____

c) Emily helps clean a local yoga studio.
She earns $8 per hour.
Last month Emily got a $10 bonus.
Her total earnings were $170.
How many hours did Emily work?

____

6.2 **2.** Write an equation that is represented by each balance scales.
Solve the equation. Sketch the steps.

a)

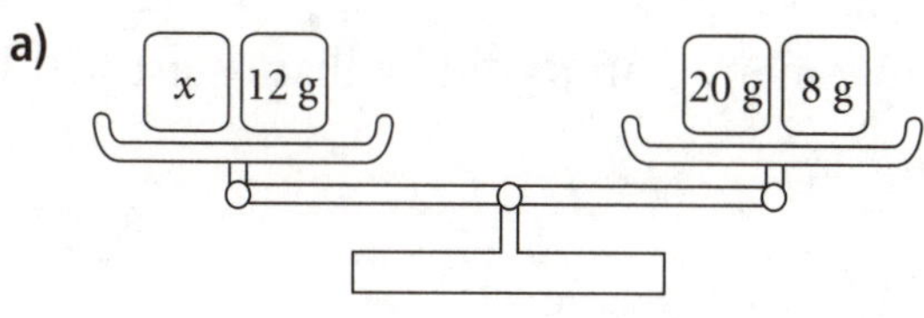

____

b)

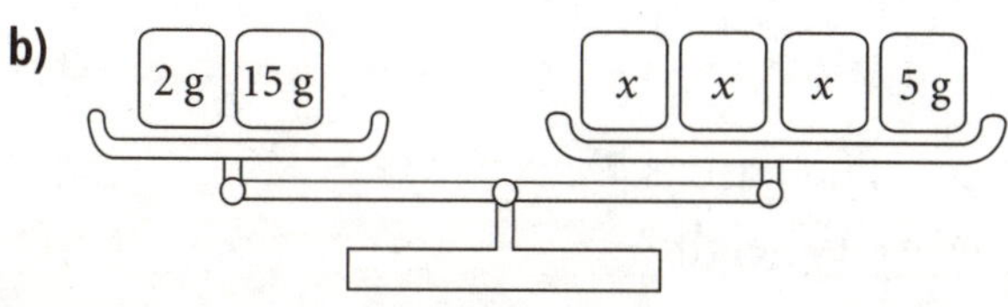

____

6.3   **3.** Solve each equation using algebra tiles. Sketch the tiles you used.
Verify each solution.

a) $x + 8 = 5$ b) $6 = x - 3$ c) $-3 = x + 7$ d) $x - 2 = -5$

_______   _______   _______   _______

4. Overnight, the temperature dropped by 15°C to –10°C.

a) Write an equation you can solve to find the temperature before it dropped.

____

b) Use tiles to solve the equation. _______________________________________

6.4   **5.** Solve each equation using algebra. Verify each solution.

a) $4n = 64$ b) $2p + 15 = 21$ c) $5r - 4 = 26$ d) $60 = q + 15$

_______   _______   _______   _______

6. Dylan starts with $40. He saves $12 a week.
After how many weeks will Dylan have each amount?

a) $100 _______________________   b) $136 _______________________

6.5   **7.** Write an equation for each problem. Solve the equation. Verify each answer.
a) A number increased by 7 is 22. What is the number?

____

b) William arranges a number of stamps into 5 groups.
There are 12 stamps in each group. How many stamps did William start with?

____

c) Six less than a number is 25. What is the number?

____

d) A rectangle has a perimeter of 38 cm. The base is 7 cm.
Sketch and label the rectangle. What is its height?

____

Data Analysis

Just for Fun

Secret Messages

QSFO K WKX K PSCR: POON RSW PYB K NKI.
DOKMR K WKX DY PSCR: POON RSW PYB K VSPODSWO.

Can you decipher this secret message?

Each letter in the original message has been replaced by another letter.
Each letter is replaced by the same letter every time.
No two letters are replaced by the same letter.
Each letter is shifted the same number of spaces.

Use the data below about how often each letter in the English alphabet is used.
Here is a table showing this information in a text of 1000 letters.

A	B	C	D	E	F	G	H	I	J	K	L	M	N	O	P	Q	R	S	T	U	V	W	X	Y	Z
73	9	30	44	130	28	16	35	74	2	3	35	25	78	74	27	3	77	63	93	27	13	16	5	19	1

Here are the frequencies of the letters in the secret message.

A	B	C	D	E	F	G	H	I	J	K	L	M	N	O	P	Q	R	S	T	U	V	W	X	Y	Z
0	2	2	3	0	1	0	0	1	0	9	0	1	3	8	7	1	5	7	0	0	1	5	2	3	0

Compare the two tables.
Shift the tallies so the greatest and least frequencies from each table match up roughly.
Each letter in the message corresponds to a letter 10 places to the left; for example, letter O in the message corresponds to E.

Decode the secret message.

____

____

Activating Prior Knowledge

Experimental Probability

$$\text{Experimental probability of an event} = \frac{\text{Number of times the event occurs}}{\text{Total number of trials}}$$

Example 1

A number cube is labelled from 1 to 6.
The cube is rolled 200 times and each outcome is recorded.
Here are the results.

Outcome	1	2	3	4	5	6
Frequency	30	40	29	28	37	36

a) What is the experimental probability of rolling a 4?

b) What is the experimental probability of rolling an odd number?

Solution

$$\text{Experimental probability} = \frac{\text{Number of times the event occurs}}{\text{Total number of trials}}$$

a) The event, rolling a 4, occurred 28 times.
The total number of trials is 200.
So, the experimental probability of rolling a 4 is: $\dfrac{28}{200} = \dfrac{7}{50}$

b) The number of times a 1, 3, or 5 occurred is: $30 + 29 + 37 = 96$
So, the experimental probability of rolling an odd number is: $\dfrac{96}{200} = \dfrac{12}{25}$

✓ Check

Use the table in Example 1 to answer question 1.

1. Find the experimental probability of each event.

a) rolling a 6: _______________________________________

b) rolling an even number: _______________________________________

c) rolling a number greater than 1: _______________________________________

Theoretical Probability

Theoretical probability of an event $= \dfrac{\text{Number of favourable outcomes}}{\text{Number of possible outcomes}}$

The outcomes of the event must be equally likely.

Example 2

A spinner is divided into congruent sectors.
The sectors are labelled from A to H.

The pointer is spun.
a) What is the theoretical probability
   of the pointer landing on C?
b) What is the theoretical probability
   of the pointer landing on a vowel?

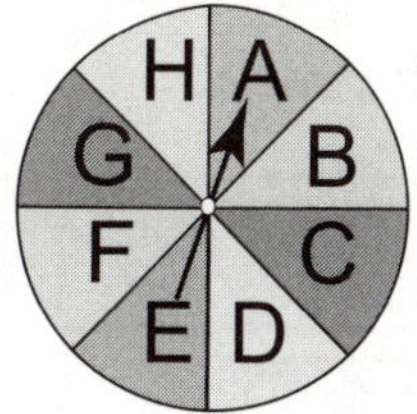

Solution

When the pointer is spun, there are 8 possible outcomes:
A, B, C, D, E, F, G, H
The outcomes are equally likely.
a) One outcome is favourable to the event of landing on C.
   So, the theoretical probability of landing on C is: $\dfrac{1}{8}$

b) There are 2 vowels: A and E
   So, 2 outcomes are favourable to the event of landing on a vowel.
   The theoretical probability of landing on a vowel is: $\dfrac{2}{8} = \dfrac{1}{4}$

✓ Check

2. Ten congruent marbles are placed in a bag.
There are 3 red, 4 green, 1 orange, and 2 purple.
One marble is selected at random.
What is the theoretical probability that the marble is green? _______________

3. A pyramid with 4 congruent triangular faces is rolled.
The faces are labelled 1, 2, 3, 4.

a) What is the theoretical probability that the pyramid lands on an odd number?

____

b) What is the theoretical probability that the pyramid lands on a number less than 4?

____

Quick Review

The **mean** is a number that can represent the centre of a set of numbers.
Here are two ways to find the mean of: 7, 5, 5, 8, 5

➤ Use linking cubes.
  Show each number with cubes:

  Rearrange the cubes to make rows of equal length.
  There will be 6 cubes in each row.
  So, the mean of 7, 5, 5, 8, 5 is 6.

➤ Add, then divide.
  Add: $7 + 5 + 5 + 8 + 5 = 30$
  Divide by the number of numbers in the set.
  There are 5 numbers in the set: $30 \div 5 = 6$
  The mean of 7, 5, 5, 8, 5 is 6.

The **mode** is the number that occurs most often in a set of data.
In the set: 7, 5, 5, 8, 5; the number 5 occurs most often.
So, the mode of 7, 5, 5, 8, 5 is 5.

Both the mean and the mode are sometimes called **average**.
The mean and the mode are **measures of central tendency**.

Practice

1. Use linking cubes to find the mean of each set of data.

a) 3, 6, 6, 1, 4 _____________

b) 1, 3, 3, 3, 5, 3 _____________

2. What is the mode of each data set in question 1?

a) _______________________   **b)** _______________________

3. Find the mode of each set of data.

a) 3, 7, 6, 7, 6, 4, 6 _______________   **b)** 8, 4, 8, 2, 4, 8, 7, 8 _______________

c) 1, 4, 1, 7, 1, 3, 1 _______________   **d)** 3, 6, 3, 6, 8, 3, 3 _______________

e) 19, 15, 14, 15, 15 _______________   **f)** 94, 16, 94, 83, 83, 94 _______________

4. Calculate the mean of each set of data.

a) 24, 16, 35, 52, 18 _______________   **b)** 150, 64, 73, 125 _______________

c) 20, 35, 14 _______________   **d)** 75, 70, 36, 51, 18 _______________

5. Here are the masses of 6 dogs: 25 kg, 30 kg, 25 kg, 20 kg, 25 kg, 25 kg

a) What is the mean mass? _______________________________________

b) What is the mode of the masses? _______________________________

6. Geraldo received these marks on 5 spelling tests: 100, 98, 97, 100, 100

a) What is Geraldo's mean mark? _______________________________

b) What is the mode of his marks? _______________________________

7. This table shows the heights and circumferences of 5 trees.

a) What is the mean height?

____

b) What is the mean circumference?

____

Tree	Height (m)	Circumference (cm)
Oak	20	65
Elm	16	82
Maple	20	60
Birch	15	82
Poplar	9	21

c) What is the mode of the heights? _______________________________

d) What is the mode of the circumferences? _______________________________

8. Jocelyn has 6 birds.
Their mean age is 10.
The mode of their ages is 8.
What might their ages be?

____

Quick Review

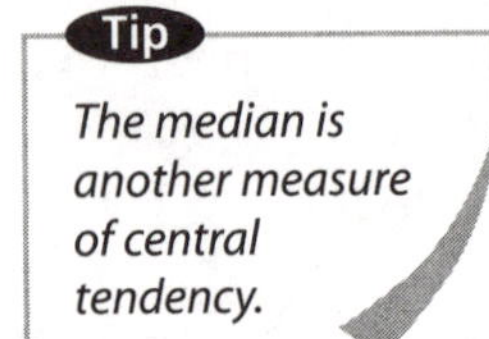

The **median** of a data set is the middle number when the data are arranged in order.

The **range** of a data set tells how spread out the data are.
It is the difference between the greatest and the least numbers in the set.

➤ Sofia caught 7 rainbow trout.
   She listed the lengths, in centimetres, from least to greatest:
   37, 39, 39, (40,) 43, 44, 44
   The middle number is 40. The median length is 40 cm.

➤ Sofia caught 1 more trout. It was 42 cm long.
   To find the new median, Sofia inserted the number
   in its correct position in the ordered list:
   37, 39, 39, 40, 42, 43, 44, 44
   Now there are two middle numbers: 40 and 42
   The median is the mean of the two middle numbers:
   $(40 + 42) \div 2 = 41$
   The median length is now 41 cm.

> **Tip**
> The median is
> another measure
> of central
> tendency.

➤ The range of the lengths is: 44 cm − 37 cm = 7 cm

Practice

1. Arrange the numbers in each set from least to greatest.
   Then, find the median and the range.

   a) 12, 18, 27, 9, 42
   From least to greatest: _______________________________

   Median: _______   Range: _______

   b) 87, 76, 93, 74, 67, 91, 79
   From least to greatest: _______________________________

   Median: _______   Range: _______

   c) 55, 45, 62, 71, 74, 58, 66, 58, 47
   From least to greatest: _______________________________

   Median: _______   Range: _______

d) 17, 12, 18, 14, 16, 11

From least to greatest: _______________________________

Median: _______   Range: _______

e) 44, 62, 17, 38, 59, 53, 48, 38

From least to greatest: _______________________________

Median: _______   Range: _______

2. Find the median and the range of these amounts: $10, $14, $9, $11, $7, $12

Median: _______   Range: _______

3. a) Measure the arm spans and the strides of 5 people, to the nearest centimetre.
Record your data in the table.

Name	Arm Span (cm)	Stride (cm)

b) What is the median arm span? ____

c) What is the median stride? ____

d) What is the range of the arm spans? ____

e) What is the range of the strides? ____

f) Measure one more person.
What is the new median arm span? ____

What is the new median stride? ____

g) Has the range of arm spans changed? If so, what is the new range? _______________

Has the range of strides changed? If so, what is the new range? _______________

4. This list shows the numbers of books 12 students read over the summer:
8, 4, 13, 2, 4, 3, 5, 17, 7, 12, 4, 5
Find each measure:

a) mean: _______________   **b)** median: _______________

c) mode: _______________   **d)** range: _______________

Quick Review

A number in a data set that is very different from the other numbers is an **outlier**.

In this set of data: 35, 37, 39, 42, 82,
the outlier is 82 because it is much greater than the other numbers in the set.

The mean and median may be affected by removing the outliers.
For example, for the data set above: 35, 37, 39, 42, 82
To find the mean, add then divide:
$$(35 + 37 + 39 + 42 + 82) \div 5 = 235 \div 5$$
$$= 47$$
The numbers are arranged in order, so the median is the third number: 39

With the outlier:
The mean is 47.
The median is 39.

Remove the outlier.
The data set is then: 35, 37, 39, 42
The new mean is: $(235 - 82) \div 4 = 153 \div 4$
$$= 38.25$$
The new median is the mean of 37 and 39: $(37 + 39) \div 2 = 38$

Without the outlier:
The mean is 38.25.
The median is 38.

An outlier may result from an error in measurement or in recording.
In these cases, the outlier should be ignored when calculating averages.

Sometimes it is important to include outliers when calculating averages.

Practice

1. Identify any outliers in each data set.

   a) 10, 20, 35, 35, 15, 95 _______________________________

   b) 3, 5, 8, 3, 2, 8, 5, 7, 4 _______________________________

   c) 10, 55, 61, 48, 60, 54, 97 _______________________________

2. For each data set in question 1:
   - Order the data from least to greatest.

   - Calculate the mean.

   - Calculate the median.

   - Remove the outliers if they exist, then calculate the mean and median again.

   a) From least to greatest: ______________________________

   Mean with outlier: ______

   Median with outlier: ______

   Mean without outlier: ______

   Median without outlier: ______

   b) From least to greatest: ______________________________

   Mean with outlier: ______

   Median with outlier: ______

   Mean without outlier: ______

   Median without outlier: ______

   c) From least to greatest: ______________________________

   Mean with outlier: ______

   Median with outlier: ______

   Mean without outlier: ______

   Median without outlier: ______

3. During one week in February, the daily snowfalls in Kingston were:
5 cm, 4 cm, 21 cm, 6 cm, 3 cm, 7 cm, 3 cm
Calculate the mean, median, and mode of the data.

Mean: ______________________________

Median: ______________________________

Mode: ______________________________

4. Use the data in question 3.

Calculate the mean, median, and mode without the outlier.

Data without the outlier: ____

Mean: _______________

Median: _______________

Mode: _______________

5. Samia has these scores on her math quizzes:
55, 89, 78, 99, 85, 83, 82, 87, 80, 78
For the mid-term report, Samia can choose between:
- using the highest average of all 10 quiz scores or
- the highest average of those scores without the outliers.

What should Samia's choice be? Justify your answer.

For all 10 scores:

Mean = ____

$\quad$ = _______________

Arrange the 10 scores in order: ____

Median = _______________

$\quad$ = _______________

Mode = _______________

The outliers are: _______________

The scores without the outliers are: ____

Mean = ____

$\quad$ = _______________

Median = _______________

$\quad$ = _______________

Mode = _______________

____

____

Quick Review

The mean, median, and mode are all measures of central tendency
of a set of data.

However, not all of the measures describe the data in the same way.

➤ Zoe's hamster has had several litters of babies.
Zoe recorded the number of babies in each litter: 17, 16, 15, 12, 5, 5, 4

There are 7 numbers in the set.

Mean: $\dfrac{17 + 16 + 15 + 12 + 5 + 5 + 4}{7} = \dfrac{74}{7}$, which is about 10.6

The mean is 10.6 babies in a litter.

The numbers of babies in order from least to greatest are: 4, 5, 5, 12, 15, 16, 17
The middle number is 12.
So, the median is 12 babies in a litter.

The number 5 occurs most often.
So, the mode is 5 babies in a litter.

Four of the 7 litters have numbers greater than 5.
So, the mode is not representative of the data.
The mean, 10.6, is not one of the data.

The median, 12, is one of the data.
The number of data greater than the median is equal to the number of data
less than the median.
So, the median would be the best measure of central tendency
used to describe the "average" litter size of the hamster.

➤ Since the mean, median, and mode are all averages, it is important to know
which one best represents the data.

• When the data represent measures such as clothing sizes, the mode best represents
the data. A store needs to re-stock the sizes that sell the most.
• When the numbers in the data set are not very different from each other,
the mean is the best average.
• When the numbers in a data set are very different, the median is the best average.

The numbers in the data set of Zoe's hamster's litter size are very different,
so the median is the best average.

1. The term "average" can refer to the mean, median, or mode.
Which average is likely being referred to in each case?

a) the average size of running shoes sold in one month ___________________

b) the average daily rainfall in Vancouver during October ___________________

c) the average amount spent in dollars by customers at a grocery store ___________

d) the average age of people buying skateboards ___________________

2. There are five numbers in a set of data.
The two modes are 0 and 2.
Both the median and the mean are 2.
Find the 5 numbers.

____

3. A cereal manufacturer says that each box of cereal contains an average mass of
50 g of raisins. A random check is made on 20 boxes.
The table shows the results.

Raisins per 400 g Box	
Amount (g)	**Number of Boxes**
48	1
49	4
50	4
51	6
52	5

a) Calculate the mean, median, and mode of the data.

Mean: _______________________________________

Median: _______________________________________

Mode: _______________________________________

b) Is the manufacturer's claim acceptable?
Justify your answer.

____

4. A radio station has a weekly Song War between the top two hit songs.
Listeners have all week to call in their votes.
Each day, the station rounds the number of calls it receives to the nearest 10
and records the number of calls.

Votes for Song A and Song B		
Day	Song A	Song B
Monday	120	200
Tuesday	100	130
Wednesday	130	90
Thursday	250	80
Friday	100	200

a) Find the mean, median, and mode votes of Song A.

Mean: ____

Median:____

Mode: ____

b) Find the mean, median, and mode votes of Song B.

Mean: ____

Median: ____

Mode: ____

c) Which song is more popular? Explain your choice.

____

____

____

____

Quick Review

When the outcomes of an experiment are equally likely,
the probability of an event occurring is:

$$\frac{\text{Number of outcomes favourable to that event}}{\text{Total number of outcomes}}$$

George has 15 bottles of flavoured water in the fridge.
He has 7 bottles of lemon, 3 bottles of orange, and
5 bottles of raspberry.
George takes a bottle without looking.

Tip

"Probability" is another name for "theoretical probability."

The probability that George takes a particular flavour of water
can be expressed as a fraction, ratio, or percent.

The number of possible outcomes is 15.

- For the probability that George takes orange:
  The number of favourable outcomes is 3.
  As a fraction, the probability is: $\frac{3}{15} = \frac{1}{5}$
  As a ratio, the probability is: 1:5
  As a percent, the probability is: $\frac{3}{15} = \frac{1}{5} = \frac{20}{100} = 20\%$

- The probability that George takes a lime-flavoured water is 0, or 0%
  because there is no lime-flavoured water in the fridge.
  This is an **impossible event.**

- The probability that George takes a bottle that contains water is 1, or 100%
  because every bottle contains water.
  This is a **certain event.**

- All possible probabilities lie between 0 and 1.

1. Suppose the pointer on this spinner is spun.

   a) What is the total number of sectors
   on which the pointer could land? _______

   b) Use a fraction, a ratio, and a percent
   to describe the probability of each event.

    i) The pointer will land on A.

    As a fraction: _____ $\frac{}{10}$ _____   As a ratio: ______ :10   As a percent: ______

    ii) The pointer will land on B.

    As a fraction: ____________   As a ratio: ____________   As a percent: ______

    iii) The pointer will land on a number.

    As a fraction: ____________   As a ratio: ____________   As a percent: ______

    iv) The pointer will land on a letter.

    As a fraction: ____________   As a ratio: ____________   As a percent: ______

    v) The pointer will *not* land on C.

    As a fraction: ____________   As a ratio: ____________   As a percent: ______

2. Gordon has some gumballs in a bag.
He has 7 red, 5 green, 2 yellow, 4 orange, 1 black, and 6 purple gum balls.
Gordon reaches into the bag without looking and pulls out a gumball.

   a) What is the total number of possible outcomes? _______

   b) Write a fraction, a ratio, and a percent to describe the probability of
   Gordon picking each gumball listed below.

	Fraction	Ratio	Percent
purple			
black			
pink			
red or yellow			

3. Find the probability of each event.
Write each answer in any form you like.

   a) Thursday immediately follows Friday. _________________________________

   b) Roll a 1, 3, or 6 on a number cube labelled 1 to 6. _________________

   c) Without looking, Julia picks a green ball from a bowl of balls

      with 7 red, 5 yellow, and 4 green balls. _________________________

4. A charity sells 1000 tickets in a draw to win a new bicycle.
Find each probability.
Write each answer as a percent.

   a) Lee buys 50 tickets.
     The probability that Lee will win is: _______

   b) Jasmine buys 20 tickets.
     The probability that Jasmine will win is: _______

5. This table shows the hair colour of 30 people.
A person is picked at random.
Find each probability.
Write each answer as a fraction.

Hair Colour	Frequency
Brown	12
Blond	11
Red	5
Black	2

   a) The person has black hair.
                         b) The person has brown hair.

    _________________________   _________________________

   c) The person does not have red hair.   **d)** The person has blond or brown hair.

    _________________________   _________________________

6. Each letter in the word BRAVO is written on a separate card.
Sarah shuffles the cards and picks one without looking.
Find the probability of each outcome, as a fraction.

                                              | B | R | A | V | O |

   a) choosing "O": _________________________

   b) choosing a vowel: _________________________

   c) choosing a consonant: _________________________

   d) choosing "Z": _________________________

Quick Review

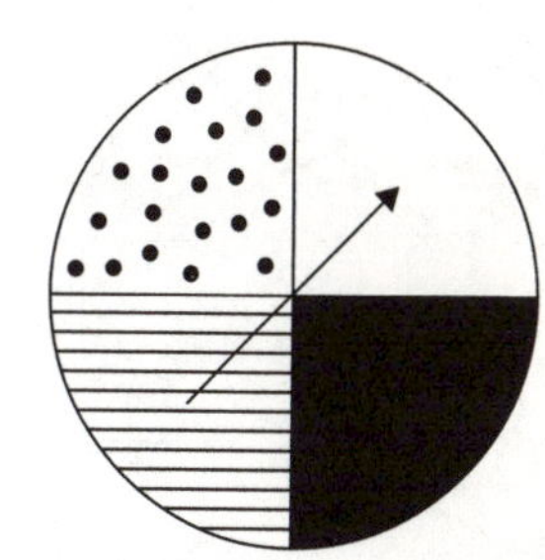

Two events are **independent** if the result of one event does not depend on the result of the other event. For example, tossing a coin and spinning the pointer on a spinner is an experiment with two independent events.

The outcomes of tossing a coin are: heads, tails

The outcomes of spinning the pointer on this spinner are: white, black, striped, dotted

You can use a tree diagram to show the outcomes of an experiment with 2 independent events.

List the outcomes of spinning the pointer. For each spinner outcome, list the outcomes of tossing the coin.

Spinner	Coin	Outcomes
White	Heads	White, Heads
	Tails	White, Tails
Black	Heads	Black, Heads
	Tails	Black, Tails
Striped	Heads	Striped, Heads
	Tails	Striped, Tails
Dotted	Heads	Dotted, Heads
	Tails	Dotted, Tails

There are 8 possible outcomes.
This set of outcomes is the **sample space**.

The **theoretical probability** of the pointer landing on a striped sector and the coin showing tails is: $\frac{1}{8}$

Ernesto carried out this experiment 100 times.

The event of the pointer landing on a striped sector and the coin showing tails occurred 11 times. So, the **experimental probability** of this event is: $\frac{11}{100}$

The fraction $\frac{1}{8}$ is close to the fraction $\frac{11}{100}$, so the experimental probability is close to the theoretical probability.

The greater the number of times an experiment is carried out, the closer the experimental probability may be to the theoretical probability.

1. The theoretical probability that a new-born child is a boy is 50%,
and the probability that the child is a girl is 50%.

a) Complete the tree diagram to show the outcomes for the births of two children.

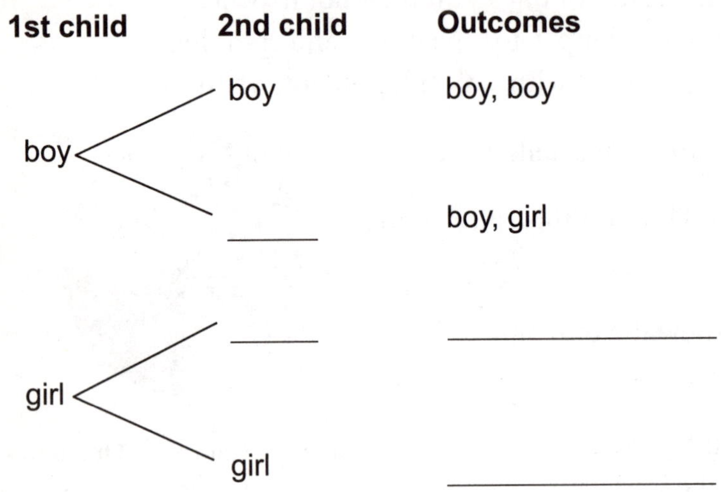

1st child   **2nd child**   **Outcomes**

boy   boy, boy

boy

                                          boy, girl

                _____

girl

                girl   ___________

b) List the outcomes from part a.

____

c) How many outcomes are there? _______

d) What is the theoretical probability of having a boy and a girl? _______________

e) What is the theoretical probability of having two girls? _______

f) In a survey of 100 families with two children, it was found that 24 families had two girls.

What is the experimental probability of having two girls? _______________

2. List the sample space for each experiment.

a) tossing a coin and rolling a tetrahedron labelled 1 to 4

b) spinning the pointer on Spinner 1 and spinning the pointer on Spinner 2

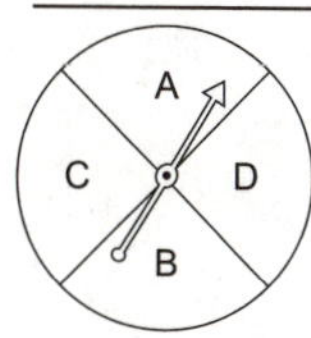 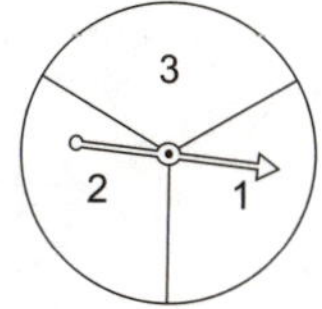

Spinner 1   Spinner 2

3. At the cafeteria, the lunch choices of the day are:
- a cheese sandwich or a peanut butter sandwich
- grapes or a banana or an apple
- milk or juice

a) Make a tree diagram to show all possible lunch orders.

b) Suppose choices are made at random.
What is the probability that an order will include:

i) a peanut butter sandwich? _________   **ii)** a banana and juice? _________

iii) a bologna sandwich? _______   **iv)** a cheese sandwich, grapes, and milk _________

4. A tetrahedron is labelled 5, 6, 7, 8.
   The tetrahedron is rolled and the pointer on this spinner is spun.

 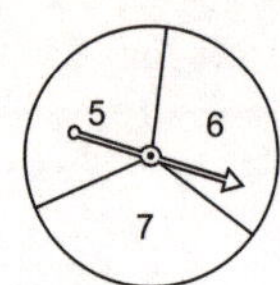

   a) Draw a tree diagram to show the possible outcomes.

   b) Find the theoretical probability of getting different numbers on the tetrahedron and

      the spinner. ____

   c) Find the theoretical probability of getting the same number on both the tetrahedron

      and the spinner. ____

   d) This experiment is carried out 50 times.
      There were 11 outcomes where the numbers were the same.
      What is the experimental probability of getting two numbers the same? ____

   e) How does the experimental probability in part d compare with
      the theoretical probability in part c? Explain.

      ____

170

In Your Words

Here are some of the important mathematical words of this unit.
Build your own glossary by recording definitions and examples here. The first one is done for you.

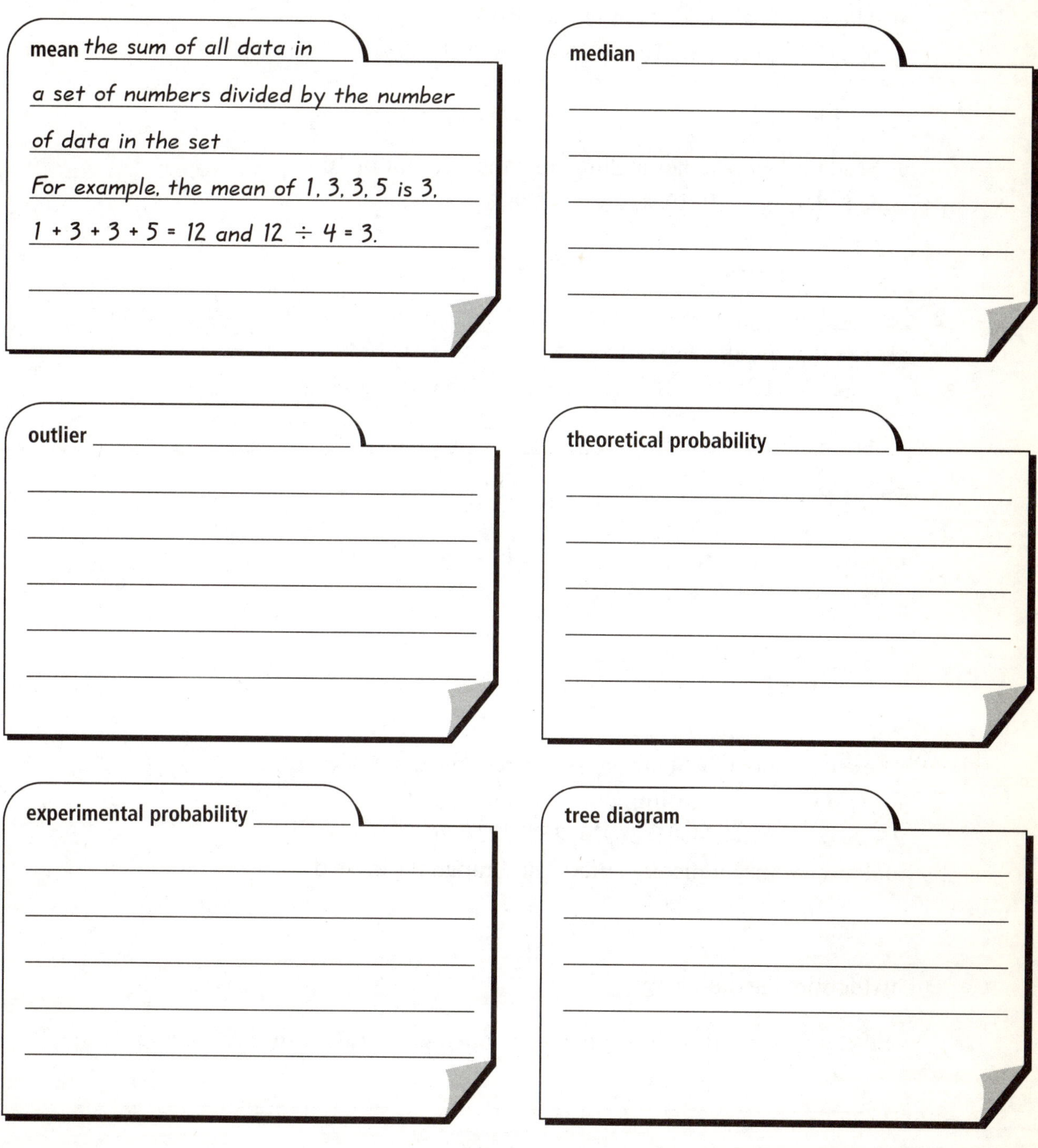

List other mathematical words you need to know.

7.1 **1.** Calculate the mean and mode of each set of data.
   a) The weekly allowances of ten students:
   $20, $25, $15, $20, $10, $20, $30, $10, $20, $0

   Mean: _______   Mode: _______

   b) Students' scores on a spelling quiz marked out of 10:
   5, 8, 8, 4, 6, 3, 10, 10, 4, 6, 7, 9, 7, 9, 9

   Mean: _______   Mode: _______

7.2 **2.** Arrange the data in each set in order, then calculate the median and the range.
   a) The heights, in centimetres, of eleven 12-year-olds:
   160, 155, 162, 152, 161, 154, 153, 160, 158, 155, 159

   From least to greatest: ____

   Median: _______   Range: _______

   b) The hours that ten grade 7 students exercised in one week:
   5, 7, 18, 5, 13, 9, 4, 12, 7, 20

   From least to greatest: ____

   Median: _______   Range: _______

7.3 **3.** These data show the daily temperatures, in degrees Celsius,
   for two weeks in the summer in Nelson, B.C.:
   23, 25, 22, 25, 28, 24, 25, 24, 25, 25, 52, 24, 20, 22
   a) Find the mean, median, mode, and range for these data.

   Mean: _______   Median: _______   Mode: _______   Range: _______

   b) Identify the outlier. _______

   Why do you think the outlier is so much greater than the other temperatures?

   ____

   ____

c) Calculate the mean, median, mode, and range without the outlier.

Mean: _______   Median: _______   Mode: _______   Range: _______

d) When reporting the average daily temperature, should the outlier be included?

Explain. ____

7.3
7.4

4. The times, in minutes, that 10 students spent walking home
from school one day are:
20, 16, 10, 12, 22, 65, 8, 12, 18, 7
a) Calculate the mean, mode, and median times for these data.

Mean: _______   Mode: _______   Median: _______

b) Identify the outlier. _______

c) Calculate the mean, mode, and median without the outlier.

Mean: ____________   Mode: ____________   Median: ____________

d) Which average best describes the data? Explain.

____

____

____

7.4
5. Cary scored these points in his last six basketball games: 5, 8, 10, 7, 15, 15
a) Find the mean, median, and mode scores.

Mean: _______   Median: _______   Mode: _______

b) Which measure of central tendency is Cary likely to use to persuade
his coach that he is a valuable player? Explain.

____

____

c) Which measure is the coach likely to use to help her decide if
Cary is a valuable player? Explain.

____

____

7.5 **6.** A basket of fruit contains 4 apples, 5 bananas, 6 oranges, and 10 kiwi fruits.
A piece of fruit is chosen at random.
Find the probability of each event. Write each probability 3 ways.

    a) An orange is picked. ____

    b) An apple or a banana is picked. _______________________________________

    c) A grape is picked. ____

7.6 **7.** Fran designs a game called *Product 24.*
She makes this spinner:
The pointer is spun twice.
To win this game, the pointer must land on
two numbers with a product of 24.

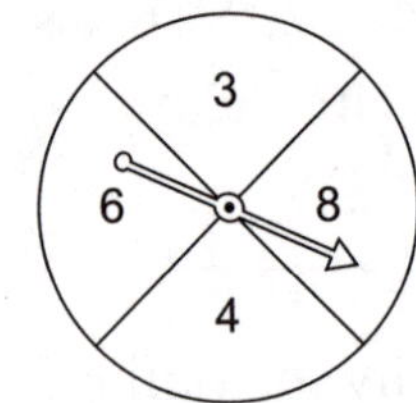

    a) Complete the tree diagram to show all possible outcomes for this game.

       1st Spin   **2nd Spin**   **Outcomes**

    b) What is the total number of outcomes? _______

    c) How many favourable outcomes are there? _______

    d) What is the probability of winning Fran's game? _____________________________

UNIT 8 — Geometry

Just for Fun

Get My Angle

Unscramble the letters in each row to form a geometry word from this unit.

LAPARLEL   ______________________

TARNSUAQD   ______________________

NMEGSTE   ______________________

SETROCIB   ______________________

GLENA   ______________________

SETCIB   ______________________

IDLUCRANEPREP   ______________________

GIINRO   ______________________

Draw It Bigger

Enlarge the cartoon.
Draw the cartoon in the larger grid.

Sum or Product?

You need two number cubes labelled 1 to 6, pencils, and paper.

Players take turns. On each turn, roll both number cubes.

If the sum of the two numbers is greater than the product of the two numbers, the player scores 3 points.
If the product of the two numbers is greater than the sum of the two numbers, the player scores 1 point.
If the sum and product are the same, the player scores no points.

Each player has 10 turns.
The player with the most points after 10 turns is the winner.

Classifying Triangles

You can classify triangles by their sides, or by their angles.

Classify by sides	all sides equal **Equilateral**	2 sides equal **Isosceles**	no sides equal **Scalene**
Classify by angles	all angles less than 90° **Acute**	one angle of 90° **Right**	one angle greater than 90° **Obtuse**

✓ Check

1. Match each triangle to its description.

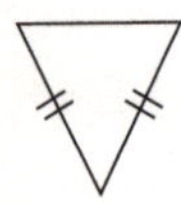
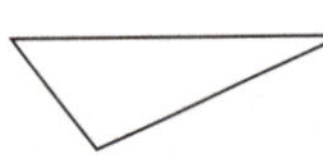
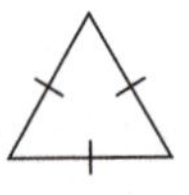
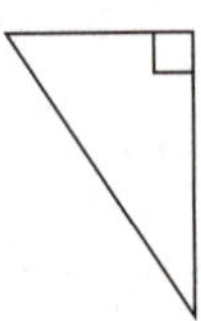

equilateral and acute   isosceles and acute   scalene and right   scalene and obtuse

2. Draw each triangle if you can. If you cannot, explain why.

a) scalene and obtuse   **b)** obtuse and acute   **c)** equilateral and acute

Properties of a Rhombus

A rhombus is a parallelogram with all sides equal.
A rhombus has:

- Opposite sides parallel
- Opposite angles equal

- Diagonals that intersect at right angles
- Diagonals that bisect each other
- Diagonals that bisect the angles

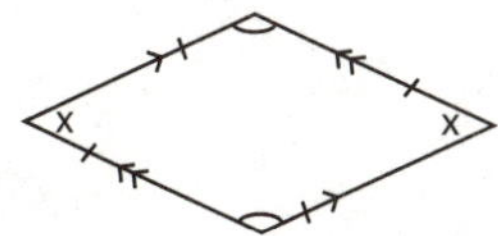
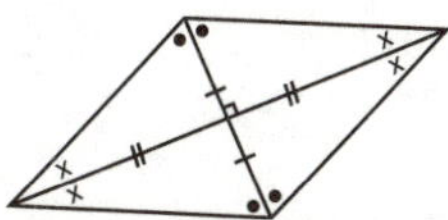

Example

For rhombus EFGH:

a) Name the opposite angles that are equal.

b) What do you know about sides EF and HG?

c) What do you know about segments EP and PH?

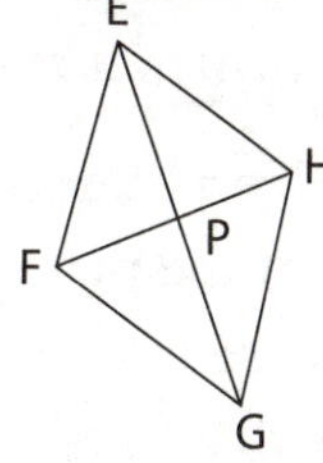

Solution

a) $\angle$FEH = $\angle$FGH and $\angle$EFG = $\angle$EHG

b) Sides EF and HG are opposite sides, so they are equal and parallel.

c) Segments EP and PH are parts of intersecting diagonals, so these segments are perpendicular; that is, they intersect at 90°.

 **Check**

3. Draw a large rhombus on this dot paper.
Label it HIJK.
Draw the diagonals of the rhombus.
They intersect at point G.

a) Name all the right angles.

____

b) What is the bisector
of HJ? ____

c) Which segment is twice the
length of IG? ____

d) Which segment is one-half
the length of HJ? __________

e) Which angle is equal to $\angle$HIG? _____________________

f) Which angle is equal to $\angle$IHK? ______

Quick Review

Parallel lines are lines on the same flat surface that never meet.
They are always the same distance apart.

Here are 2 strategies for drawing a line segment parallel to line segment AB.

Using a ruler and a protractor

➤ Choose a point C on line segment AB.
Place the centre of the protractor
on C. Align the base line of
the protractor with AB.
Mark a point D at 90°.
Repeat this step at point E
to mark point F.
Draw a line through FD.
Line segment FD is parallel to AB.

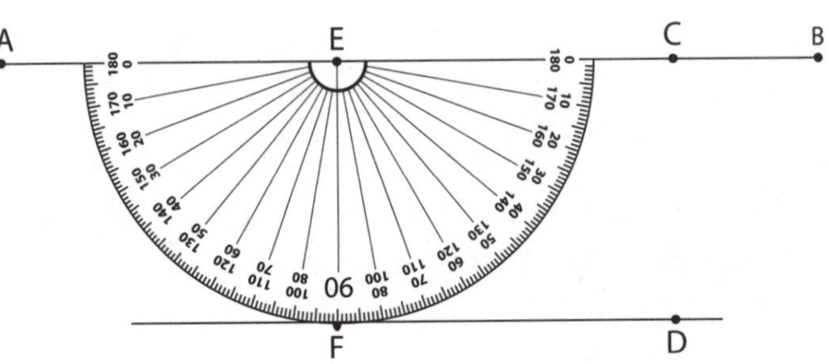

Using a ruler and a compass

➤ Mark any point D on line segment AB.
Place the compass point on D.
Draw an arc to intersect AB at E.
Place the compass point on E.
Draw an arc to intersect AB at F.

➤ Place the compass point on F.
Draw an arc below AB.
Place the compass point on E.
Draw an arc below AB. This arc
should intersect the arc drawn
from F, at G.
Place the compass point on D.
Draw an arc below AB to intersect
the arc drawn from E, at H.

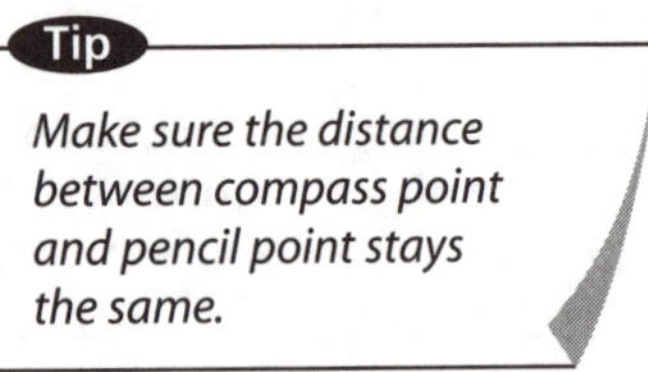

➤ Draw a line through GH.
Line segment GH is parallel to AB.

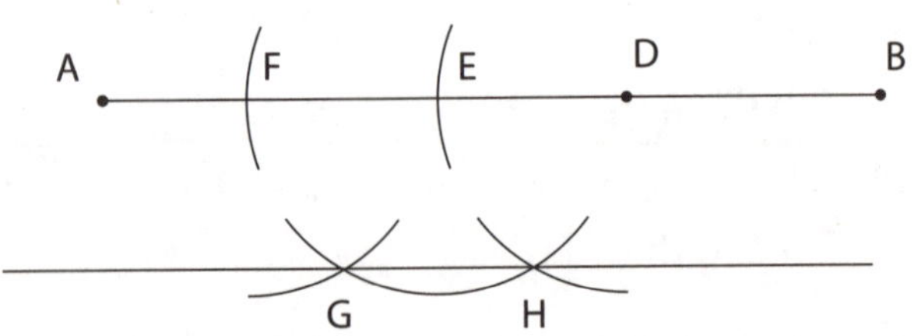

1. Are the line segments in each pair parallel?

a) _______

b) _______

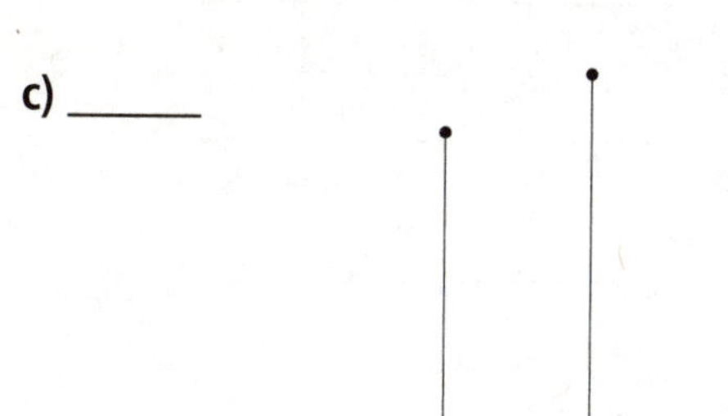

c) _______

d) _______

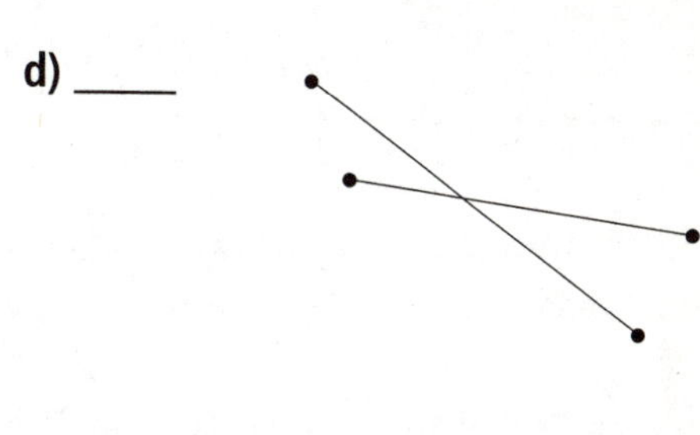

2. Draw a line segment.
Use any method you like to draw a parallel line segment.
Explain your strategy. How do you know the lines are parallel?

____

____

____

____

3. Look around you for examples of parallel line segments. List 6 examples.

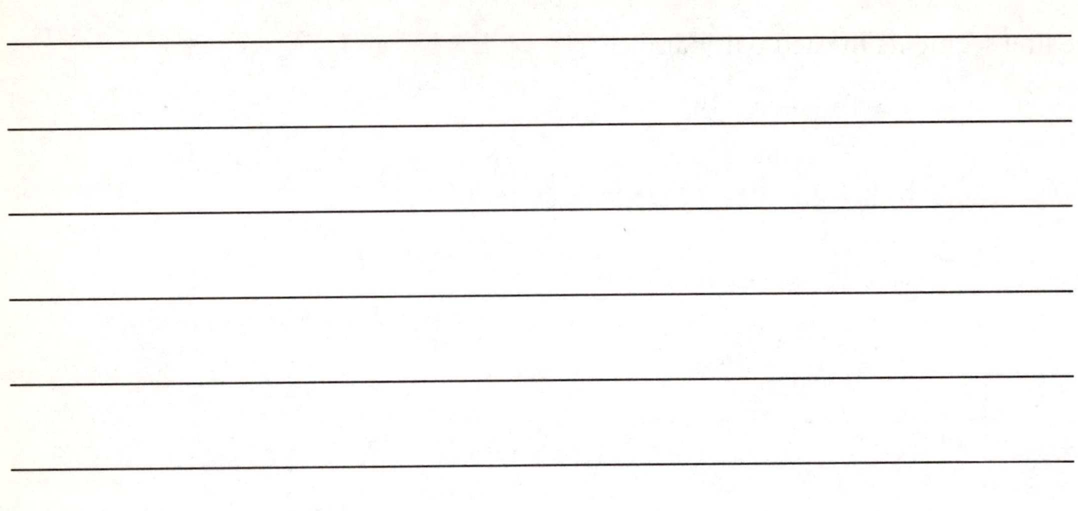

4. Draw a line segment parallel to each segment shown.

a) 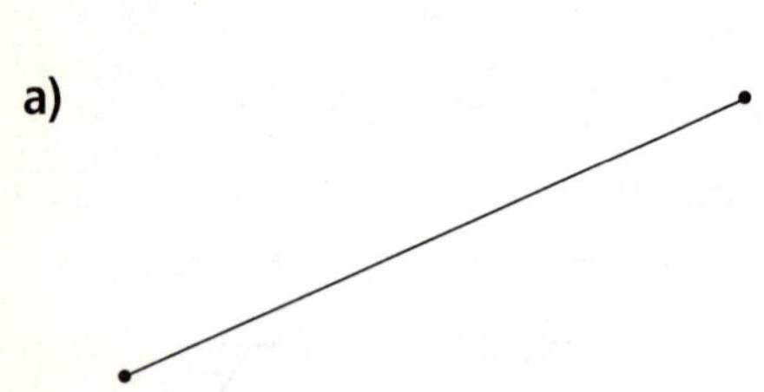

b) 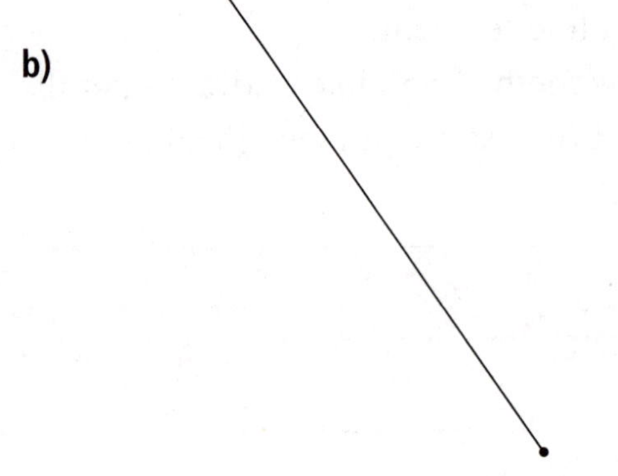

c) 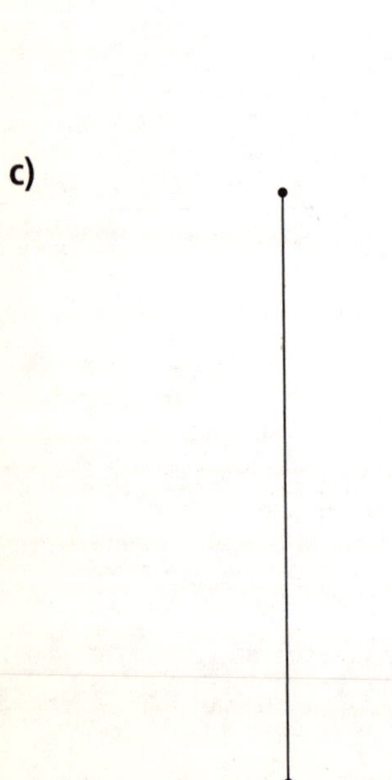

d) 

5. How do you know these line segments are parallel?

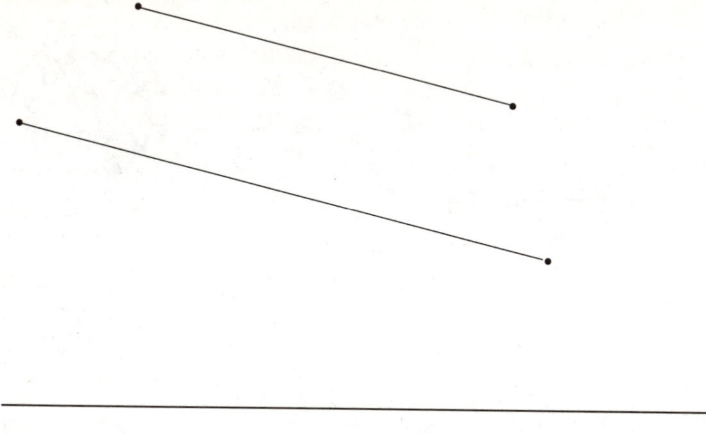

____

____

____

____

6. Look at the diagram below.
Find as many pairs of parallel line segments as you can.

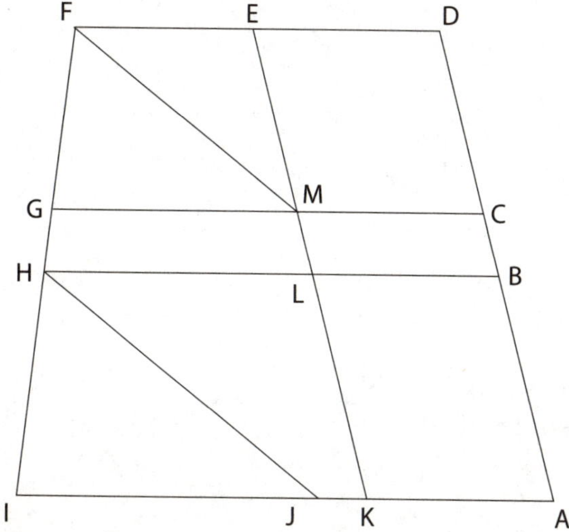

____

____

____

Quick Review

Two lines are perpendicular if they intersect at right angles.

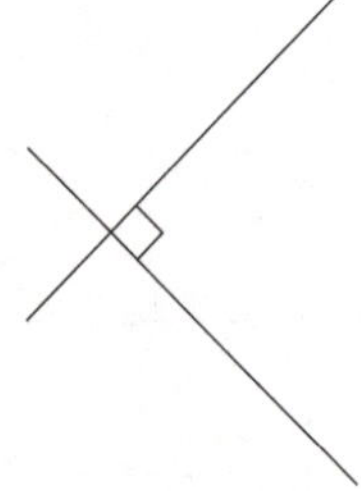

Here are 2 strategies to draw a line segment perpendicular to line segment AB.

Using a plastic right triangle

➤ Place one of the shorter sides of the triangle along line segment AB.
Draw line segment CD along the other shorter side.
Line segment AB is perpendicular to CD.

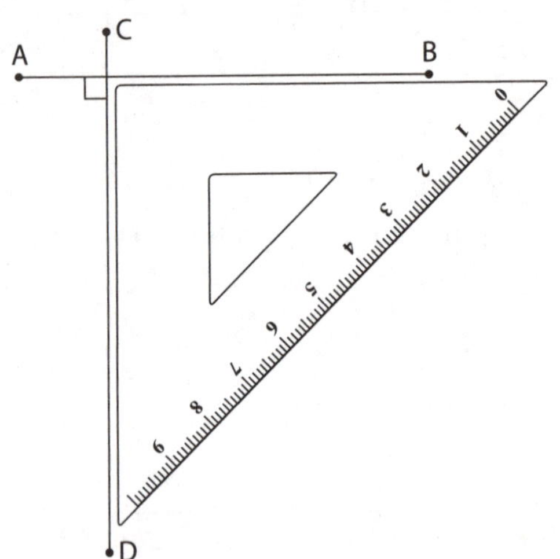

Using a ruler and a compass

➤ Mark a point C on line segment AB.
Set the compass so the distance between the compass and pencil points is greater than one-half the length of AC.
Place the compass point on A.
Draw a circle that intersects AB.
➤ Place the compass point on C.
Draw a circle to intersect the first circle you drew, at D and E.
➤ Draw a line through DE.
Line segment DE is perpendicular to AB.

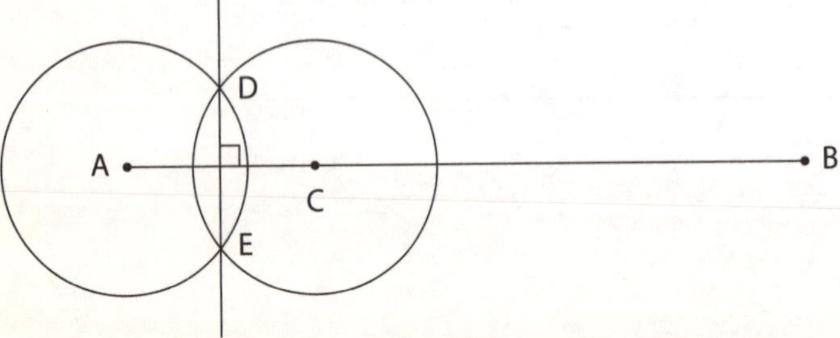

1. Are the line segments in each pair perpendicular?

a) ______ 

b) ______ 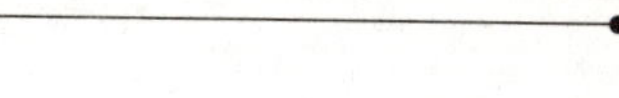

c) ______ 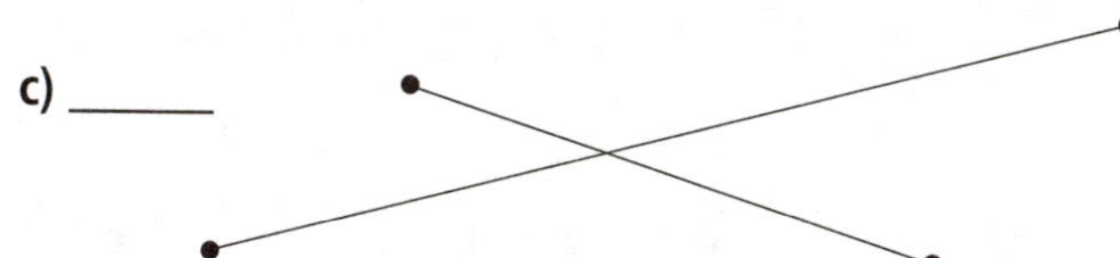

d) ______ 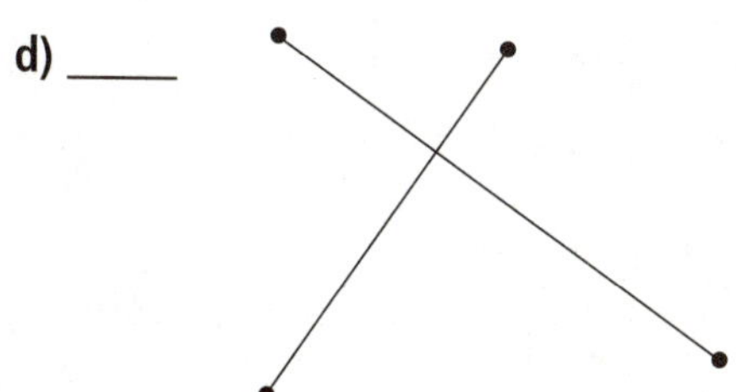

2. Draw a line segment.
Use any method you like to draw a perpendicular line segment.
Explain your strategy.

____

____

____

3. Look around you for examples of perpendicular line segments. List 6 examples.

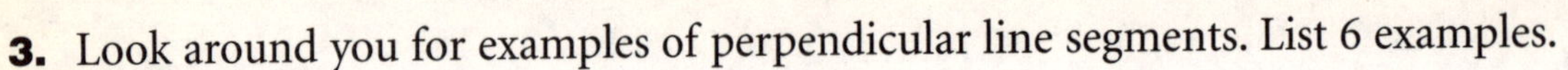

4. Draw a line segment perpendicular to each segment shown.

a)

b)

c)

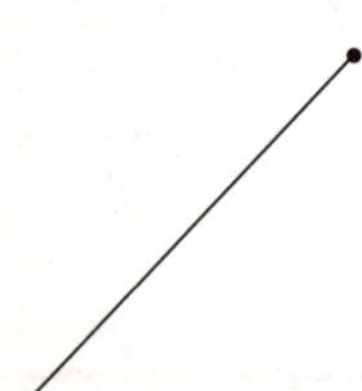

d)

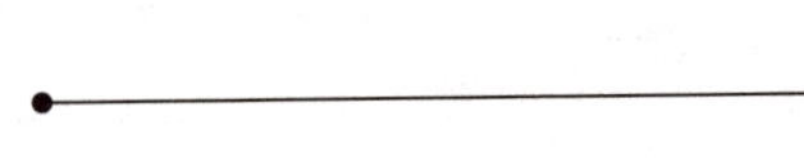

5. How do you know these line segments are perpendicular?

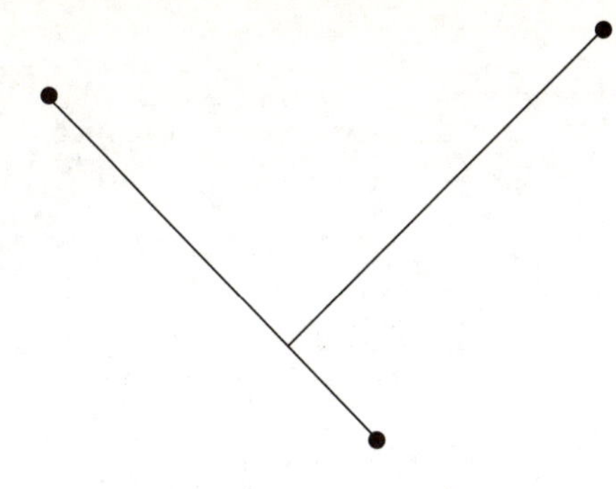

____

____

____

____

6. Look at the diagram below.
Find as many pairs of perpendicular line segments as you can.

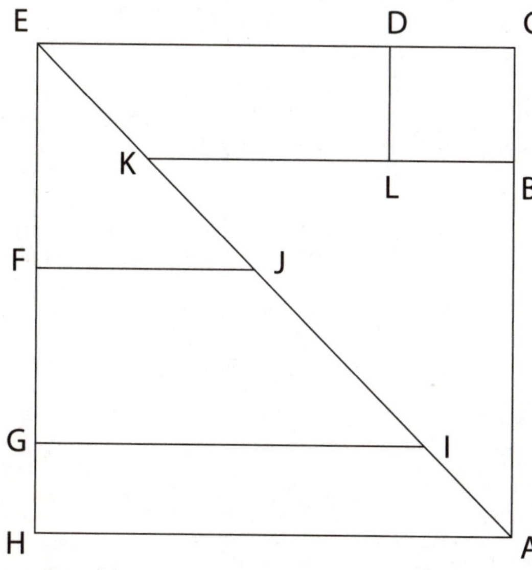

____

____

____

____

Quick Review

When you draw a line to divide a line segment
into two equal parts, you *bisect* the segment.
The line you drew is a *bisector* of the segment.

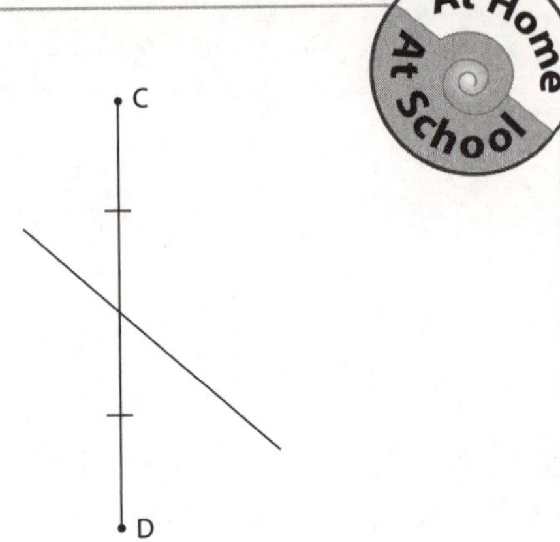

When the bisector is drawn *perpendicular*
to the segment, the line is the *perpendicular*
bisector of the segment.

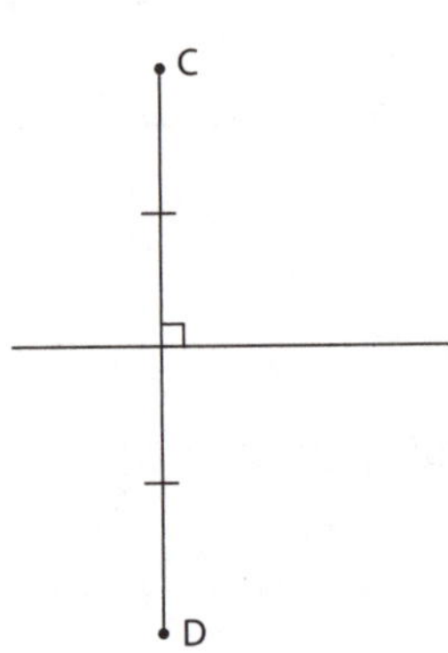

Here are 2 strategies to draw a perpendicular bisector of line segment AB.

Using paper folding
Fold the paper so that point A lies on point B.
Crease along the fold.
Open the paper.
The fold line is the perpendicular bisector of AB.

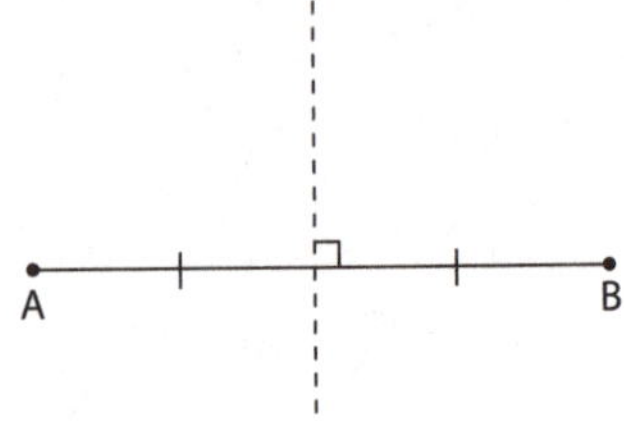

Using a ruler and a protractor
➤ Use the ruler to measure the length of AB.
   Mark its midpoint C.

➤ Place the centre of the protractor on C.
   Align the base line of the protractor with AB.
   Mark a point D at 90°.

➤ Draw a line through CD.
   The line through CD is the perpendicular bisector of AB.

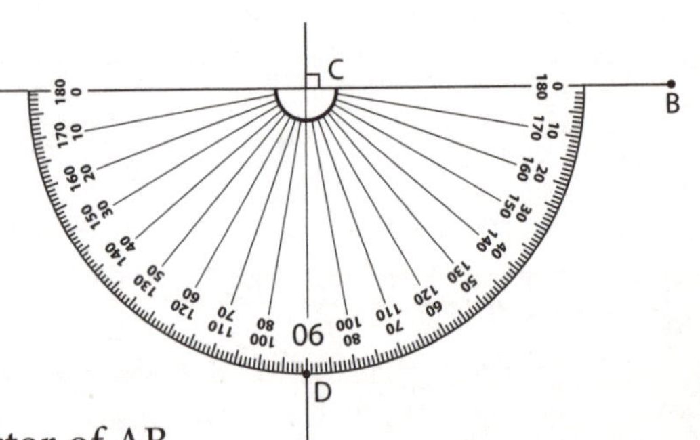

1. Match each term with its definition.

a) right angle

a line segment that joins two vertices of a shape, but is not a side

b) bisector

a 90° angle

c) perpendicular bisector

a line that divides a line segment into two equal parts

d) diagonal

a line that is perpendicular to a line segment and divides the segment into two equal parts

2. Identify the perpendicular bisector in this kite.
How do you know the segment you identified is a perpendicular bisector?

____

____

3. Draw any line segment MN.
Use any method you like to draw the perpendicular bisector of MN.
Explain your strategy.

____

____

____

4. Has each line segment AB been bisected?
How do you know?

a)

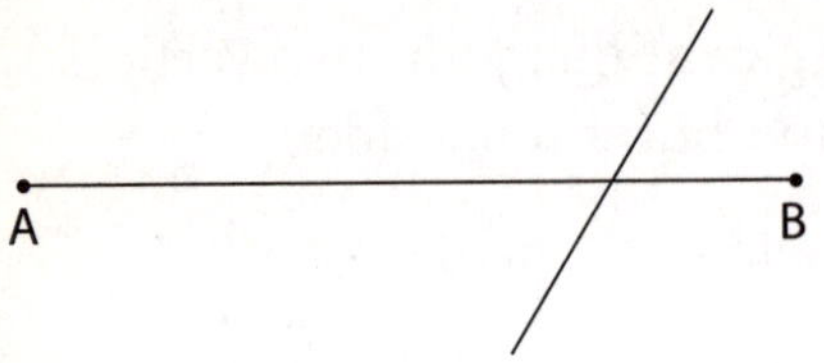

b)

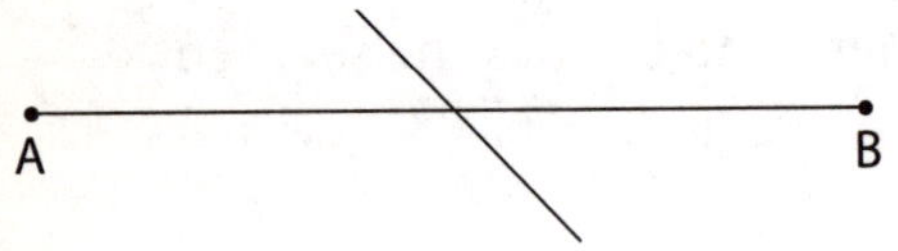

c)

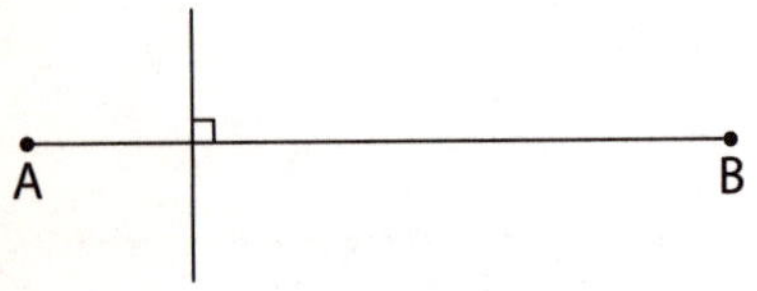

d)

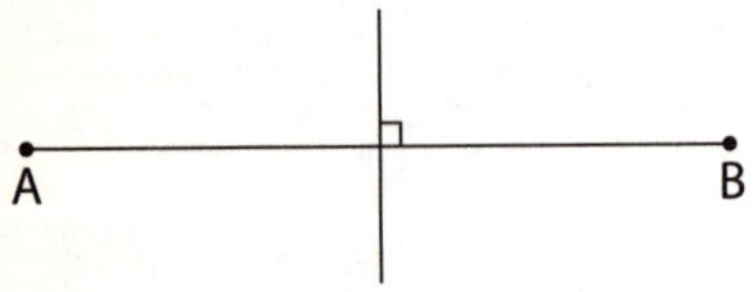

5. Look around you for examples of perpendicular bisectors. List 2 examples.

6. Draw the perpendicular bisector of line segment GH.
Draw a bisector of line segment JK.

G ————————————————— H   J ————————————————— K

a) Why does a line segment have many bisectors?

____

____

b) Why does a line segment have only one perpendicular bisector?

____

____

7. Draw line segment PQ 10 cm long.
a) Draw the perpendicular bisector of PQ.

b) Choose three different points A, B, and C on the bisector.

i) Measure PA and QA. _______________________

ii) Measure PB and QB. _______________________

iii) Measure PC and QC. _______________________

iv) What do you notice about the measures in parts i, ii, and iii? Explain.

____

____

Quick Review

The bisector of an angle divides the angle into two equal parts.
Line segment QS is the bisector of ∠PQR because ∠PQS = ∠SQR.

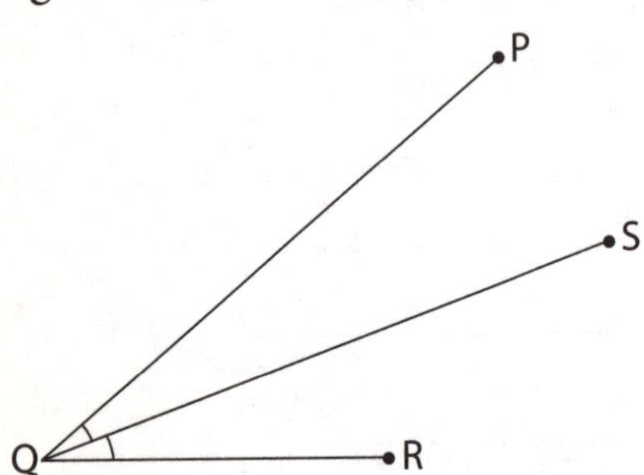

Here are 2 strategies to draw the bisector of ∠ABC.

Using a Mira

Place the Mira between the arms of the angle so that
the reflection of one arm lies along the other arm.
Draw line segment BD along the edge of the Mira,
through the vertex of the angle.
Line segment BD is the bisector of ∠ABC.

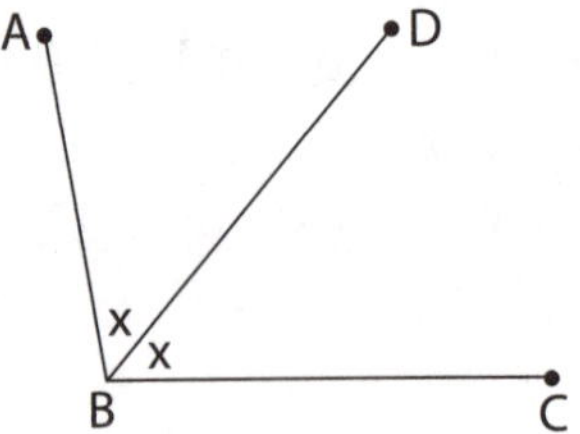

Using a ruler and compass

i) 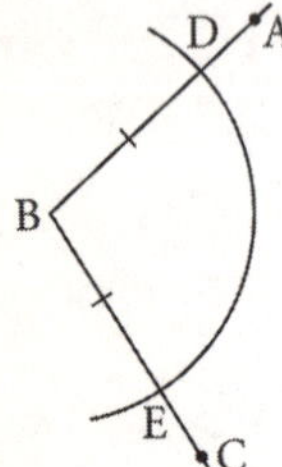

ii) 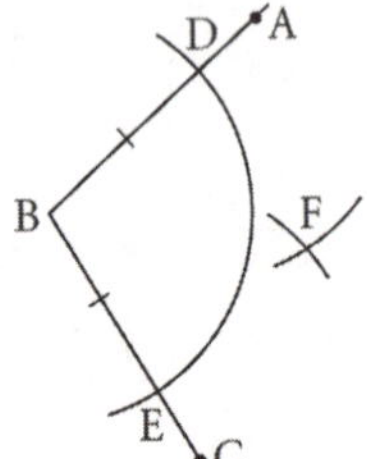

iii) 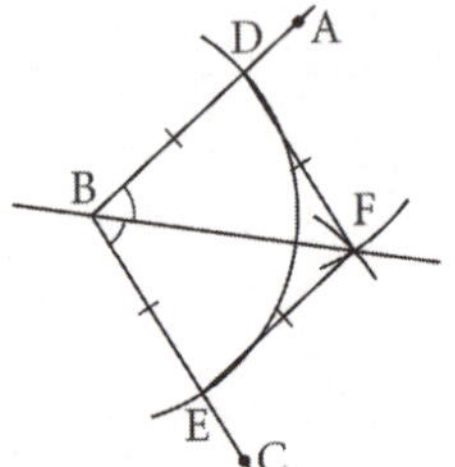

i)   Place the compass point on B. Draw an arc to meet BA at D and BC at E.

ii) Place the compass point on D. Draw an arc between the arms of the angle.
     Keep the distance between the compass and pencil points.
     Place the compass point on E. Draw an arc to meet the previous arc at F.

iii) Join BF.

BF is the bisector of ∠ABC.

1. For each ∠DEF, is EG a bisector?

a) ___

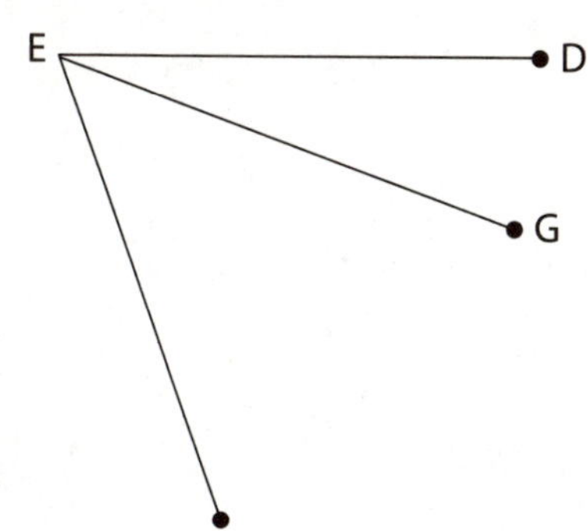

b) ___

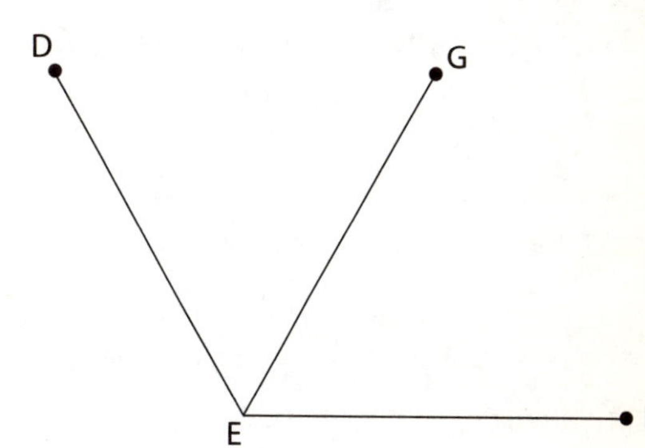

c) ___

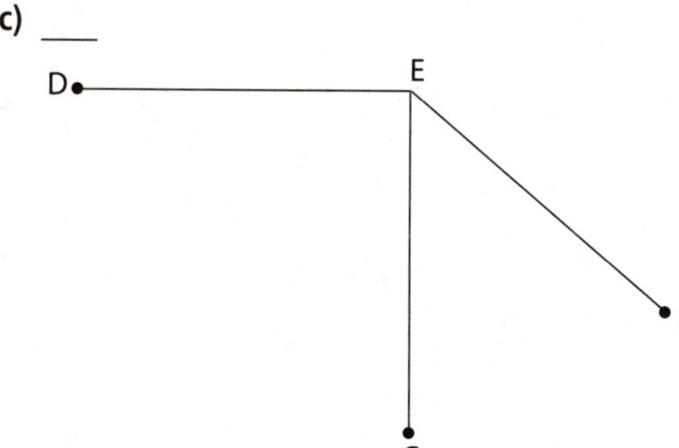

d) ___

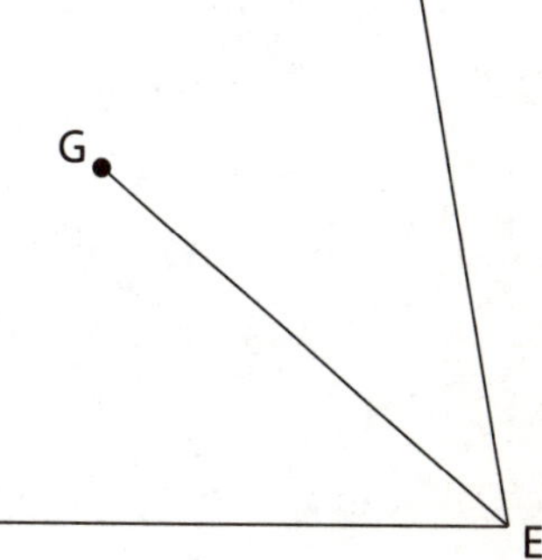

2. Draw any acute ∠MNP.
Use any method you like to draw the bisector of ∠MNP.
Explain your strategy.

3. How can you check that the bisector you drew in question 2 is correct?

____

____

4. Use a plastic right triangle to bisect ∠BCD.
Use a ruler and compass to bisect ∠EFG.

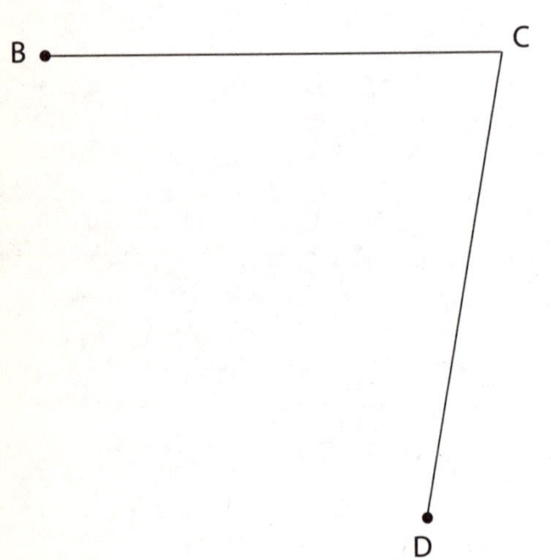

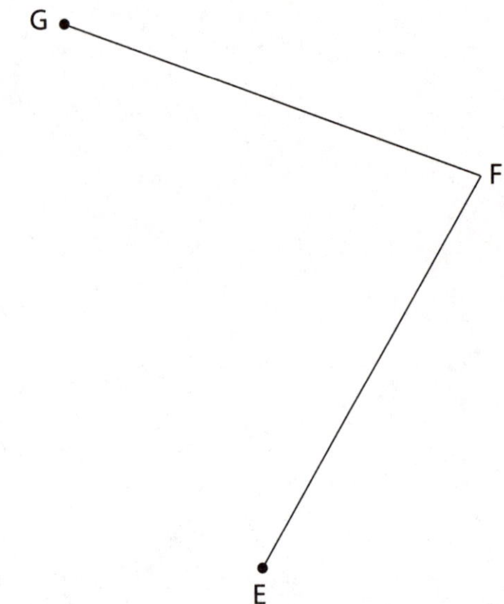

Measure the two angles formed by each bisector.

a) Measures of angles formed by bisector of ∠BCD: __________

Measures of angles formed by bisector of ∠EFG: __________

b) What do your answers from part a tell you about ∠BCD and ∠EFG?

____

5. Use a ruler and compass to draw
the bisector KB of ∠ABD.
Then draw the bisector MB of ∠DBC.
Use a protractor to measure ∠KBM.

What do you notice?

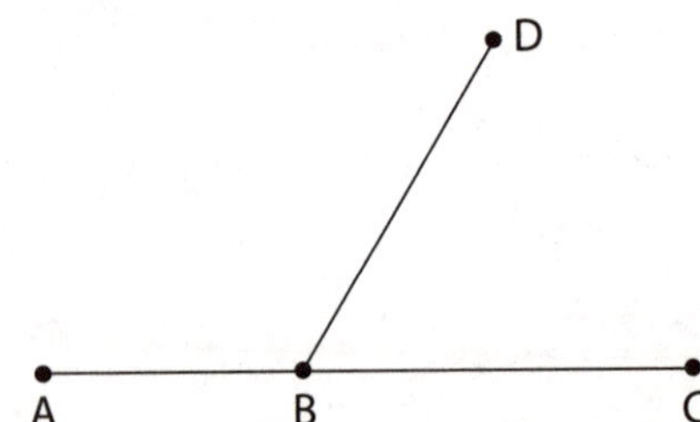

____

Quick Review

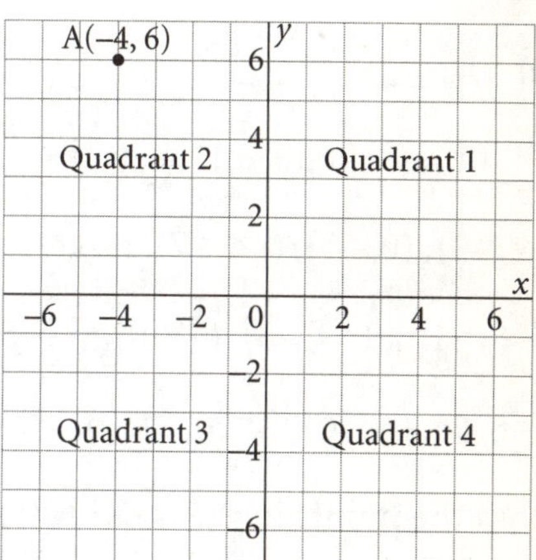

➤ A **coordinate grid** is formed when a horizontal number line and a vertical number line intersect at right angles at 0.

➤ The horizontal number line is the **x-axis**. The vertical number line is the **y-axis**. They meet at the **origin**.

➤ The axes divide the grid into 4 **quadrants** numbered 1, 2, 3, and 4 counterclockwise.

➤ Points on the axes do not belong to any quadrant.

➤ A point on a coordinate grid is located by an **ordered pair** of numbers. The first number, the x-coordinate, tells how far left or right of the origin the point is. The second number, the y-coordinate, tells how far up or down from the origin the point is. For example, (−4, 6) is 4 units left of the origin and 6 units up.

Practice

1. Use each letter once. Complete these descriptions for points in the diagram.

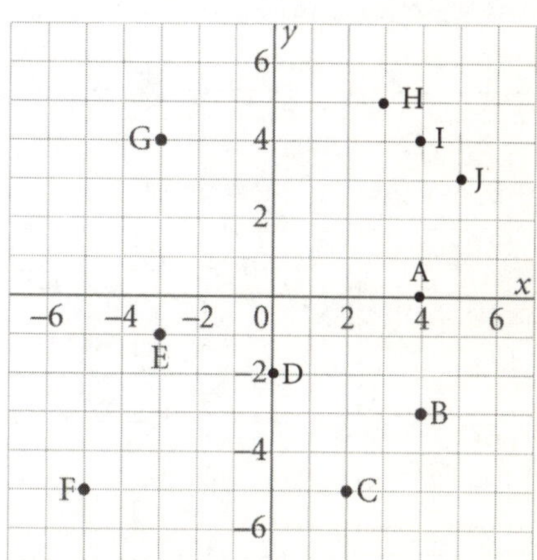

a) Point _______ is 3 units right of and 5 units up from the origin.

b) Point _______ is 5 units right of and 3 units up from the origin.

c) Point _______ has x-coordinate 0.

d) Point _______ has y-coordinate 0.

e) Points _______________________ have the same x-coordinates.

f) Points _______ and _______ have equal x- and y-coordinates.

g) Points _______ and _______ are in Quadrant 4.

2. Use the diagram in question 1.
Write the coordinates of each point.

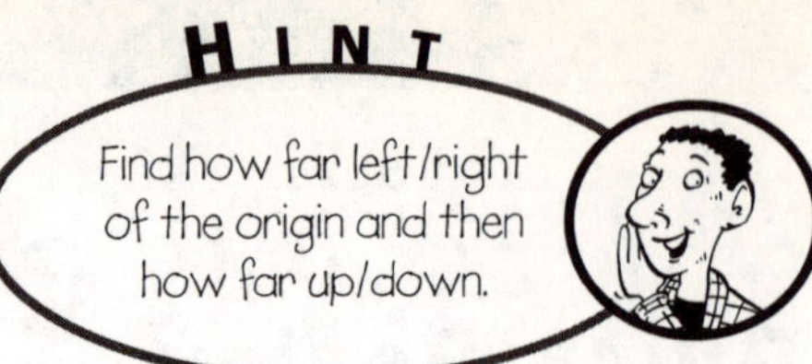

a) A (4, _______)

b) B (_______, –3)

c) C _____________

d) D _____________

e) E _____________

f) F _____________

g) G _____________

h) H _____________

i) I _____________

j) J _____________

3. Plot these points on the grid.

(2, –9), (0, –5), (–4, –7), (–6, –10),

(–8, –10), (–9, –8), (–7, 0), (–5, 5),

(–6, 7), (–3, 6), (2, 3), (4, 0), (8, –4)

Join the points in the order listed.

Which animal's head did you draw?

____

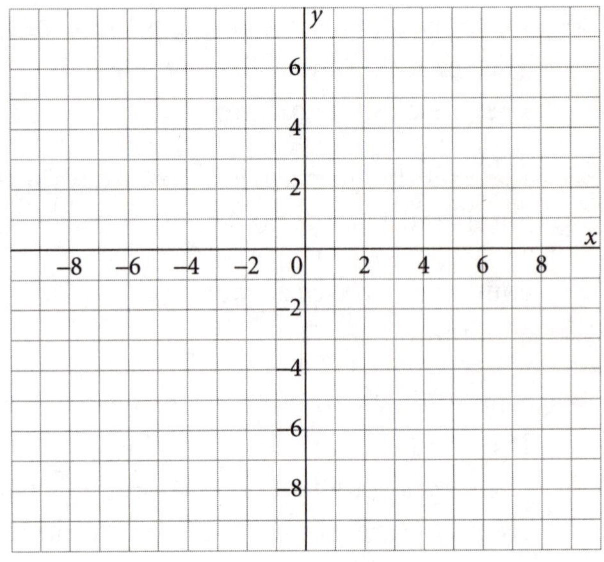

4. Graph each set of points. Join the points in order. Then join the last point to the first point.
Name the geometric shape you drew.

a) (5, 3), (5, –3), (–5, –3), (–5, 3)

b) (–4, 0), (2, 0), (5, 3), (–1, 3)

____

____

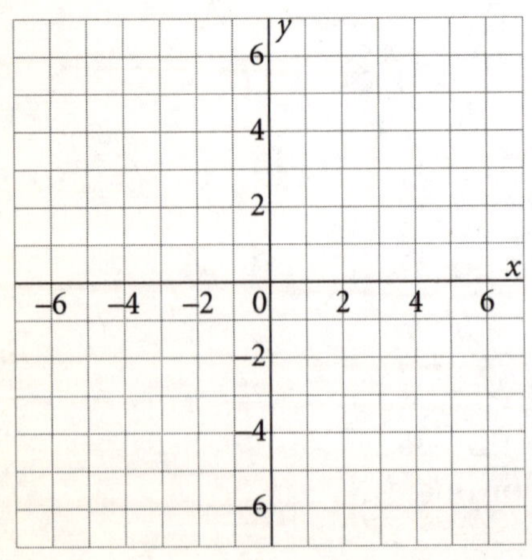

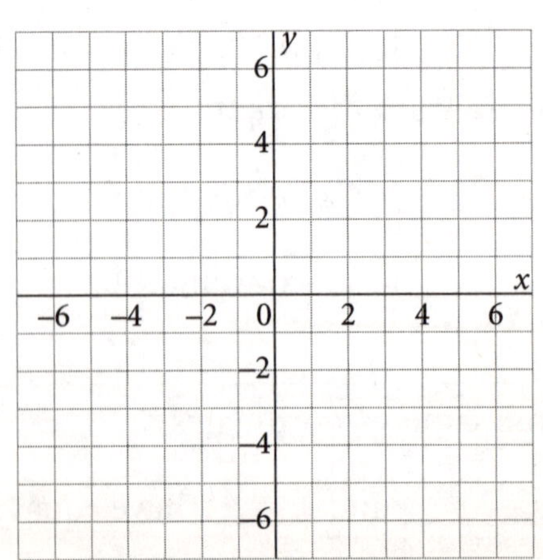

c) $(-3, 4), (2, 4), (4, -2), (-4, -2)$

d) $(5, 1), (-2, -2), (-5, 1), (-2, 4)$

__________________________   __________________________

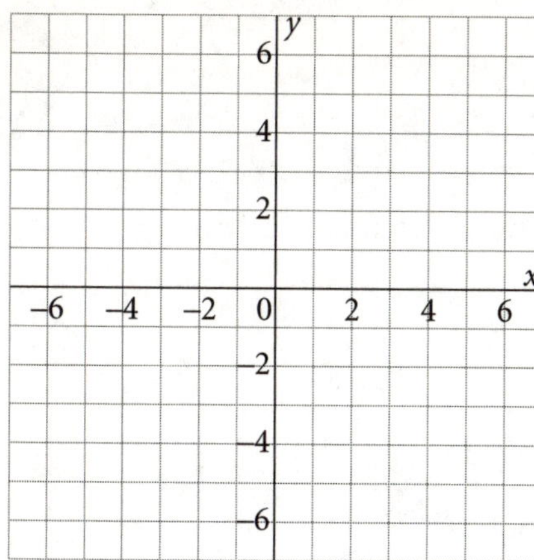

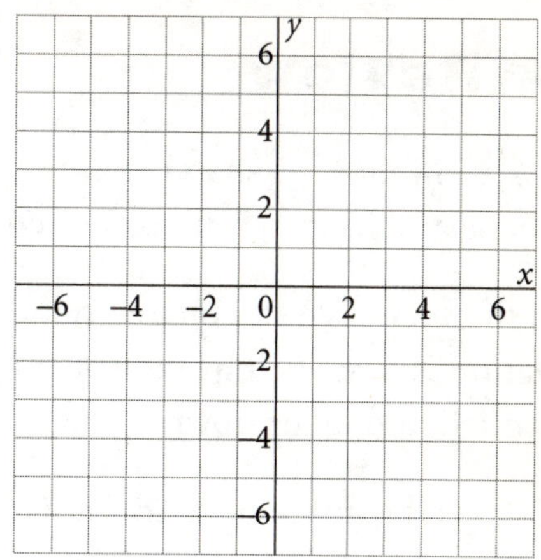

5. a) A($-4, -2$), B($-4, 5$), and C($3, 5$) are 3 vertices of square ABCD.
Graph these points on the grid.

b) What are the coordinates of point D?

____

Graph this point on the grid.
Join the points to form square ABCD.

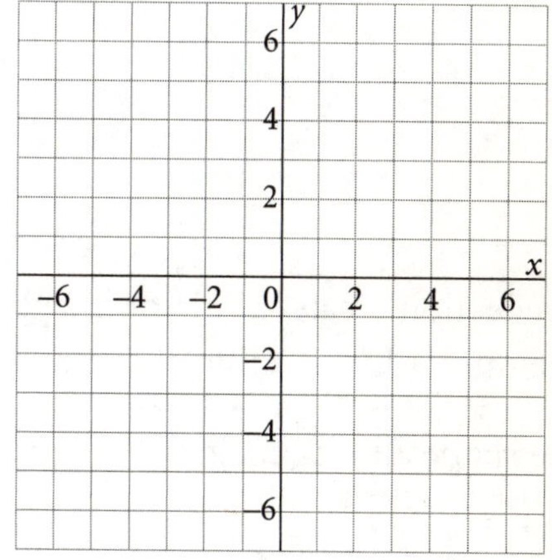

c) Find the area and perimeter of square ABCD.

The side length of square ABCD is _____________ units.

The area of square ABCD is _____________ square units.

The perimeter of square ABCD is _____________ units.

Quick Review

➤ A translation moves a shape in a straight line.
The shape and its image are congruent, and have the same orientation.

When the shape is on a square grid, the
translation is described by movements
right or left and up or down.

$\triangle A'B'C'$ is the image of $\triangle ABC$ after a
translation 7 units left and 4 units up.

Both $\triangle ABC$ and its translation image
$\triangle A'B'C'$ are read clockwise.

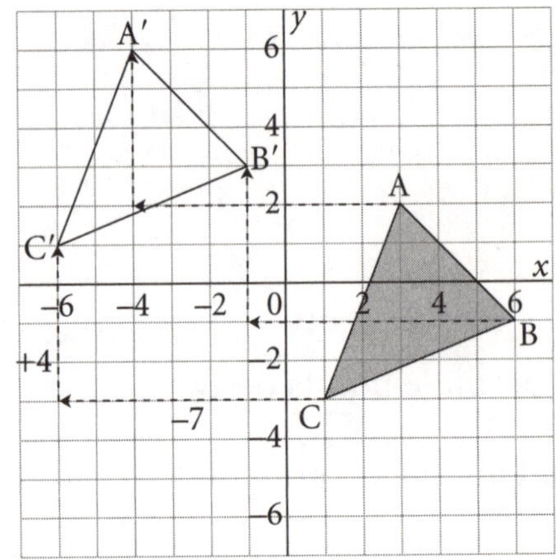

➤ A reflection creates a mirror image of a shape.
The mirror line is a line of symmetry for the shape and its image.

The shape and its image are congruent, but have different orientations.

$\triangle A'B'C'$ is the image of $\triangle ABC$ after a reflection in the x-axis.
$\triangle A''B''C''$ is the image of $\triangle ABC$ after a reflection in the y-axis.

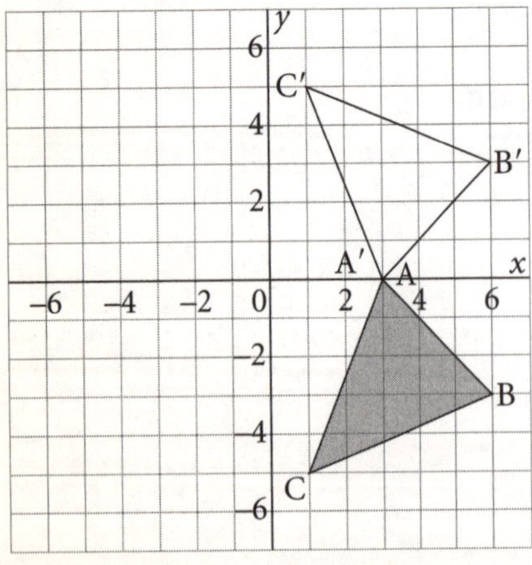
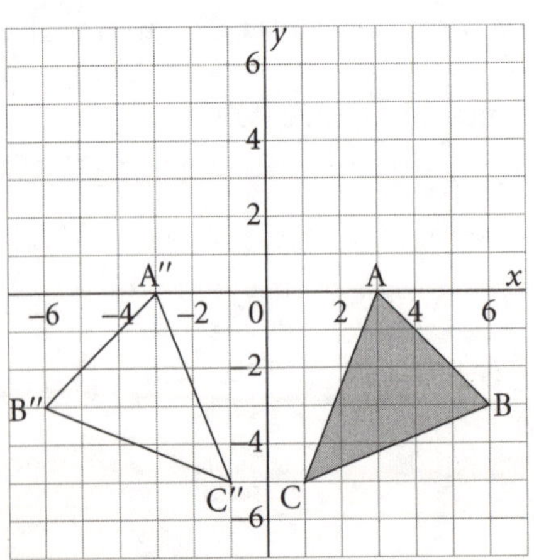

$\triangle ABC$ is read clockwise.
Its reflection images $\triangle A'B'C'$ and $\triangle A''B''C''$ are read counterclockwise.

1. Which triangles are translation images of the shaded triangle? Which are reflection images?

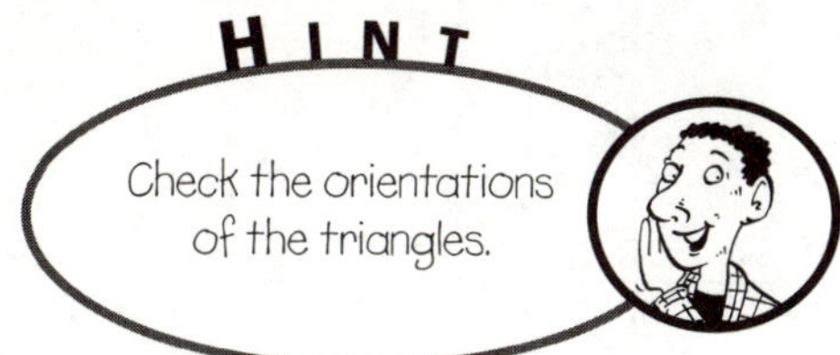

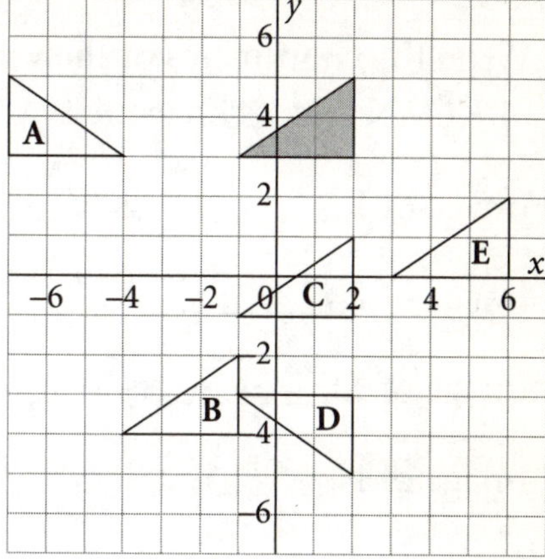

Triangles _____________ are translation images.

Triangles _____________ are reflection images.

2. a) Draw the image of △ABC after a translation of 5 units left and 3 units up.

b) Write the coordinates of the vertices of △ABC and its image △A′B′C′.

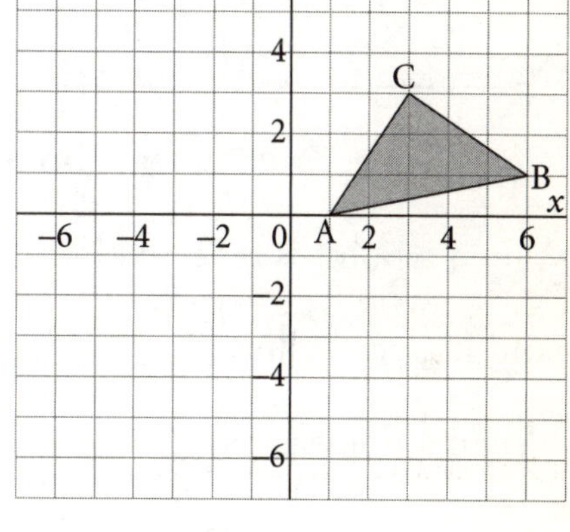

The image of A(1, 0) is A′(−4, 3).

The image of B(6, 1) is B′ __________

The image of C________ is C′__________

c) For a translation 5 units left and 3 units up,

the *x*-coordinate _______________ by 5,

and the *y*-coordinate _______________ by 3.

3. Quadrilateral W′X′Y′Z′ is a translation image of quadrilateral WXYZ.

a) Describe the translation.

____

b) Write the coordinates of the vertices of the quadrilateral and its image.

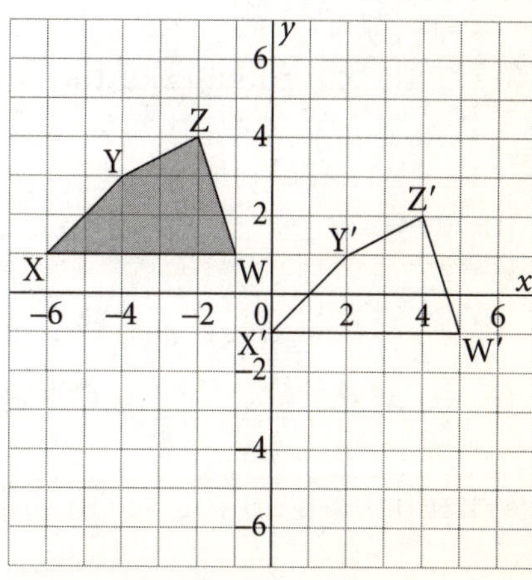

The image of W________ is W′________

The image of X ________ is X′________

The image of Y ________ is Y′________

The image of Z ________ is Z′________

4. a) Draw the image of quadrilateral KLMN:

- after a reflection in the *y*-axis. Label the image K′L′M′N′.
- after a reflection in the *x*-axis. Label the image K″L″M″N″.

b) Write the coordinates of the vertices of KLMN and its image K′L′M′N′.

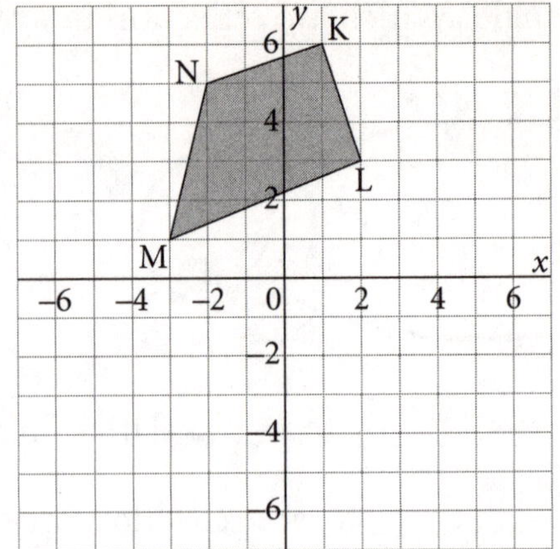

Image of K_________ is K′_________

Image of L_________ is L′_________

Image of M_________ is M′_________

Image of N_________ is N′_________

c) Write the coordinates of the vertices of KLMN and its image K″L″M″N″.

K_________   K″_________   L_________   L″_________

M_________   M″_________   N_________   N″_________

d) Complete each statement about reflection.

When a point is reflected in the *y*-axis, its *y*-coordinate _______________________

and its *x*-coordinate _________________________.

When a point is reflected in the *x*-axis, its *x*-coordinate _______________________

and its *y*-coordinate _________________________.

5. a) Draw the image of $\triangle$ABC after a reflection in the line through P(−3, −3), O(0, 0), and R(3, 3).

b) Write the coordinates of the vertices of $\triangle$ABC and its image $\triangle$A′B′C′.

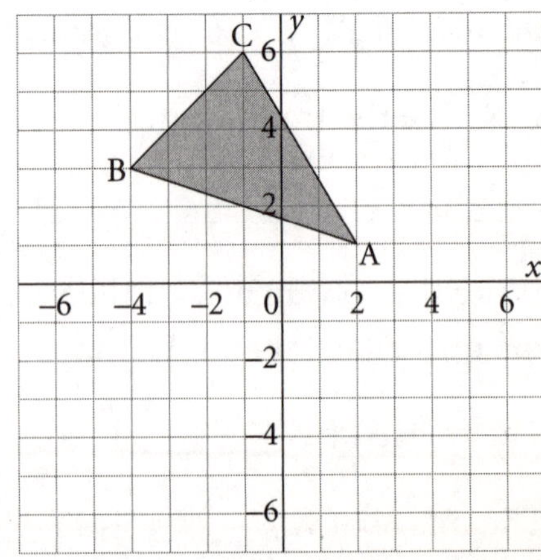

Image of A_________ is A′_________

Image of B_________ is B′_________

Image of C_________ is C′_________

c) What pattern do you see in the coordinates of each point and its image?

____

____

Quick Review

➤ A rotation turns a shape about a point of rotation.

➤ Rotations can be clockwise or counterclockwise.
A counterclockwise rotation is positive.
A clockwise rotation is negative.

➤ You can use tracing paper to draw the images of a shape after a 90°, 180°, or 270°
rotation about the origin on a coordinate grid.
• Trace the original shape and the axes.
• Label the positive y-axis on the tracing paper.
• Place a pencil point at the origin. Rotate the tracing paper counterclockwise until
the positive y-axis coincides with the given axis.

Rotation	Positive y-axis coincides with . . .
90°	negative x-axis
180°	negative y-axis
270°	positive x-axis

• Mark the vertices of the image with a sharp pencil through the tracing paper.
• Join the vertices to draw the image of the original shape.

This diagram shows the images of a shape after rotations of 90°, 180°, and 270° about
the origin.

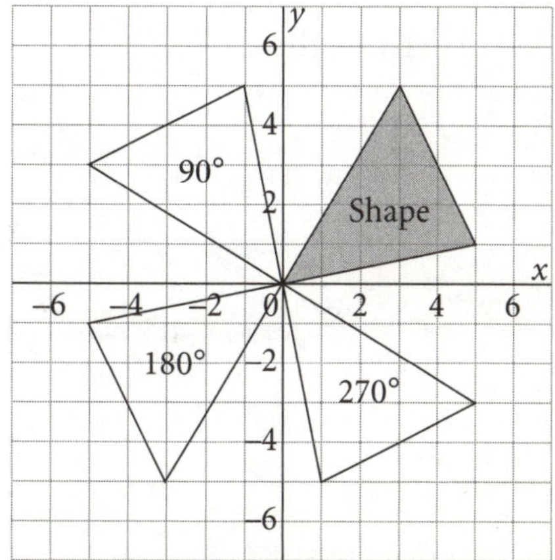

➤ Each image is congruent to the original shape.

1. Match the image with each transformation of the original shaded triangle.

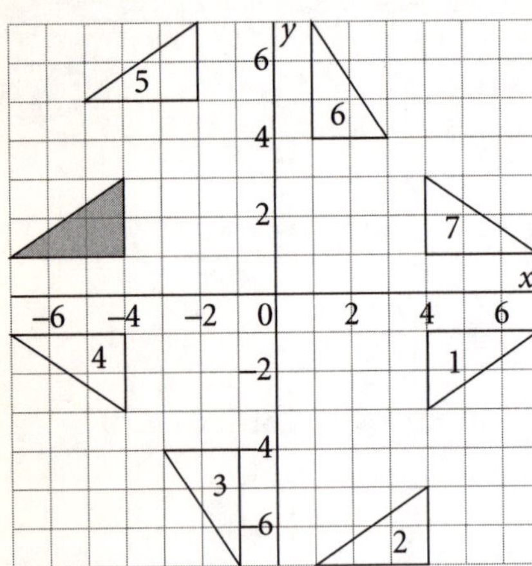

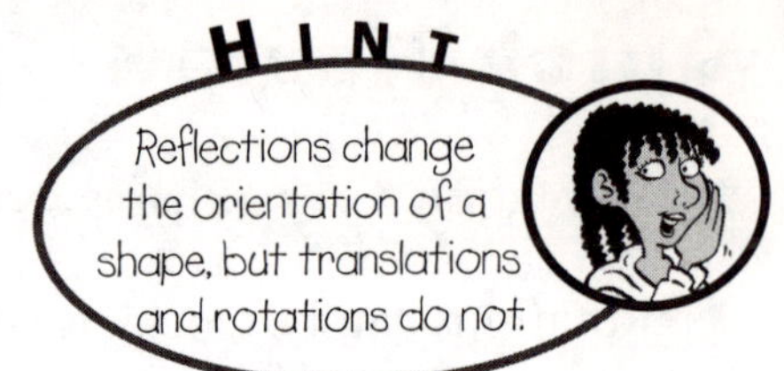

Image	Transformation of Original Triangle
1	rotation of 90° counterclockwise about the origin
2	reflection in the *x*-axis
3	translation 2 units right and 4 units up
4	reflection in the *y*-axis
5	rotation of 180° about the origin
6	rotation of 90° clockwise about the origin
7	translation 8 units right and 8 units down

2. a) Draw the image of quadrilateral WHAT after a rotation of 90° about the origin.

b) Write the coordinates of the vertices of the original shape and its image.

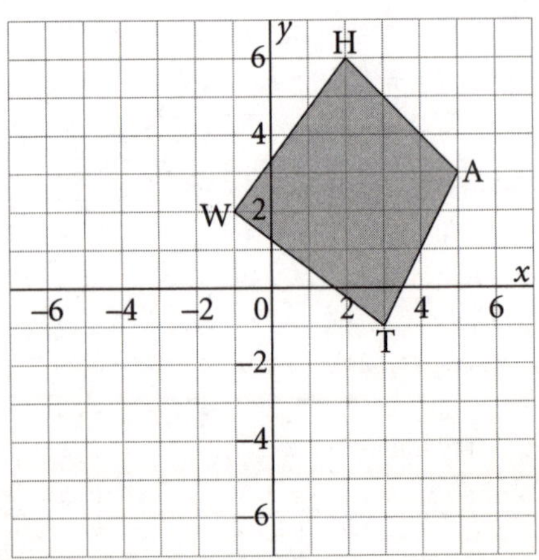

W_________ → W′_________

H _________ → H′_________

A _________ → A′_________

T _________ → T′_________

What pattern do you see in the coordinates?

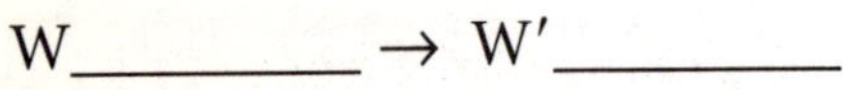

____

____

3. a) Draw the image of quadrilateral WHAT after a rotation of 180° about the origin on the coordinate grid in question 2.

b) Write the coordinates of the vertices of the original shape and its image.

W__________ → W″__________

H __________ → H″__________

A __________ → A″__________

T __________ → T″__________

What pattern do you see in the coordinates?

____

____

4. a) Draw the image of quadrilateral WHAT after a rotation of −90° about the origin on the coordinate grid in question 2.

b) Write the coordinates of the vertices of the original shape and its image.

W__________ → W‴__________

H __________ → H‴__________

A __________ → A‴__________

T __________ → T‴__________

What pattern do you see in the coordinates?

____

____

> **Tip**
>
> *A clockwise rotation is shown by a negative angle. A rotation of −90° is the same as a rotation of 270°.*

5. Use the patterns from questions 2 to 4 to predict the coordinates of the image of K(−5, 1):

a) after a rotation of 90° about the origin. ______________

b) after a rotation of 180° about the origin. ______________

c) after a rotation of 270° about the origin. ______________

6. Write the coordinates of the vertices of the image of △ABC after a rotation of 90° about the origin.

A(3, 2) → A′__________   B(5, −4) → B′__________   C(−6, −1) → C′__________

In Your Words

Here are some of the important mathematical words of this unit.
Build your own glossary by recording definitions and examples here. The first one is done for you.

parallel lines *are lines on the same flat surface that never meet; the lines on this file card are parallel*

perpendicular lines ______________

perpendicular bisector ______________

angle bisector ______________

coordinate grid ______________

ordered pair ______________

List other mathematical words you need to know.

____

Unit Review

8.1
8.2

1. Draw line segment FG.

   a) Draw a parallel line segment. Label it HJ.

     Explain your strategy for drawing the parallel segment.

     ____

     ____

   b) Draw the perpendicular bisector of HJ. Label it KM.

     Explain your strategy for drawing the perpendicular segment.

     ____

     ____

     ____

     ____

8.3
8.4

2. $\angle PQR$ is an obtuse angle.

   Draw the bisector of $\angle PQR$.

   Label it KQ.

   Draw the perpendicular bisector of QR.

   Label it MN.

   MN intersects QR at J.

   a) What do you know about $\angle PQK$?

     ____

     ____

   b) What do you know about segment QJ?

     ____

     ____

8.5

3. Use the diagram at the right.

a) The coordinates of D are ___________.

b) The coordinates of F are ___________.

c) Point ___________ has coordinates $(2, 6)$.

d) The coordinates of the origin are _______.

e) Point ___________ has y-coordinate 0.

f) Point ___________ has x-coordinate 0.

g) Point ___________ is in Quadrant 2.

8.6
8.7

4. Plot these points on the coordinate grid:
A$(0, 4)$, B$(6, 5)$, and C$(7, -2)$.
Join the points to form $\triangle$ABC.
On the same grid, draw the image of
$\triangle$ABC after each transformation.

a) A translation 9 units left and
7 units down
Label the image $\triangle$A'B'C'.
Write the coordinates of the vertices
of $\triangle$A'B'C'.

A'_________ B'_________ C'_________

b) A reflection in the y-axis
Label the image $\triangle$A"B"C". Write the coordinates of the vertices of $\triangle$A"B"C".

A"_________ B"_________ C"_________

c) A rotation of $-90°$ about the origin
Label the image $\triangle$A‴B‴C‴.
Write the coordinates of the vertices
of $\triangle$A‴B‴C‴.

A‴_________ B‴_________ C‴_________

Tip

A clockwise rotation is shown by a negative angle such as $-90°$.

How are the images alike? Different?_______________________________________

____

____